COMING ALIVE
FROM NINE TO FIVE

EMILIO LOMBRE

12-27-89

COMING ALIVE
FROM NINE TO FIVE:

THE CAREER SEARCH HANDBOOK

THIRD EDITION

Betty Neville Michelozzi
Corralitos, California

MAYFIELD PUBLISHING COMPANY
Mountain View, California

Library of Congress Cataloging-in-Publication Data

Michelozzi, Betty Neville.
   Coming alive from nine to five: the career search handbook/
Betty Neville Michelozzi.—3rd ed.
     p. cm.
   Bibliography: p.
   Includes index.
   ISBN 0-87484-825-3
   1. Vocational guidance.   2. Job hunting.   I. Title.
HF5381.M46 1988
650.1′4—dc19   87-25945
                                           CIP

Manufactured in the United States of America
10 9 8 7 6 5 4 3 2 1

Mayfield Publishing Company
1240 Villa Street
Mountain View, California 94041

Sponsoring editor, Franklin C. Graham; production editor, Linda
Toy; manuscript editor, Victoria Nelson; art director and cover
designer, Cynthia Bassett; text designer, Juan Vargas; illustrator, Liz
Callen. The text was set in 10/11 ITC Garamond Book by The
Clarinda Company and printed on 50# Finch Opaque Book by
George Banta Company.

C O N T E N T S

CHAPTER 6

WORKPLACES AND WORK STYLES: SCANNING THE SUBTLETIES   151

CHAPTER 7

THE JOB HUNT: TOOLS FOR BREAKING AND ENTERING   191

CHAPTER 8

DECISIONS, DECISIONS: WHAT'S YOUR NEXT MOVE?   225

CHAPTER 9

WORK AFFECTS THE SOUL: THE FINAL ANALYSIS   257

PREFACE

Coming Alive from Nine to Five is a unique handbook that develops, demystifies, and integrates between two covers all the various facets of career search and choice. It is meant to be a comprehensive handbook: a handy reference book drawing together into one practical, easily usable and reusable source the essentials of the career search process. Flexible enough to be adopted in whole or in part, in individual counseling sessions, in workshops, or in semester-long courses, this book is used in colleges and high schools, in industry and business, by people concerned about their own career development or that of others.

Primarily the handbook is intended for anyone who is making a life change. Though the text focuses specifically on careers, this topic can be translated into "meaningful life activity." *Coming Alive from Nine to Five* contains valuable material for all phases of career choice, even into retirement. Previous editions have been used by a broad population ranging from high school students to persons approaching retirement, from managers of households to managers of corporations, from job trainees to career-changing professionals in transition. This updated and expanded edition focuses on career preparation not only for the 1990s but for the next century as well. Using the same personal approach as earlier texts, the third edition expands awareness of the quality of workplaces and work styles as they relate to the whole of one's life. The dilemma of unemployment is addressed as well as trends that will shape the future.

Writing a third edition has once again provided an opportunity to develop new material, integrate overlapping exercises, and eliminate what seemed less helpful as well as update innumerable bits of data. Feedback from those who used the first two editions has been most helpful and supportive in the revision process.

Specifically, the three exercises leading into the Job Group Chart found in Chapter 4 have been integrated into one, greatly simplifying the Job Group Chart and making it much more effective. Focus on the decision-making process has also been streamlined by combining two exercises into one. As always, data on trends as well as on workplaces and work styles were revised. A section on tips for starting a small business was added. New material added to the leader/instructor's manual includes source material on the new inventories and Job Group Chart; more exercises, readings, exam questions, research; pages that can be easily made into transparencies; a career program development guide; material to be used for Vietnamese- and Spanish-speaking students, and other materials to assist students with their career choice.

Use of this handbook is most fruitful when the searcher approaches it in a relaxed, lighthearted manner. But a serious career search calls for commitment and motivation—and so does the handbook. The text is most helpful to those who become thoroughly involved in it. They will experience greater clarity about their lives and new confidence in themselves. Their goals will be easier to recognize and to reach. The career search will become a journey of personal growth on the path toward self-actualization.

—B.N.M.

. . . .

A C K N O W L E D G M E N T S

Private: Please do not read this.

Acknowledgments are a very personal thing. They point up the fact that it is impossible to accomplish anything of importance all alone. Thanks to:

Peter, my husband, for his caring support, endless proofreading, and "thought-full" suggestions. He helped me keep perspective on life's deeper meaning when a sea of paper and words threatened to engulf me.

All the caring, careful typists who contributed 'way back, most especially my neighbor Ruby Garcia, who goes beyond neighborliness to heroism; Kay Koyano at West Valley College, whose patience with the first manuscript was unmatched; and Jerry Johnson, who guided me, step by shaky step, into the computer world.

Supportive colleagues at West Valley and Mission Colleges who read, reviewed, and gave helpful feedback: Bill Allman, Veronese Anderson, Chloe Atkins, Don Cordero, Ken Gogstad, Tom Heffner, Carolyn Hennings, Michael Herauf, Jo Hernandez, Sharon Laurenza, Joyce McClellan, Gladys Penner, Richard Przybylski, Pat Space, Jill Trefz, Pat Weber, and Jan Winton; Dave Fishbaugh and the Mission library staff who helped check references.

Staff and students in many places who attended workshops and lectures on this material and gave generous feedback.

Aptos, Santa Cruz, and Watsonville library staff who at the drop of a phone call searched out many details and even called back—in minutes! The staff at the Department of Labor, Bureau of Statistics and Bookstore in San Francisco for their hospitable response to many questions.

West Valley and Mission college students who taught me to teach Careers and Lifestyles and shared the beauty of their lives and their journeys.

Career people who share their stories and give support and resources to career searchers; company people who share their workplaces with those who seek information.

Colleagues and resource people in many places who have been supportive, have given assistance and information: Judy Shernock for her work on the Personality Mosaic, Cora Alameda, Judy Appelt, Sally Brew, Dorothy Coffey, Denise Douglas, John French, H. B. Gelatt, Bobbie George, Phyllis Hullett, Barbara Lea, Gene Malone, Ritchie Lowry, John Maginley, Lillian Mattimore, Stephen Moody, Ruth Olsen, Julie Pitts, Alex Reyes, Kay Ringel, Ed Watkins.

Instructors who shared class time to test materials—too numerous to mention by name but remembered with gratitude.

People (past and present) at Mayfield who have been so great to work with: Naomi Angoff, Liz Currie, Bob Erhart, Laraine Etchemendy-Bennett, Frank Graham, Pat Herbst, Yaeko Kashima, Carol Norton, Don Palm, Nancy Sears, Linda Toy, and Pam Trainer.

Manuscript editors Carol King and Victoria Nelson, who have contributed above and beyond the call of duty.

My family and friends, who gave me "living love."

You have all enriched me.

Betty

COMING ALIVE
FROM NINE TO FIVE

INTRODUCTION

Career search can be a special, very precious time to orient and organize your life. It can be a time when you look deeply at yourself and what you have been doing. It can lead you to question how you intend to spend your life for a time, or your time for the rest of your life: to keep or not to keep certain goals, to change or not to change certain behaviors, to aspire or not to aspire to certain positions—all with a view toward greater life enrichment.

Career search involves more than simply figuring out what job might suit you best. That is the short-range view. The perspective expands when you ask yourself what you want that job to do for you. Very quickly you may find yourself face to face with some of your deepest values. Do you want power, prestige, profit? Peace, harmony, love? Are some values incompatible with others? Can you have it all?

Can you work 60 hours a week moving up the corporate ladder, nurture loving relationships with family and friends, grow your own vegetables, recycle your cans on Saturday, jog daily, be a Scout leader, meditate, play golf at the country club, and do yoga? How fully can all your interests and values be actualized in the real world? What is the purpose of work? What is the purpose of life?

Career search, then, can be a profound journey of personal growth—not just a superficial job hunt. A career can be a vital means of self-expression—not just a job. Besides providing a living, a career can satisfy some of your deepest longings.

Because it is important, some people approach a career decision with fear and trembling lest they make a mistake. Others avoid the process altogether, certain it will nail them down to a lifelong commitment they can never change. Still others feel that any job will do just to get them started on something! And then there are those who feel that even if they did a thorough career search, it would turn up absolutely nothing. In reality, a careful career search can help everyone. It can help *you* to see many possibilities, and in turn give you flexibility and a great deal of confidence. It can even help people who have made a career decision better understand themselves and their connection to the work world. The result can be greater career/life satisfaction.

What process should you use in making a "thought-full" career decision? Many people choose their career using the "muddle-about method." They consider subjects they've liked in school: if it's math, then they'll be mathematicians; if it's history, they'll be historians. They consider the careers of people they know and ask the advice of friends. Uncle Jim the firefighter is a family hero, and a new crop of firefighters is launched. If they fry hamburgers at McDonald's for a time, they're tempted to judge the whole world of business through the sizzle of French fries. If models and airline pilots capture their attention, they long for a glamorous life. An opportunity crops up; they grab it and years later ask, "Is this all there is?"

Many people spend their whole lives muddling about, like Hobart Foote, who describes it this way:

> I'm from Alabama, my wife and kids are Hoosiers. I was gonna work a few years and buy me a new car and head back south. Well, I met the wife now and that kinda changed my plans.
>
> I might've been working in some small factory down south or I might have gone to Detroit where I worked before or I might have gone to Kalamazoo where I worked before. Or else I mighta stuck on a farm somewheres, just grubbing off a farm somewhere. You never know what you woulda did. You can't plan too far in advance, 'cause there's always a stumblin' block.[1]

Other folks make very early decisions: "I knew when I was two that I wanted to be a chimney sweep." Career choice can sometimes seem trivial. Adults ask six-year-olds what they want to be when they grow up. Are they going to sell shoes at Kinney's or invade the corporate complex of IBM? Will plumbing be their outlet or travel tours their bag? Yet many adults aren't always sure what their next job will be.

At least occasionally, however, the image of life's wholeness flashes before us and we catch a glimpse of the time and energy that we will invest in work. We see that work will affect our lives in many ways. Unless we keep a tight lid on it, the ultimate question will eventually present itself: "What's it all about,

Alfie?" If we deal in depth with career choice, we are bound to slip into philo-sophic questioning of life's meaning. To do otherwise is to trivialize a profound experience.

Since you are reading this book, you're indicating that "muddling about" is not the way you want to approach your career decision. Begin by looking at the stages and steps in the career search process. The search has four stages along a career choice continuum. For many people, the journey begins at ground zero with not an idea in sight. But as you gather career information, you reach a midpoint where you seem to be engulfed in too many ideas. In other words, things seem to get worse before they get better. Eventually you must begin to lighten the burden by choosing. You simply can't follow every career in one lifetime. The calmer you stay, the more easily you will arrive at your decision point. Where are you on the Career Choice Continuum? Mark your position with a plus ($\sqrt{}$) sign.

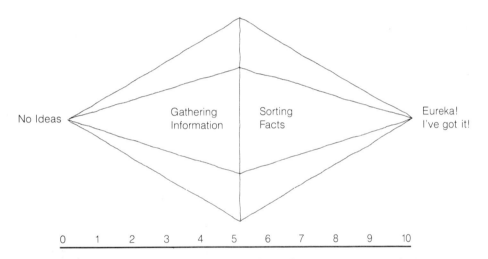

Mark a ✔ on the scale from 0 to 10 to show where you are *now* on the Career Choice Continuum.

The steps to be taken must be part of a *system* that is clear and demysti-fied, that can be used many times in a lifetime—for one decision may lead to another, which is part of the process of testing ideas out. What kind of a system should this be? First, a system that helps people articulate who they are and what they do well. Second, a system that describes the work world as simply and completely as possible. Third, a system that helps searchers see where their personal characteristics fit into that world of work. Fourth, a system that "em-powers" them to secure the job they have chosen by increasing their job hunt-

. . . .
Career Planning: Breaks Barriers, Builds Bridges

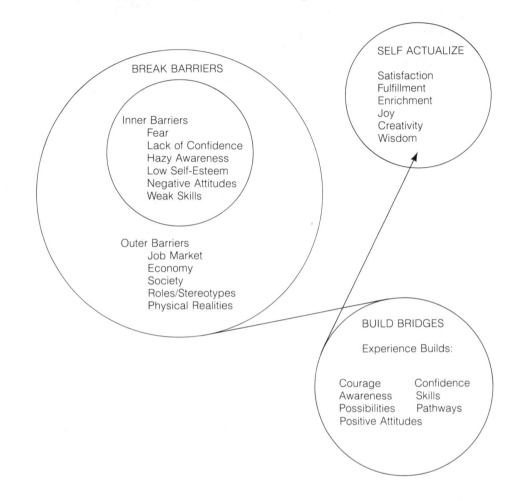

ing skills. Fifth, a system that raises their consciousness about work as only one part of their personal journey, one aspect of their total lifestyle. And finally, a system that addresses issues of global concern, showing how work is part of the world picture with its many challenges and how solutions to these challenges are provided by our work.

In *Coming Alive from Nine to Five* you will find such a system. It is based on identifying clear values that lead to good decisions. At first glance this book may look like a conventional careers manual. Read the book, fill in the blanks, and (even if you're already over forty) you'll know what you want to be when you grow up.

VELEY Reprinted with permission from the Saturday Evening Post Society, a division of BFL&MS Inc. © 1987.

You *will* find blanks to fill in as part of the step-by-step process of getting to know yourself and the job world. You *will* explore your needs, wants, and values. You *will* discover your personality orientation. You *will* examine your past and select the activities you've enjoyed as well as skills you've developed over the years. A job group chart will help you to put *you* and *work* together in a meaningful way. And a final inventory will collect all this "you data" and help you to see it as a unified whole.

This book also touches on some of the heavier issues of life. How can you fulfill your potential? Be happy? Be content? It deals with such things lightly—sometimes whimsically—because life is meant to be joyful. But after a good chuckle we get serious and *think* again because our lives are also important and sometimes sad.

The career search is really a time to *stop out* to see who you are and where you're *growing*. This text is written for those who are in transition and would like the opportunity to learn a thought-full career decision process: graduating seniors, parents no longer needed at home, the newly divorced or widowed, job changers, the disabled, the unemployed, grandmothers and grandfathers kicking up their heels, corporate tycoons stopping to smell the flowers, people in midlife crises, veterans, ex-clerics, people becoming parents and providers, persons retiring, and all others willing to let go of behaviors that are no longer appropriate and risk new ones.

A book about career choice is inevitably a book about life and all its stages, from nineteen to ninty-nine.

The Career Search Guide

Most people base career decisions on incomplete information. As you begin your career search, it may help to focus on some important questions. Check (√) the items you feel are already answered satisfactorily for you.

1. Self-Assessment: A Guide
   a. Needs, wants, and shoulds
      What do you *need* to survive? What do you *want* to enrich your life? Do your *shoulds* help you or hold you back?
   b. Interests and values
      The choices you've made over your lifetime have developed into a strong pattern of interests. These reflect what you value most in life. Are your values clear?
   c. Roles
      What *roles* do you play now? What expectations do you and others have about these roles? Do you wish to change or adapt these roles?
   d. Skills
      Analyze your most enjoyable activities. Through repeated choices in your areas of interest, you have developed many skills. Of all the skills you have, which do you enjoy using the most?

2. Job Market Exploration: Where to Start
   a. Research the job market
      Interest and skill inventories lead you to an overview of the entire job market. What jobs fit your self-image?
   b. Trends/workplaces
      Check the job market outlook and relate it to *trends* in society. Will there be a need for people to do the job you'd like? What workplaces will you choose? Do you have alternatives?

    c. Information interview

       Have you talked to people in careers that interest you? Have you surveyed and evaluated possible workplaces? Does the survey show that you need to reevaluate your choices?

    d. Tools for the job hunt

       Do you know how to portray yourself effectively through résumés, applications, interviews, letters? Can you talk fluently about yourself?

3. The Final Analysis: Wrap-Up

    a. Decisions: Finalize your decision.

    b. Goals: Set realistic goals with time lines.

    c. Strategy: Develop a strategy for action.

    d. Values/philosophy: Review the whole picture to make sure it fits your value system, your philosophy of life and work.

NEEDS, WANTS, AND VALUES: SPOTLIGHTING YOU

F O C U S

Examine important values in your personal and work life.

Develop a broader understanding of work.

Identify steps in making desired changes in your life.

• • • • •

To start the career process at its roots, ask yourself what you *really* need. A genuine need is something you must have to survive, something you cannot live without. After these basic needs are identified, begin to look at your *wants.* Wants can enrich life beyond the level of needs. Then look at *shoulds* because sometimes they create confusion about what we really want. What we want reflects our *values* and gives meaning to our lives. Looking at needs, wants, shoulds, and values, at the roots of a career search, can open a new phase of personal growth.

Four need levels are adapted here from the well-known hierarchy of psychologist Abraham Maslow: physical, emotional, intellectual, and altruistic or spiritual. Minimal survival needs on each of these levels are the basis for becoming a fulfilled and self-actualized person. All human beings have basically the same needs, with variations appropriate to innate capacity and stages of life.

Physical needs are the most basic. Without food, for example, we would not survive many days. Gandhi said, "Even God cannot talk to a hungry man except in terms of bread." Air, water, food, clothing, shelter, health maintenance, exercise, and the transportation required for these necessities are the elements of our physical need system. Accompanying our physical needs is the need to feel reasonably secure in order to carry out our life tasks. It would be hard to concentrate on reading a great book in a burning building. The world arms build-up is an attempt to increase feelings of security. Our physical safety can be threatened in many remote ways, too—by worry, for example. We can let ourselves worry about nuclear attack, illness from air pollution and chemical additives, being cared for in old age, meeting new and unfamiliar situations, and job security. Such continued worry can shrivel our present physical well-being.

Yet we've heard stories about infants whose physical/safety needs were met but nevertheless died mysteriously. We've heard of old people "dying of loneliness" or of a person dying after hearing of the death of a loved one.[1] Human beings seem to need love, some kind of faith and assurance that they are lovable, someone to give them courage. People's self-esteem and life energy can be diminished by real or imagined deprivation of love. Some level of emotional nurturing, then, is real and necessary for even the most basic physical survival and growth.

Our minds also need to know and to grow to ensure our survival. People learn in different ways. Those who relate best to the physical world seem to "learn through their hands." Some learn best through their ears, some through their eyes. Some learn best from the emotion-laden words of people they love. And media lovers learn easily from books, pictures, diagrams, and other symbols.

On the altruistic or spiritual level, human beings at times put their own desires aside to care for others. The survival of an infant depends upon this sort of self-sacrifice. The very survival of our planet may demand the same of all of us. Human survival would be endangered if we totally disregarded the needs of others. Imagine your daily commute. The freeway would become a free-for-all!

If you have survived modern life thus far and are reading and understanding this book, a good share of your basic needs have already been fulfilled. Many people have contributed to your well-being on all levels along the way. But someday, or maybe even now, you may face a situation in which your physical needs are threatened. You may be next in line for a layoff; you may have friends losing their jobs and the unemployed losing their benefits. Unpaid bills, a baby on the way, and ailing parents can bring Mike Mechanic in Michigan or Martha Millhouse in North Carolina close to panic.

Lower minimum needs must be taken care of first, Maslow says, and you couldn't agree more. Concerns about emotional, intellectual, and altruistic needs can fly out the window! But perhaps this is the time to gather some emotional support, resources, and ideas, to use every bit of intelligence and knowledge to carve out a survival path. It may seem foolish to do career planning during a crisis, when it seems that any job will do. But the insights gathered may be just what you need to boost confidence and morale and open up unsuspected possibilities. In any case, to lead a balanced and satisfying life you need to develop your potential as far as possible in all areas.

NEEDS RELATE TO WANTS

Very soon in life you begin to move beyond mere survival to a place of enriched choice where you actualize your wants. It's important to differentiate between needs and wants.[2] Needs are absolutely necessary for life. A cup of water, a bowl of rice, and a few sprouts will do, but humans have discovered thousands of additions to that survival menu called wants. Risks such as changing jobs are less frightening when you know that you can survive on very little. Once your needs are satisfied, you can work more calmly toward achieving your own set of wants. But sometimes your wants can lead you far from your goals. You can choose things, relationships, and activities that are either nurturing or harmful. It has been said that "everything you own owns you." So you must plan your journey carefully. You don't want to find yourself halfway down the block without realizing you've turned the corner.

NEEDS AND WANTS RELATE
TO FEELINGS AND SHOULDS

How did your own individual set of wants evolve? Basically, they come from two divergent areas: what feels good to you and the reasoned and not-so-reasoned judgment of others.

Running free feels good to a child, but the reasoned judgment of an adult says that a busy street is not a good place to exercise this freedom. The child learns to curb good feelings by using reasoned judgment, sometimes known as common sense. But if not-so-reasoned judgment and excess caution inspire anxiety about every venture, the child will lose the joy of trying new things. He or she will become a slave to shoulds, according to college counselor Carolyn Hennings. When you say "I should," you are implying that you neither need nor want to do this thing, but some force or some person outside of you is saying you must. Shoulds are energy drains because they create a feeling of resistance and apathy. They cause you to shift responsibility for your choices somewhere else. When you make life changes, it's important to know if your shoulds are value-inspired. A should thus explored will either evaporate as unimportant or, if value-related, will be owned as a want.

So ask yourself, in regard to what you want and value, if you tend to act solely on feelings and thus sabotage your real needs by not using reasoned judgment or common sense. Or have you absorbed judgments of others that no longer fit you, losing touch with what would give you joy? Are you afraid of your feelings or have you exchanged true feelings for unreal fear or frustration?

Sometimes it's difficult to sort out all of these feelings and judgments by yourself. They may seem to be leading you into unproductive and even damaging behavior. Carl Rogers, the psychologist who first used the term "unconditional positive regard," believes that a person grows best and most positively when he or she can explore feelings freely in a caring, nonjudgmental atmosphere. Since feelings are a physiological response to the environment, they serve as useful indicators. By focusing directly on these feelings, experiencing them, and exploring them with a trusted guide, you can learn to channel your emotional energy in a positive way to accomplish your goals.

NEEDS, WANTS, AND FEELINGS RELATE TO VALUES

What you *need* is an absolute survival minimum on the physical, emotional, intellectual, and altruistic levels. What you *want* goes beyond survival to a place of enriched choices. Changing shoulds to wants and getting in touch with what you *feel* clarifies your needs and wants and helps you to consider what you really *value.*

Becoming aware of what you really value and cherish is a lifetime process. To find out whether an action of yours truly reflects a value, ask yourself:

• Did I have a choice?
• Did I weigh my choices carefully?

- Did I choose freely?
- Am I happy with my choice?
- Has my choice become a part of my life pattern?

Values are what you *do,* not what you *say.* Your struggles, disappointments, worries, hopes, and dreams are all indicators of value areas because they show what is important enough for you to be concerned about. A true set of values is indicated when you feel confident, enthusiastic, and clear about yourself and others, and about your choices.

On the other hand, murky values can result in many conflicts. We see these conflicts in people who are apparently turned off, confused, changeable, complaining, hostile, alienated, or "lazy." The person who overconforms or overrebels probably has problems in clarifying values.

If you are clear about your values, you won't let your wants disguise your needs. When people substitute possessions for love needs, for example, they acquire all sorts of status symbols. They are hoping for attention and love, but they may alienate those they are trying to impress. A person with clear values goes right to the heart of the matter and works on improving relationships by good communications and caring.

The values each person cherishes are an individual expression of self. For King Midas, gold was everything. Most people are astounded when someone leaves a million dollars to a pet cat. All aspects of life are value laden: family, love and friendship, religion and virtue, work and leisure.[3]

Values Influence Your Lifestyle/Act as Motivators

The values you esteem will lead you to make decisions about the whole of your life, not just your career. All the elements of your lifestyle, including family, friends, home and work environments, religious preference, education, and recreation, will reflect your values. So too the career that you choose, with its attendant values, will influence your lifestyle in many subtle and not so subtle ways. You will learn new skills, change some behaviors to fit your new role, make new friends, and learn a new vocabulary. Your work can lead to new involvements, new values, and even new ways of seeing yourself.[4] In fact, work roles can be so overpowering that some people find it hard to relate to a new acquaintance without knowing what they do for a living, seeing only the role and not the person.

It may seem difficult or impossible at times to align all your lifestyle elements with your values. Life is not always that obliging. The Great American Novel may be on your dream agenda, yet you find yourself typing engineering specs. The reality may be that at present you value feeding yourself and your family over feeding your love for art. Being clear about your values and the order of preference can eliminate a great deal of conflict. When you have realistic goals, both immediate and long term, you will have a far greater possibility of actualizing your dreams.

The work you choose will fulfill many of your needs and wants, and directly reflects your values. To do work requires motivation because we humans don't act without it. Our motivators are our needs and wants. Most people work for money to fulfill their various needs in Maslow's hierarchy. Those with enough resources to fulfill their basic needs then work for other reasons. A housewife works to care for husband and children. Her rewards may vary from love and mutual support to avoidance of disapproval.

Some people work because the work is intrinsically satisfying to their personalities. Others go to work to be with people, get noticed, be approved, and for a whole host of unique and individual enticements. Clarifying your values will help to uncover your motivations. In this book you will be clarifying many values as you learn about yourself and your characteristics. You will be making decisions based on those values. This process is bound to enhance your personal growth.

Personal Growth

Getting acquainted with yourself—your feelings, needs, wants, and most cherished values—as you transform your shoulds is a continuous process. But at certain stages of life the quest for self becomes imperative. You find that you have outgrown familiar roles: child, student, nurturer, business dynamo, provider, supermom. Life has a way of forcing us to make changes. When children start school, and especially when they leave home, a person can no longer be a parent in the same old sense. When a young person graduates from college, takes a job, marries and has children, he or she can no longer be a carefree young adult. When a person achieves success in a job and reaches the top, or realizes she or he is not going to reach the top, what then?

Growing as a person means changing, adjusting to both inner and outer reality. The need for growth on all levels is a powerful force within us. It means expansion into new and exciting areas of life. And never before in the history of humankind have people had such opportunity for growth at all stages of life. Many people are living longer, are more affluent, have access to vast amounts of technology, and are more aware of possibilities.

There are new dimensions to life that were not present even twenty years ago. People are going back to school at ages seventy and eighty, getting degrees, starting businesses, publishing their first books, painting, initiating nationwide

The Flowering of Personal Growth

The flowering of our growth brings
aliveness, effortlessness
individuality, playfulness,
completion, richness.

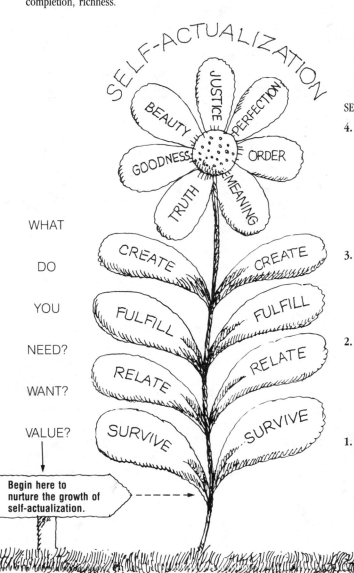

SELF-ACTUALIZATION

BEAUTY · JUSTICE · PERFECTION · GOODNESS · ORDER · TRUTH · MEANING

WHAT

DO

YOU

NEED?

WANT?

VALUE?

CREATE · CREATE
FULFILL · FULFILL
RELATE · RELATE
SURVIVE · SURVIVE

**Begin here to
nurture the growth of
self-actualization.**

SELF-ACTUALIZATION

4. ALTRUISTIC NEEDS: We all
must interact with others to
survive, but to live life fully is
to have that generous, loving
spirit that promotes truth,
goodness, beauty, justice, perfection, order, meaning, and
all that is noble and good in
the world.

3. INTELLECTUAL NEEDS: A degree of knowledge and understanding are necessary for survival, but a truly developed
mind is one in which wisdom
and creativity flourish.

2. EMOTIONAL NEEDS: Basic
caring from others is necessary for our growth. Rich relationships bring us joy and
the courage that comes from
emotional support, love, and
respect.

1. PHYSICAL NEEDS: We all have
needs for food, clothing, shelter, safety—the things that
keep us alive. Our carefully
chosen wants enrich us and
enable us to simplify our lives
and feel self-sufficient.

political action groups, teaching swimming! We are confused. Whatever happened to that obsolete object, the rocking chair? People are discovering that their powers are about as strong as their attitudes: physical (including sexual) ability, the ability to learn, to develop new ideas. My mother went to work at a publishing company at age seventy with little training or work experience. Her success at correcting material and supervising other workers was a source of amazement and delight to her.

All personal growth activities are aimed at understanding yourself better in relationship to others and the environment. When you understand yourself better, you learn to take responsibility for what you feel. Instead of blaming others for your feelings, you may realize that your troublesome reactions are largely based on past experiences instead of present realities. You may catch yourself misinterpreting another's words or actions and thinking the worst, without checking the facts.

Self-deception results when one feeling masks another. Suppose you feel angry at a meeting when someone speaks intelligently, expressing an idea that you couldn't put into words. Your anger may mask hurt pride. Your hurt pride may mask feelings of inferiority and insecurity, which in turn mask a profound feeling of being unesteemed by others. If you learned to recognize the truth, you might say, "I feel profoundly unesteemed when others articulate ideas well." This statement puts you in touch with an absurdity and helps you to become aware of your esteem needs. You may then find ways to meet your needs. And, incidentally, you may become aware that you seldom, if ever, compliment or grant esteem to others.

If you care about your relationships with others, you will share your feelings with them when appropriate, in an honest and caring way. You will take responsibility for the feelings, and experience them without denial or delay so that you can deal with them clearly. You will be neither timid nor aggressive but *assertive*. Both the timid and the aggressive person create dissonance wherever they go: one by "nitpicking around the bush," and the other by bulldozing the bush out of existence. And who wants to spend a lifetime "picking nits or dozing bulls"? (Some of us alternate between the two extremes: first being polite while suppressing feelings, then exploding.) The assertive person, then, is a growing, balanced person who is centered within self, feels comfortable with life, has little need to fear or control people, and is more able to love and value self and others. In turn, such a person will be loved and valued.

We can create our own happiness and solve our "feeling problems" by changing what can be changed and then changing our attitude about the unchangeable. Negative emotions can be rechanneled if we catch them at the first inkling. They are all related. We begin by wanting something that we think we need. If it doesn't come easily, we begin to fear we won't get it. This anxiety can turn to frustration and anger and even hate for others who seem to block our path. If we choose to let those emotions overwhelm us, judgment gets fogged up. Used well, however, strong feelings can be a source of good power.

It takes practice. But since feelings so often get in the way of effective action, it can be worth the effort. We have a choice. *We can actually select our feelings!* Some people find it helpful to talk to a counselor when they are experiencing strong emotions. It's difficult to make decisions about careers when you feel overwhelmed by other problems.

The alternative to growth is: a diminished life that closes out self by put-downs, lack of confidence, many shoulds; closes out others by bitter angry thoughts, blaming/projecting, many demands; closes out life by tension, guilt, anxiety, and finding fault on all sides.

The process by which we grow is not always easy. Author Bill Cane asks, "Is it possible to accurately plot out a lifetime without budgeting in the possibility of change, darkness, and personal pain?"[5]

So personal growth means: not getting stuck but moving on; not clinging to an obsolete role but trying on new ones until one fits; not denying but accepting reality. Growth can be defined as increasing the number of things we: (1) find out for ourselves, (2) decide for ourselves, (3) do for ourselves.[6]

Many people find it helpful, when making life changes, to review their past experiences. An important clue to your skills and interests is to become aware of what you've been doing all your life. Your "free spirit" years are especially important. Those are the years beginning at about five or six when you started to be independent enough to cross the street alone and make some choices. During that time you may have chosen friends and activities without too much parental guidance. You weren't as worried about what people thought as you might have been as you reached the ten- to twelve-year-old stage.

Pay attention to what gave you satisfaction then. Your disappointments are important too, since they wouldn't be disappointing if they meant nothing to you. Some people find great motivation striving for success in a so-called area of failure. Timid speech students conquer their fear and become noted speakers; inept Little Leaguers make up their minds to become strong athletes.

Times of transition are fearful periods when life seems so empty that we'd give anything not to face reality. But when we do face it, we are amazed at how much more there is of all good and joyful things, especially love for ourselves and others. We gradually begin to see life differently. In the words of Ken Keyes, Jr., a humanist who developed a system for handling strong feelings, we thus create our own world, and "a loving person lives in a loving world."[7] Self-awareness leads to self-acceptance, which leads to self-confidence. We are on the way to self-actualization.

A self-actualizing person might be described as follows:

- Authentic, open, doesn't hide behind roles or masks
- Is ruled neither by ego nor emotion
- Simple, natural, with little need for status symbols
- Autonomous, centered, not pulled along by every fad

- Able to make decisions, take responsibility
- Takes life seriously with a generous touch of whimsy
- Can see through the "put-ons" of others with a benign view and maybe even a chuckle
- Emotionally balanced, enjoying peak experiences, delighting in people, art, nature, yet able to "get the job done"
- Not burdened with the anxiety, guilt, or shame that go with shoulds
- Spontaneous, passionate, creative, enjoyer of life—yet moral, ethical, concerned
- Sees all useful work as dignified and treats all workers with respect
- Takes time for self-renewal and relaxation
- Can be alone or in a group with equal ease
- Values privacy yet feels one with humankind
- Tends to form deep personal relationships based on love and caring with other self-actualizing people
- Has a basic set of beliefs, a philosophy of life
- Acts not out of greed, fear, or anger but out of love and caring for the whole world

So when minimal needs are fulfilled on every level, when our wants are becoming reality, when our shoulds have dissolved or turned to wants, when our feelings are helping rather than hindering the process, it seems that endless vistas of growth open up for us. As Maslow said, "We may still often (if not always) expect that a new discontent and restlessness will soon develop, unless the individual is doing what he's fitted for. A musician must make music, an artist must paint, a poet must write, if he is to be ultimately at peace. What a person can be, he must be. This need we call self-actualization."[8]

Some persons even seem to go beyond self-actualization. Heroic deeds based on minimal needs make up the fabric of their joyful lives. So when people "have it all," where do they go next? Service to others motivated by natural altruism or spirituality is the highest form of self-actualization. For example, Joseph P. Sullivan, the successful rescuer and chief executive officer of Swift and Company, one of the world's largest meat packing concerns, seemed to "have it all." But after putting this company in the black, to the chagrin of his colleagues he resigned. A deeply spiritual man, he needed to make a contribution to society on a deeper level instead of pursuing ever more prestige, power, and profit. A friend says this was "a natural part of his growth and development." One of the groups who will profit from Sullivan's talents is the American Refugee Committee as well as the Board of Trustees of Mundelein College.[9] In the same vein, successful architect John Law changed the thrust of his work to develop housing for low-income people. The profit will go to support a medical clinic in a ghetto neighborhood.

In telling the story of hero Jeff Wiser who rescued several people from a burning auto wreck, *Prevention Magazine* tells us that such altruism may be a genetic necessity. Our ancestors may have said, "I'll save you from this saber-toothed tiger if you save me from the next one." Ed Piszek, a multimillionaire, says he knew he didn't want to leave this earth without "doing something meaningful for society."[10]

So the more talents you develop, the more self-actualized you are on all levels from physical through emotional, intellectual, altruistic/spiritual, the more you will be making a positive contribution to the world you live in. This world is filled with challenges. It is work that provides many of the options and solutions.

· · · · · · · · · ·

THE UNEXAMINED

life is not worth living.

SOCRATES

· · · · · · · · · ·

A GLOBAL/PHILOSOPHIC
VIEW OF WORK

What is work? There are many definitions, including some that overlap or contradict. Without getting too technical and precise, let's say that work is activity that provides goods and services to others while providing some reward for the worker. But along the way, work must also be useful to others. "Work is the way that we tend the world, the way people connect. It is the most vigorous, vivid sign of life—in individuals and civilization."[11]

· · · · · · · · · ·

WITHOUT WORK

all life goes rotten.
But when work is soulless,
life stifles and dies.

ALBERT CAMUS

· · · · · · · · · ·

Day and night the world hums with the activities of people and machines making goods for one another. Mines and forests, oceans and fields yield raw substances to make a myriad of *things*. Wood and metal, coal and cotton, thousands of other materials are baled and baked, pounded and pummeled, mixed and milled, cut and checked, piled and packed for delivery to the world. Trucks and trains, ships and planes move endlessly huffing and hauling it all to other factories and farms, stores, and homes.

Things! They are bought, sold, used, recycled, worn out, and finally discarded to become mountains of debris. Some of it returns to the earth, some of it remains to pollute and plague us. Technology, ever more sophisticated, makes marvelous things and in the process saves industrialized people from many back-breaking tasks.

Along with the production of goods, work involves those often intangible "services rendered." From answering phones and directing traffic to designing systems and supervising workers, more and more people are involved in transactions, interactions, communications, "deals." We seem to be struggling into a new era that emphasizes information, ideas, and people over mere things. In two centuries we have moved from an agrarian society, based on simple necessities, to a high-tech age in which the new product is *information*.

Many affluent people made prosperous by this revolution in technology, cluster in suburbs and gentrified city areas, believing they are "average Americans," while the true average American looks mighty prosperous to much of the rest of the world. Though only one-sixth of the world's population, the United States has entered an era of unprecedented affluence and high living standards. Many ordinary children own television sets, stereos, video games, calculators, computers, ten-speed bikes, and other magical gadgets that would be the envy of emperors of old. And our powerful influence causes others to rush to imitate US, a process that bears examining since we use the most energy and resources per capita of any country, about one-third of the total consumed each year.

The information society, in which information jobs predominate over production jobs, accounts for only a small percentage of the world's population. Some human beings do not survive because they lack even food, clothing, shelter, and the transportation necessary to bring them basic goods. Every 24 hours, 35,000 human beings die as a result of world hunger and starvation[12] even though the world grows more than enough food for everyone. Societies that were once self-sustaining, now dislocated by expanding technologies, are no longer able to supply their own necessities for many complex reasons, from social to economic to political. The high-tech age seems light years away to such people.

But the provision of goods and services (called *work*), to those willing to pay for them, is costly in more than dollars and souls. It is costing us dearly in terms of irreplaceable energy and resources and in irreversible damage to the environment, to say nothing of arousing the envy of the rest of the world's people. The United States seems to be leading the world on a collision course with nature and its inhabitants.

Decisions are needed, but we don't see clearly what to decide. Every possible choice causes some group somewhere to protest as we try to clarify needs, wants, and values and find our own personal direction. Work affects our souls! We are at an exciting crossroads where careful choices could create a better world. But there are no simple answers. So far, some individuals' suggested alternatives sound strange and unworkable to many people: appropriate technology, economic democracy, and sustainable ecology.

We might agree that work should be a self-fulfilling, leisurely, meaningful activity that produces worthwhile products and services through peaceful, non-polluting, resource-conserving methods. We are surprised that not everyone agrees what these products and services shall be. Such issues have social, political, and economic ramifications. For example, *peaceful* means "peace-keeping" to many people. And thus the national defense budget consumes over three-fourths of the personal income tax collected yearly.[13] We may agree to provide goods and services to the weaker members of the world: the needy, the disabled, the elderly, the unwanted young, the uneducated, the poor, the imprisoned. But then our tax bill comes and we rebel. According to the United Nations Center for Disarmament,

> The money required to provide adequate food, water, education, health and housing for everyone in the world has been estimated at about $18.5 billion a year. It is a huge sum of money . . . about as much as the world spends on arms every two weeks.[14]

In the extreme view, we are caught in a bind of building/producing/providing more and more of what we could perhaps use less and less of. We exhaust ourselves and the environment to keep the economy going. When we get to the ultimate point (the one just before "no return"), will we have to start paying to dismantle it all? Garrett DeBell fantasizes this happening in "A Future That Makes Ecological Sense." Maybe it has already started: A parking lot in Yosemite National Park has been turned into a meadow.[15]

At any rate, a national and global clarification of values continues. Your individual soul-searching will add to the pool of collective wisdom. Again, how much of what things do you want and need? How do your choices fit the global view? How do these choices affect your soul?

THE WORK ETHIC:
A PERSONAL PHILOSOPHIC VIEW

An integral part of our value system and a reflection of our personal growth is our attitude toward work, our *work ethic.* Is work really necessary? Is it valuable? Is it demeaning? Enhancing? Often we are ambivalent. Vocational educator Terrence E. Carroll says, "Work is necessary, of course, and sometimes enjoyable. However, there is no intrinsic virtue in work in and of itself. Virtue is attached to it by individual attitudes that have been learned, and the fact that a great many individuals in our society share that attitude does not mean either that all people should share it or that it is even a healthy attitude for all who do. The human personality is capable of enjoyment and was meant to enjoy, not merely to consume; to create, not merely to produce."[16] Edward Kennedy recounts how, during his first campaign for the U.S. Senate, his opponent said scornfully in a debate, "This man has never worked a day in his life!" Kennedy says that the next morning as he was shaking hands at a factory gate, one worker leaned toward him and confided, "You ain't missed a goddamned thing."[17]

Not everyone shares Carroll's attitude toward work, of course. (Thar's them 'ats fer it, 'n them 'ats agin it.) The strong work ethic in America stems from early colonial days, when the maxim "idleness is the Devil's workshop" was a truth not to be questioned, nor was Ben Franklin's dictum, "Time is money." Americans value those who have "made it" and look down upon poor achievers with feelings ranging from compassion to moral outrage. People should do their work as a God-given duty, they believe, and only then can they expect a just reward: happiness and a home in the suburbs. So goes the common thinking. Thus, by and large, we are work addicts—striving, struggling, even being ruthless and immoral to succeed. (Work itself sometimes becomes the Devil's workshop!)

The backlash from our national policies and attitudes has been vividly described in *Work in America,* a Special Task Force report to the Secretary of Health, Education and Welfare:

> Because work is central to the lives of most Americans, either the absence of work or employment in meaningless work is creating an increasingly intolerable situation. The human costs of this state of affairs are manifested in worker alienation, alcoholism, drug addiction, and other symptoms of poor mental health. Moreover, much of our tax money is expended in an effort to compensate for problems with at least a part of their genesis in the world of work. A great part of the staggering national bill in the areas of crime and delinquency, mental and physical health, manpower and welfare are generated in our national policies and attitudes toward work. Likewise, industry is paying for its continued attachment to Tayloristic practices* through low worker productivity and high rates of sabotage,

absenteeism, and turnover. Unions are paying through the faltering loyalty of a young membership that is increasingly concerned about the apparent disinterest of its leadership in problems of job satisfaction. Most important, there are the high costs of lost opportunities to encourage citizen participation: the discontent of women, minorities, blue-collar workers, youth, and older adults would be considerably less were these Americans to have had an active voice in the decisions in the workplace that most directly affect their lives.[18]

Mainly, however, we seem to be in a period of rising expectation about ourselves and about work, even in a frequently shaky job market. As T. George Harris, former editor of *Psychology Today,* once said, "We were doing all right until some idiot raised the ante on what it takes to be a person and the rest of us accepted it without noticing."

Well, why not? Why not expand our vision? "The true person is as yet a dream of the future." Why keep that idea forever in the future? Why not begin to make it a present reality? The premise of this manual is that work—and maybe even life—can be a joy! For the first time in history we can allow ourselves the luxury of considering work as fulfilling. And each person will find that fulfillment in a unique and special way.

If we can find a place where we feel some measure of success, some value, we shall find new energy to put into our work. Dr. Hans Selye describes the relationship between aging, work, and stress: "Work wears you out mainly through the frustrations of failure. Most of the eminent among hard workers in almost any field lived a long life. Since work is a basic need of man, the question is not whether to work but what kind of work is play."[19] And Yehudi Menuhin expresses it well when he says, "All my life I have reveled in the sound of the violin."

We have many resources of mind and spirit. Can we move to a place of greater joy in work and in life? Personal growth is essential. Each person can help by expanding his/her awareness of self and others. We seem to long for a less pressured, more serene life, with less frantic activity. Busy people are asserting their need for daily meditation, yoga, exercise, or other forms of relaxation to help them get in touch with deeper values.

We have merely touched the surface of a few of the concerns, global and personal, that relate to work. But each individual must garner the courage to fashion a meaningful existence, to find the balance between personal needs and the needs of others. We are responsible to ourselves for the quality of our own lives. We can be friends or enemies to ourselves by the choices we make, which in turn make up the lives we live. Real caring about ourselves is the first step in caring for others and in solving global concerns.

May your career choice contribute to your dream of the future.

---

*Standardization/mechanization of work duties, time, and tools.

Self-Assessment Exercises

The following exercises are designed to help you with your inward search. Use *only the ones that are useful to you. You may not need to do them all.* Chapter 9, "Work Affects the Soul: The Final Analysis," has been set aside for summaries of some of the Self-Assessment Exercises. You may note the results of your surveys there as you finish each chapter. Or you may wait until you reach the end of the book and then go back and collect them all. It's up to you.

1. Tapping into Feelings

How do you habitually respond to life situations? Do feelings get in your way and block your effectiveness? What would you like to change?

> a. Place a check (√) in front of any words in the following list that describe your habitual responses.
> b. Place an X in front of those words that describe feelings and attitudes you would like to eliminate.
> c. Place a plus (+) in front of those words that describe responses you would like to expand.

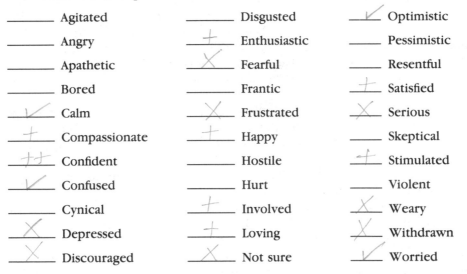

	Agitated		Disgusted	✓	Optimistic
	Angry	+	Enthusiastic		Pessimistic
	Apathetic	X	Fearful		Resentful
	Bored		Frantic	+	Satisfied
✓	Calm	X	Frustrated	X	Serious
+	Compassionate	+	Happy		Skeptical
++	Confident		Hostile	+	Stimulated
✓	Confused		Hurt		Violent
	Cynical	+	Involved	X	Weary
X	Depressed	+	Loving	X	Withdrawn
X	Discouraged	X	Not sure	✓	Worried

Most people have feelings that contradict each other. You can feel discouraged and optimistic at the same time. Even when change takes place, old habits pop up when least expected. Not too many people are perfect! Begin where you feel most comfortable by picking *one* improvement you'd like to make. Describe some specific, practical steps you can take to carry it out. Then take the key

Well, what have we here?

word from the list and write it in a prominent place as a reminder, e.g., on the bathroom mirror. Write all your changes here.

    a. I'd like to stop being so: _____ *Serious* _____

    b. I'd like to become more: _____ *Confident - Happy* _____

2. Life Problems Checklist

    a. Identify the factors holding you back. Rate the items listed on the next page by checking the appropriate columns: I am happy with; I am managing with; I'm having trouble with. Year + = this problem has been going on for a year or more; chronic = this problem has been constant for a great deal of my life.

	Happy	Managing	Trouble	Year +	Chronic
1. Parents/brothers/sisters	✓				
2. Spouse/children				✓	
3. Family closeness	✓				
4. Friends/relationships/love	✓				
5. Privacy/freedom				✓	
6. Dwelling		✓			
7. Work				✓	
8. Finances		✓			
9. Personal achievements/success			✓		
10. Confidence					✓
11. Health		✓			
12. Diet/drugs/drinking/smoking	✓				
13. Exercise			✓		
14. Your appearance		✓			
15. Physical well-being	✓				
16. Hectic lifestyle		✓			
17. Recreation/hobbies			✓		
18. Spiritual/religious well-being	✓				
19. Emotional/mental well-being				✓	
20. Status	✓				
21. Intellectual ability	✓				
22. Artistic ability		✓			
23. Education		✓			
24. Social concern		✓			
25. Political concern		✓			

b. Circle the number of the items you would like to change. Perhaps see a counselor to discuss your feelings. It's easier to make a good career decision if anxieties are not getting in the way.

3. Needs, Wants, Shoulds, and Values: Dream Your Goals

a. Survival Needs Plus: Your Enriched Wants Reflect Your Values

What lifestyle is important to you? Dream—let your imagination soar—describe your ideal.

Your home _Comfortable, lg (not hudge), warm, nice things w/shrubs + bkg_

Your clothing _in style - be able to have the right thing for each occass._

Your food _not elaborate, well balanced - healthy_

Your family _Close, happy, loving, sharing_

Your friends _" " " " "_

Your associates _Support, guidance for growth,_

Your transportation _Jaguar " -_

Your pets/plants _none - maybe later_

Your gadgets and playthings _VCR - CD player,_

Your activities _tennis, travel, school_

Other _____

b. People Needs

What do you expect from each group around you, e.g., family, friends, associates? What would you like to change?

to be there when I need them & know they may need me. To feel love + respected. I wish family could be together more often -

c. Fulfillment Needs/Wants

Dream again! If you could instantly be in the career/lifestyle of your choice, already skilled and trained, what would you do:

1. To amaze your family and friends and delight yourself?

glamorus executive in fashion world
or art world –

2. To improve the world:

teach, counsel, head up charities
for poor

d. List and examine the shoulds that hold you back. Are they related to values? Can you drop or change them to wants?

_____

_____

e. Take charge! Today, what specific steps, little or big, can you take to improve your life?

Counseling, exercise, school

_____

_____

_____

f. Today, what immediate and specific steps, little or big, can you take to make your world a better place?

Start at church – youth, needy

_____

_____

g. Check the balance in your life. What do you do, over and above absolute need, to contribute to your well-being on each of the following four levels?

Physical _Started Jogging_

Emotional _seeking Counseling_

Intellectual _____

Altruistic _involved heavily in church – ministry_

4. Rating Values

Here are six incomplete sentences that encourage you to think about values. In the lists that follow each one, check (√) *every* word that finishes the statement correctly *for you* as you or your life are *now*. Put a plus sign (+) in front of every word that describes things you would like to *develop more.* Feel free to add, delete, or change words on each list.

a. Career values: In my career, I do (√); I would like to (+):

_____ Create ideas	_____ Create beauty
_____ Make things	_____ Explore ideas
_____ Design systems	_√_ Follow directions
+√ Help people	_____ Take responsibility
_√_ Perform physical tasks	_+_ Experience variety
_+_ Organize things	_+_ Improve society

b. Result values: I have (√); I'd like to have (+):

_+_ Adventure	_√+_ Money
_√_ Beautiful surroundings	_√_ Pleasure
_√_ Comfort	_____ Power
_+_ Fun	_√_ Possessions
_+_ Happiness	_+_ Prestige
_+_ Independence	_+_ Security
_+_ Leisure time	_√_ Structure

c. Personal qualities: I am (√); I'd like to be more (+):

_√_ Accepting	_√_ Honest
_+_ Ambitious	_√_ Intelligent
_√_ Affectionate	_+_ Joyful
_√_ Balanced	_√_ Kind
_√_ Brave	_√_ Loyal
_√_ Caring	_√+_ Mature
_____ Competitive	_√_ Neat
_+_ Confident	_√_ Needed
_√_ Conscientious	_+_ Peaceful
_√_ Cooperative	_√_ Poised
_√_ Courteous	_√_ Prompt

_+_ Creative   _++_ Self-accepting

_++_ Decisive   _✓_ Sensitive

_✓_ Disciplined   _+_ Strong

_✓_ Efficient   _+_ Successful

_✓_ Enthusiastic   _✓_ Trusting

____ Famous   _✓_ Understanding

_✓_ Good looking   _✓_ Verbal

_✓_ Healthy   _✓_ Warm

_✓_ Friendly   _++_ Wise

d. People satisfiers: I have (√) good relationships with; I'd like good relationships with (+):

_+_ Spouse/lover   _✓_ Children

_✓_ Relatives   _✓_ Friends

_✓_ Parents   _✓_ Neighbors

_✓_ Siblings   _✓_ Colleagues

_+_ In-laws   _++_ Supervisors

e. Personal growth satisfiers: I am satisfied with my development in (√); I'd
like to develop more in (+):

_+_ Physical   _+_ Intellectual

_+_ Emotional   _+_ Altruistic/spiritual

f. Global values: I am working toward (√); I would like to work more toward
(+):

_+_ Arms control   ____ Industrial development

_✓_ Brotherhood   _+✓_ Peace

_+_ Economic   ____ Prosperity
    development

_+_ Environmental   ____ Technological
    preservation   development

_✓_ Harmony   _+_ World food supply

_+_ Human rights   _+_ World order

g. Star (*) your top three values in each section a–f. Tell someone (or write a paper, perhaps your autobiography in Exercise 8), describing who you are using these value words. Explain any value contradictions.

5. Drawing a Self-Portrait

a. Your Free Spirit Years

Between the ages of five to ten, what activities did you enjoy the most? Remember various seasons, indoors, outdoors; remember friends you played with. Check (√) the things you enjoyed the most.

b. Your Life Line

Beginning with the "young childhood" period, draw a "life line" representing the ups and downs of your experience at various times of your life. Draw your first impressions without concern about detail.

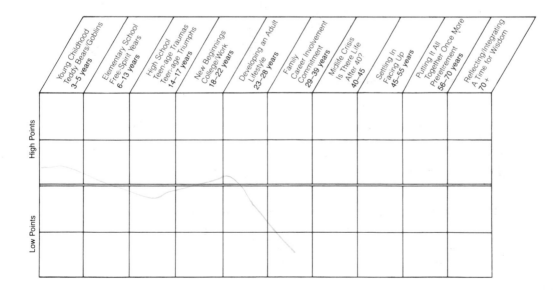

1. List the low points/disappointments:

low self esteem - parents fighting
not "popular" - shy
ardesissive - marriage fail -
financial burden

2. List the high points/successes:

intellectual stimulation - new love
life, giving more self confidence

3. List your most important life decisions:

go to college
to get married
have a child
grow up on my own!
becoming Catholic

4. List three to five people who influenced you the most at each stage (include teachers, authors, etc.). Tell what they did. Rate the importance of their influence now by:

   1 = Very important   3 = So-so

   2 = Important   4 = No longer important

mom - encouraged   1
michael - love   1
Teacher   encouraged   2
Fr. Dave - Spiritual Growth 1

6. Candid Camera—3-D

Each activity you've chosen to do contains important clues about you, your skills, and your interests. This exercise will be one of the first steps on the road to career decision making. It is also the first step toward preparing a résumé and getting ready for an interview. Your life in 3-D will help you discover who you are, decide your goals, design your strategies.

Spend an intense hour doing this exercise as outlined here. Use scratch paper. Then save it and add to it, refine it, and organize it according to the exercises that follow.

1. *Loves:* Make a list of activities you love to do, not *like or should* but *love.*
2. *Jobs:* List every job you've held for pay, way back to babysitting/lawn mowing.
3. *Other:* List extracurricular activities, community volunteer jobs, hobbies done at home or on vacation, sports, anything you've done that is important to you.

Then take a separate sheet of scratch paper for each of these items and begin to list what you did to accomplish each activity. For example, if skiing is on your list, you might say: buying equipment, doing fitness exercises, deciding where to go, making reservations, budgeting funds, what else?

Become aware of the times when you are dealing with People and Things. Notice when you are dealing with ideas and information alone—as, for example, in reading analyzing, and organizing material, just what this exercise requires. You will see that in dealing with people and things, you always need ideas and information. Then code each activity D, P, or T.

P = activities when you deal directly with PEOPLE
T = activities when you deal directly with THINGS
D = activities when you deal with IDEAS and INFORMATION alone, called DATA

7. Your Data File

Here are some examples of file cards done by students. They summarize activities performed in various jobs, some of them volunteer. Notice that any activity can be expanded with more detail. Make a file card for each of your important jobs and activities.

Drug Abuse Prevention Center
374 Snow Valley Lane
New Castle, DE 19720
(302)555-1212

Supervisor:
Virginia Anderson
Salary: volunteer
Dates: Jan 1988
to the present

Title: Community worker
- Screen clients
- Lead groups
- Design publicity folders
- Give talks to high school/junior high
- Refer to other agencies
- Handle hot line

INK, Inc.
53 Route 128
So. Deerfield, MA 01373
(413)555-1212

Supervisor: Bozo Brown
Salary: $19,800
Dates: Apr 16, 1986- present

Job Title: Material Planner- Production/Inventory Control
- Initiate purchases
- Plan projects
- Count Inventory
- Process MTX on computer
- Balance inventory accounts
- Write out paperwork for assemblies
- Coordinate buildings of assays
- Write old and new reports on computer
- Pull kits
- Fill shortages
- File paperwork
- Write up TR cards
- Research shortages
- Research processing errors

Flora Fauna Wood
436 Eureka Canyon Road
Pendleton, OR 97801
(503)555-1212

Owner/mgr Quin Hill
Salary: $30,000
Dates: 1956 - Present

Job Title: Sales Manager

- Administered warehouse/market orders
- maintained and expanded old business
- Bid on new contracts with public agencies, private companies
- Resolved customer complaints
- Arranged for demonstration of products
- Hired/trained sales personnel

8. Creating an Autobiography

Many people find that creating an autobiography is a valuable way to rediscover themselves. Use one of these suggestions.

a. Simply write the story of your life.

b. Write a summary of Exercise 5b, "Your Life Line."

c. Using Exercise 5b, "Your Life Line," write about the people who influenced you. What were their messages to you?

d. Make a poster or collage out of magazines or old pictures that illustrate you and your life line.

e. Use the three circles as a basis for an autobiography. Discuss each item in the past, present, and future circles as it applies to your life.

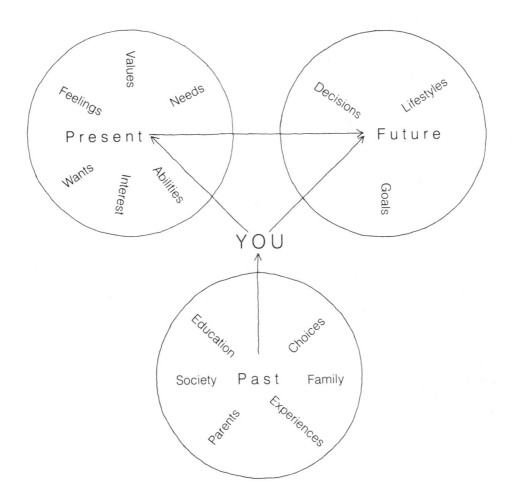

f. Create a personal "I Wheel" like the one shown here.

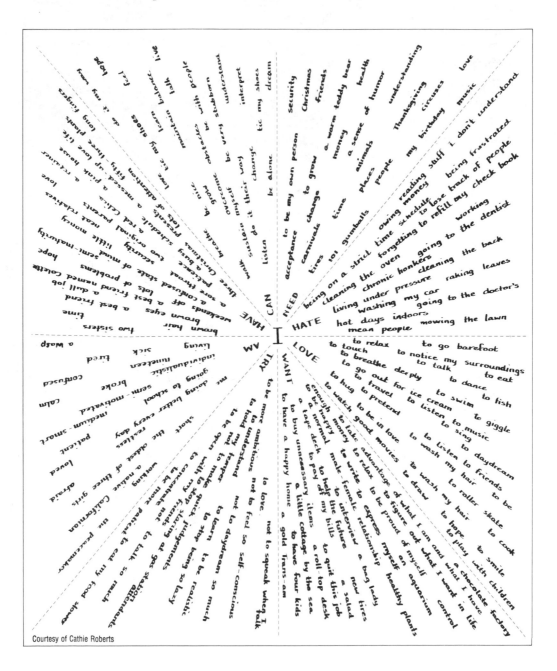

Courtesy of Cathie Roberts

Group Discussion Questions

In addition to these group discussion questions, share with others the exercises in this and all the chapters.

1. What is the connection between our needs and wants and the work we and others do?

2. What limits and demands do your personal wants place on your career choice?

3. Name the last five items you've purchased. What basic needs did they fulfill? What wants? Could you get along without them for a year?

4. List all the devices in your home that use electricity. On a scale of 1 to 10, rate how necessary each appliance is to you. If you could use only five, which ones would you choose? Is electricity a basic human need?

5. Fantasize about the changes you would make if you had to keep all your discards and throw nothing away. How would your lifestyle change? Do we ever *really* throw anything away completely? Explain.

6. What products do you consider useless? Harmful? What would happen if people stopped buying them? What would happen to workers making them? What is the solution?

7. How were seven basic workplace functions carried out in early human societies: business, industry, education, entertainment/communication, health, government, and military? What are the major differences in the way work was carried out in prehistoric times and now?

8. Do the basic human needs change over time?

9. How can meeting the needs of all the earth's people increase our personal security?

10. Give as many answers as you can to this question: Why do we work?

2

ROLES AND REALITIES: SINKING THE STEREOTYPES

F O C U S

Review common stereotypes.

Examine roles that people play.

Consider changes/attitudes about roles.

39

• • • • •

It's easy to overlook some important factors in making a career decision. One of these, deeply imbedded in your being, motivated by your needs and wants and closely related to your values, has to do with the *roles* you play. Everyone functions in a variety of roles: male, female, mother, father, spouse, child, student, senior citizen, disabled, minority, immigrant/refugee— plus career roles, from accountant to zookeeper. People play these roles for many reasons. Some roles they're born into, others they feel pressured to assume, and still others they choose freely. Years and years and layers and layers of conditioning can cause stereotypes to limit your thinking about these roles.

People seldom feel they make decisions based on stereotypes, but everybody does. Stereotyping is a way of understanding and organizing information. Here are some obvious and useful stereotypes: A doctor can fix your sagging back, a carpenter can fix your sagging door. But some stereotypes are based on faulty assumptions: For example, women can't handle engineering because they can't do math and are "too emotional"; men should always know how to fix things and should never, never cry!

One very pervasive stereotype that still influences career and lifestyle choice is that of the "American Dream." Evolving after World War II, it indicated that just about everyone would live in a cozy house in the suburbs with two cars in the garage and two bright, healthy children: an older boy and a younger girl. Father commuted to work in a proper suit and tie and worked hard supporting his family as a successful manager. His loving wife "did not work" but stayed at home, dusting up a bit, attending to child problems, preparing each day for her husband's return to their little nest. If she ever worked, it was at a "feminine" position and only temporarily, until she could entrust herself to the care of a man. Marriage meant "living happily ever after."

But since the mid-1960s, there have been sweeping changes in the institutions of marriage and family: more divorce, remarriage, single parenthood, delayed marriage and postponed childbearing. More people, especially the elderly, the disabled, minorities, immigrants, and refugees, are poor and isolated from the mainstream of society. Societal problems of increased permissiveness, irresponsible sex, drugs, crime, violence, and a shaky economy can make a person timid about career and lifestyle decisions. Thus the American Dream, which we had assumed was the "average American" way of life, turns out to be the 7 percent stereotype and therefore a myth for most people.

OLD IMAGES, NEW IMPERATIVES

Every person, no matter what his/her roles, has hopes and dreams that can be actualized through career and life choices. In this chapter you can look at each role as it relates to you and those around you. You can gain an understanding of the struggles that others experience in achieving their goals. You may be able to pinpoint ways to avoid some of these problems for yourself.

Male/Female Roles

At every age and every stage of life, male/female roles are most basic. Daniel J. Levinson writes, in *The Seasons of a Man's Life,* "During the last several hundred years, there has been a slow reduction in the ancient gender distinctions. There is greater recognition that women are not categorically different from men, that they have much the same desires as men and can develop much the same skills."[1] No one has ever been able to prove how many of our male/female attitudes and behaviors derive from societal expectations and how many from our physical makeup. But almost everyone has strong opinions about this issue. Consider the battle to pass the Equal Rights Amendment. It has touched on the deepest issues about the ways in which men and women view themselves. It has raised questions that we will be trying to answer for years to come.

Our experience tells us that both male and female behavior can be found all along a spectrum. This spectrum ranges from the Victorian myth of the fragile, fainting female to the tough "Annie, Get Your Gun!" figure; from the "Little Lord Fauntleroy" sissy male, getting sand kicked in his face on the beach, to the gun-toting, mighty, macho male. In the case of both males and females the range runs from timid to tough.

You play your role according to a variety of images you've absorbed over time. Where are you on the Timid/Tough Spectrum (Figure 2-1)? As people become more educated, they tend to move somewhat toward the middle. Most realize that they need to balance these extreme qualities to survive modern life. Yet many tough men and women feel they need to fight the world to protect themselves, and many timid men and women run and hide for protection. But it can be just as dangerous to your personal safety to be armed to the teeth for battle as it is to be cowardly.

No matter how wide a range of behavior both men and women display, the truth is that in today's job market men are wa-a-a-ay ahead of women in earnings and job status. Early expectations have encouraged men to aim for success and prestige and women to downplay their role as achievers. Women typically say things like, "I could never do math!" or, "I'm so helpless around machinery!" and finally, "I'm just a housewife!" But frustration over past inequities is beside the point. Let's look at some facts about the status of women in relationship to men today—facts that don't fit the stereotype in the American Dream. Of necessity, the discussion will focus on the dilemma of being female in the workplace.

Women's Work: Cut Out for Them. The statistics on women and men show a discouraging picture for women. Rarely have women's rights come easily. The

• •
FIGURE 2-1 The Timid/Tough Spectrum

Here are some words to describe people along the Timid/Tough Spectrum.

The Fragile, Fainting Female The "Little Lord Fauntleroy," Sissy Male	The Humorous, Humane Human	The Mighty, Macho Male The "Annie, Get Your Gun" Female
Timid	**Assertive/Balanced**	**Tough**
soft	strong	powerful
cowardly	confident	tough
dependent	equal	superior
gives up	persistent effort	keeps going beyond reason
aloof	cooperative	competitive
overwhelmed by harsh feelings	accepts all feelings	denies tender feelings
motivated by approval	self-motivated	motivated by power/money/fear
acts emotionally	blends intuition and logic	acts rationally
sacrifices all	asks for what is needed	demands all
manipulates	cooperates	dominates
withdraws	negotiates	attacks
inept, insecure	learning, open, growing	knows all, can do all
rigid	spontaneous	reckless

The Timid Person	The Assertive Person	The Tough, Aggressive Person
is	*is*	*is*
indirect, inhibited, self-conscious, unsure	direct, clear, open, centered, accepting	direct, overbearing, domineering, controlling, insensitive
and feels	*and feels*	*and feels*
tearful, shaky, angry, hurt	strong, buoyant, self-respecting, confident	angry, explosive, superior, demanding, pseudo-confident
and experiences	*and experiences*	*and experiences*
uncertainty, domination, disregard, disrespect, annoyance from others.	acceptance, clarity, respect, cooperation from others.	lack of cooperation, isolation, confusion, anger, hurt, guilt from others.

Where are you on the Timid/Tough Spectrum?
Where would you like to be?

◄———————————————————————————————►
TIMID   BALANCED   TOUGH

Keeping Up

"Very pleased to meet you. What does your husband do?"

early history of the United States saw women struggling for their place as achievers and movers in the larger society. Abigail Adams, for example, wrote to her husband John, the country's second president (1797–1801), interceding for women's rights. At age seventy-two, Elizabeth Cady Stanton, speaking to the International Council of Women, said, "The younger women are starting with great advantages over us. They have the results of our experience; they have superior opportunities for education; they will find a more enlightened public sentiment for discussion; they will have more courage to take the rights which belong to them. . . . Thus far, women have been the mere echoes of men. Our laws and constitution, our creeds and codes, and the customs of social life are all of masculine origin. The true woman is as yet a dream of the future." Somehow that quotation sounds more recent than 1888! In the 1980s, the true

• • • • • •   **Men and Women in the Workplace: Fifteen Facts**

1. Fifty-one percent of the U.S. population is female; 49 percent is male. Forty-four percent of all workers are women. Fifty percent of black, 44 percent of white, and 39 percent of Hispanic workers are women.

2. More than 90 percent of all women work sometime in their lives, two-thirds out of economic necessity because they are single, divorced, widowed, or married to men earning less than $15,000 per year.

3. Women accounted for nearly 66 percent of the increase in the civilian labor force between 1970 and 1984—about 18 million women compared with more than 12 million men.

4. The life expectancy of a female born in 1982 is 78.8 years. In 1920 it was 55 years. The life expectancy of a male born in 1982 is 71.5 years. In 1920 it was 54 years.

5. The average woman worker 16 years of age in 1979-80 could expect to spend 29.3 years in the labor force, compared with 39.1 years for a man the same age. The length of work tenure is closer to men's for younger women.

6. The average woman worker is as well educated as the average man worker; both had completed a median of 12.8 years of schooling as of March 1985.

7. Many women tend to cluster in low-paying, dead-end, nonpensioned jobs. Eighty percent work in administrative support (including clerical), with only 8 percent in precision production, craft, and repair. They were 69 percent of all retail and personal services sales workers, but only 36 percent of all executives, administrators, and managers. They were 6.4 percent of all apprentices in 1985. As a result, the average woman worker earns only 64 percent of what a man earns, even when both work full time year round, and this discrepancy is shrinking slowly if at all. A man, then, earns 156 percent the salary of a woman.

8. Fifteen percent of women workers are unionized. These women earn 33 percent higher salaries, have better benefits, and have recourse to grievance procedures.

9. The median income in 1984:

All women	$14,780	All men	$23,218
White women	14,904	White men	23,962
Black women	13,720	Black men	16,940
Hispanic women	12,545	Hispanic men	16,636

10. Percent of unemployment:

Teenagers (16–19)		Adults (20 years +)	
Black men	41	Black men	13.2
Black women	39.2	Black women	13.1
Hispanic men	24.7	Hispanic women	9.9
Hispanic women	23.8	Hispanic men	9.1
White men	16.5	White women	5.7
White women	14.8	White men	5.4

11. One percent of women and 12 percent of men earn more than $25,000 a year.

12. Women tend to change occupations more often in order to obtain some of the better jobs opening up for them.

13. About 28 percent of all women workers in nonagricultural industries held part-time jobs, (less than 35 hours per week) in 1985, 76 percent of this number on a voluntary basis. More than 66 percent of all part-time workers were women.

14. A nurse with 14.2 years of education earns 5.8 percent less than a deliveryman. A secretary with 13.2 years of education earns less than a truck driver with 9 years of education. Salary based on comparable worth, equal pay for equivalent work, is being adjusted slowly, piece by piece, in a small number of places.

15. According to the United Nations' Women's Conference (1980), two out of every three illiterates in the world are women. Although women account for one-third of the labor force, they put in two-thirds of the work hours, earn one-tenth of the world's income, and own less than 1 percent of the property.[2]

woman is still a "dream of the future."[3] Today women still have little voice in government decision and policy making.

Eighty percent of women still tend to cluster in low-paying, low-status, stereotypical jobs. They still receive different education, training, and counseling than men. They work less overtime because of such factors as family care. They get started later in their careers for the same reason. Many women lack confidence in their abilities, and experience fear and ambivalence. Men's salaries increase dramatically with a BA or BS degree, women's only modestly. Only with advanced degrees does the gap narrow.

In the 1970s and early 1980s, inflation accelerated the movement of women into the workplace. Many older women who had been neither socialized nor educated to see themselves in careers have headed for low-paying, dead end jobs. But younger women have begun to have a different perspective. Planning for a career is higher on their agendas. Older women with experience are also moving up in the workplace. The general trend is toward improvement and opportunity for working women. Though people are concerned that men will be pushed out of jobs if too many women come into the labor market and also that wages will fall, women must work mainly because they must to survive. Their economic condition has improved little in the last two and one half decades, even as their needs have increased. Barbara R. Bergman, speaking on the economics of the women's movement, estimates that if the 40-hour work week fell to 31, all potential workers could be accommodated and end up with more leisure. She adds that working women use more goods and services, not fewer, thus further increasing productivity.[4] Many inequities must be addressed before equality in the workplace is a reality. By 1990, 72.4 percent of women between the ages of 25 and 54 will be working, mostly at traditional jobs. They will comprise 45 percent of the workplace.[5] Yet by the year 2000 women will be known as the "new poor."

New Directions for Men.   While women are trying to define new roles, men also face dilemmas because their roles have been geared to a timetable that did not always fit personal needs. Because society says their careers are primary and their families secondary, men have to keep on working and moving up the ladder of success until they are forced to retire. But we are becoming aware that a man's whole future isn't determined when he chooses a career, and the white male executive doesn't always rise to the top in an easy, direct ascent if he rises at all.

Levinson writes in *The Seasons of a Man's Life* that male adult development takes place in three overlapping, age-linked eras marking early, middle, and late adulthood. Many men experience traumatic crises as they make the thirties, forties (midlife), and sixties transitions. During these times, many men reevaluate at least two and possibly three components of their lifestyles. Career is most important as a vehicle for contributing to society and fulfilling a person's dream about himself. Marriage and family are usually an integral support for this dream. Friendships/peer relationships, ethnicity/religion, and sometimes leisure—especially sports—come in for their share of scrutiny.

Decisions made at these times are linked to values and are highly interrelated. Salary, prestige, commuting time, overtime, pressure, travel, and colleagues all have an impact, positive or negative, on family life. Approaching the final settling-down period of life with a life structure that doesn't live up to expectations can prove intolerable for many men.[6]

Much energy goes into the daily competition for success in the marketplace. Men who have made it have to work to keep it. For men, making business contacts is as natural as breathing. Or is it? The stereotype is that the old boys' network begins at age six with the soccer team and works its way up to the college/military fraternity. The hearty handshake and exchange of business cards isn't the road to success for every male, however, and images like these put needless pressure on many men to achieve, especially minorities with little access to the power structure. Many feel hostile at now having to share a piece of the pie with women and, in some cases, to be passed by while a woman is promoted. Often men come to a dead end where no more promotions are possible, and they have to relinquish their life amibitions. The same old job has become too familiar; all the challenge is gone. Like many women, many men feel trapped in monotonous, demanding, or demeaning jobs. Many workers of both sexes seem dissatisfied with their jobs.

Unfortunately, career success does not prevent the crisis. Some men achieve their long-sought goals only to ask, "Was it worth it?" Perhaps they have moved up into administration and now find themselves in prestigious positions they do not enjoy. Sometimes these jobs involve long hours, trips away from home, and frequent moving. The result may be alienation from the family—a loss of nurturing that can be critical, especially in times of crisis. Many marriages don't survive this stress.

In the past, whether equal to the task or not, men have had full economic responsibility for their families. Often they were expected to spend weekends and vacations doing heavy work at home, with little time for rest and recreation. As children grew older and required less care, a husband may have resented a wife who stayed home enjoying her leisure and playing cards with her friends. Culturally conditioned to deny many human feelings, men are allowed to get angry but not to show fears or tears. The successful man as well as the unsuccessful may be leading a life of quiet desperation.

Yet some of these alternatives may seem frightening. Changing careers may mean stepping down, with a resulting loss of income and possibly a sense of defeat. Instead of retraining for a new line of work, the dissatisfied working man may decide to "stick it out" until retirement or to look for a new company with a fresh outlook. He seems to have fewer choices than his wife, who can change her life dramatically by going back to college or taking a job outside the home. In most instances the immediate goal for both husband and wife is not

A Man Speaks

I followed all the rules this culture of the mid-twentieth century laid down for a man to follow. Many choices, many moves, many promotions, many setbacks later I faced divorce and starting over. Funds needed to get a business going well were absorbed in the settlement. The business and I struggled on for two years, finding the drastic and unwanted change of lifestyle almost too much. A rest, a reassessment, a different career, a new marriage bring me into the present. I am in my fifties and already the promotion brings new duties that are stressful. Major family problems and worry about retirement bring new levels of confusion.

I feel that a man over fifty is supposed to know everything and be there for everyone to lean on. My "shoulds" include the dictum that a man cannot show emotion, a man cannot cry, a man cannot be weak. These are my unwritten laws. They were molded into the framework of this growing manchild from birth. To change them is sacriligious—unheard of. A man with unwritten laws hanging over his head, yet he has to learn how to cry and show emotion. He has to learn to deal with his anger. And most of all, a man has to learn to say, "I really don't know everything about that subject." It is not easy being a man in a man's world that is being *invaded* [italics added] by women. The rules have changed. To survive, a man must change.

Leo L. Pavlovich

self-actualization but paying off the mortgage, educating the children, and caring for elderly parents.

But midlife can be a special time, a time to realize that *dis*-illusionment means seeing more clearly. It is a time to reorder values, build confidence, face areas of deficiency, and develop neglected segments of life. Midlife can be a healing time, a time for growth, a time to befriend yourself by putting your world into perspective—a time to ask, "What do I really want out of life?"

As they face the issues and *grow* through this crisis, some men develop a new, deeper, more mature outlook that restores their energy and vitality. Some are surprised to learn that they need better skills in human relations and communications, instead of a new job or a new kind of work. Some find the courage to make needed changes in work or home life, go back to school, break out of old patterns. The need to let go of the past is a common human experience that can bring us closer to the real meaning of life. Learning this and not feeling that you should "have it all together" once and for all can be liberating. Both men

"It seems like only yesterday I was on the verge of getting it all together."

and women need support when they are experiencing these critical periods in the normal course of human development.

DON'T LET LIFE

discourage you;
everyone who got where he is
had to begin where he was.

—RICHARD L. EVANS

Family, Career, or Both. Each person has to resolve basic questions involving family versus career while attempting to fulfill needs and wants. In the past, men found themselves on a career path early in life, supporting a wife who reared the children. But the questioning sixties seemed to turn all the guideposts around as choices multiplied. These issues are many and complex. Their solutions will be found by the usual muddling that takes place in human existence. And for the majority, the results will continue to be unclear.

FAMILY PORTRAITS: U.S.A.

- Only 7 percent of American families have a working father, a dependent mother, and two children.

- From 1970 to 1985, nonfamily households increased 62 percent while family households decreased 13 percent.

- The number of working wives increased from 40 percent in 1972 to 54 percent in 1984. In 1984, the median income for two-earner families was $34,668 compared to $23,582 for married-couple families without the wife in the paid labor force.

- Some 1984 median incomes:

White family	$27,686
Black family	$15,432
Hispanic family	$18,833

- Sixty-two percent of women with children under 18 and 54 percent with preschool children were working as of March 1985. Eighty-four percent could find no government licensed day care in 1980; its availability has decreased even further since 1981. Six million children under age thirteen do not have access to child care.

- Fifty-one percent of all working women are married; 49 percent are single, widowed, or divorced, many with dependent children.

- Fewer Americans got married in 1985 than at any time in nearly a decade, and the divorce rate edged upward by 2 percent. The divorce rate was half the marriage rate.

- One year after divorce, women and minor children in their households experience a 73 percent decline in standard of living and men a 42 percent rise.

Family life fulfills some of the deepest longings of men and women. It fulfills needs and wants on many levels for physical, emotional, intellectual, and altruistic/spiritual support and growth. Families are those people who, theoretically, see a person through the ups and downs of life and are enduringly present in a special way.

Today we see people opting for all sorts of new family lifestyles: from traditional marriage to live-in roommates; from large families to delayed families or no children by choice; from single parents to remarried parents, communal parenting to househusbanding. Divorce rates reach 50 percent of new marriages. But the questions men and women ask are vastly different. Women wonder if and how they can combine a family with a career. Men, remaining career

• Only about one-third of households with children and without fathers receive child support and one-third of these live in poverty. In 1984, fathers
owed $4 billion in child support per year.

• In 1984, 26 percent of children under eighteen were living in single-par-
ent families, mostly headed by women. In 1970, the comparable figure was
15 percent.

• Fifty-nine percent of all U.S. children born in 1983 will experience divorce
of parents before age eighteen. With 18.4 percent born out of wedlock,
the number of children spending childhood with both natural parents will
be a minority.

• Overall, 11.6 percent of families were living in poverty in 1984; 61 percent of all persons 16 years old and over living in poverty were women.

• Women maintained 8 percent of all families between 1940 and 1960. In
1984 the percentages of women heading families were:

All families	17%
Poor black	73%
Poor Hispanic	49%
Poor white	38%

Almost half of households headed by women are below the poverty line.
Though three-fifths of the women work, they earn 50 percent less than
men who head families.[7]

oriented, wonder if they need a family, especially one that might include a very
liberated wife.

Historically, a great number of American women do not marry and thus
must support themselves. In the early eighties, this figure was about 16 percent.[8] Many women, especially minorities and immigrants, have always worked
in factories and service jobs. Cottage industries were a way of life before the
industrial revolution, and even as late as the 1940s, farms (where women
worked beside men) claimed 25 percent of the population.

But it was only after World War II that the mythical woman whose stereotype still lingers evolved in the American Dream. Content to stay at home,
she was first a wife, next a mother, rarely herself as a woman. Her life was

defined by the roles of others, and she served their needs. Betty Friedan called this new role limitation, this problem that has no name, "the feminine mystique."[9] But it gradually began to occur to many that this American Dream person was not the "true woman." Certainly it described only a small percentage of women.

So even though it is still quite acceptable for a man to be career oriented, the ambivalence remains for a woman. She may forego marriage and children, opting for a full-time career. The struggle to "make it" is still greater for women than for men. If a woman chooses to marry and have children, she will be largely responsible for their care. Though in 1950 about 80 percent of American women had at least one child before they reached thirty, today it is only 60 percent and falling. Because of career and economic considerations, 20 percent of married women will never have a child.[10]

In most cases working wives and mothers can expect to carry the burden of household chores and child care. Working women don't have wives at home. Alice Cook, Cornell Professor and scholar in residence at Stanford University's Center for Research on Women, surveyed nineteen nations and published a report entitled *The Working Mother* in 1976. Her conclusion: "The husband spends very little more time assisting the wife and mother with household tasks when she works outside the home than when she does not."[11] A 1982 *Better Homes and Gardens* survey found most working women still caring for household tasks. Some younger and better-educated couples are an exception, but not yet numerous enough even today to affect the statistics significantly. More men are taking custody of children after divorce, a 30 percent increase from 1980 to 1984, but this is still miniscule since it represents an increase of children living with father of only 1.7 to 2.2 percent.[12]

Eve Steadman, a wife who returned to school, wrote this fantasy about men and housework:

Women have always worked. The term "working women" usually indicates that these women are working for pay and that they have some choice about the kind of work they will perform. Many years ago, when I felt trapped in a future of endless diapers, dishes, and debris, I used to speculate about what would happen if the work situation pushed upon women were also applied to men. First of all, men could have no choice; every man by virtue of his biology would have exactly the same work. Second, this work would be comparable with that of women, that is featuring monotony, drudgery, and repetition. Suppose, I thought, every man regardless of talents and interests were forced to be a ditchdigger. The man would not only dig all day, but every night while he slept someone would come by and push all the dirt back into the ditch! When he faced the dirt next morning, he would be expected to look glamorous and cheerful. Under these conditions, the Men's Revolution would not have been long in coming!

In the small nuclear family of today, full-time child rearing can be expected to take only seven to ten years of a seventy-five year existence. If a woman remains at home until age thirty-five or forty, she still has twenty-five to thirty years to fill with some kind of activity before she reaches retirement age. Men, even wealthy men, work. Why not women? The nuclear family makes even grandmothering a part-time job—if babysitting is needed at all, since grandmother and grandchildren may be living in widely separated geographic areas. Where kids once played and coffee flowed freely among friends, an empty nest in daytime-desolate suburbia can become the lot of the nonemployed middle-class woman.

Skills can get rusty and confidence eroded while women stay at home. Just getting dressed and leaving the house in the morning can be invigorating for some, especially when childrearing is finished. Work offers opportunity for personal growth and may make for happier wives and mothers than those who feel trapped at home.

Yet another question asks if paid work is the only activity that leads to fulfillment. Family and community involvement can also be enriching despite its financial sacrifice. Creative homemaking, generous volunteering, and meeting with like-minded people can be interesting and stimulating for some women, and even some men. Sometimes the items that are sacrificed by not working are simply those that "everybody has" and might not be all that necessary. Whether *things* are a good substitute for parental attention can be an important question. And parents have to weigh the advantages of being at home with children at those special and irreplaceable moments versus leaving them to someone else. And for the woman finished with childrearing, the empty nest may be a delight of peace and quiet after years of mothering.

For the mother with children still at home, working can sometimes be a bowl of lemons. One working mother, after dropping off her children in the morning at different schools, taking one to the dentist during lunch hour, and making a trip to the shoe store with another after work, arrived home at 6:30 to find her husband late and the refrigerator empty. She asked herself, "Is this liberation?"

Many women who have chosen motherhood are exploring viable ways to do it well and still have successful careers. Some employers let women work part time for a few years, share a job with another person, or act as consultants during the child rearing period. Studies show increased productivity as a surprising result of this flexibility.

Many husbands welcome the increased economic security that a wife's income provides. One man remarked that he "loves being dependently wealthy!" Both partners in the relationship can benefit from a more balanced lifestyle. Some men whose wives enjoy working are cutting down on their own work hours, again moving toward a better balance. Perfection in any one area may have to go by the wayside. Others feel threatened by the thought of a working wife. Long accustomed to seeing themselves as "sole providers," they see their main role in life eroding. But Bess Myerson, a nationally prominent woman of many careers, says, "When it comes to machismo versus mouths to feed, machismo is a luxury no family can afford."[13] Self-fulfillment also may be a necessity, not a luxury.

Even if a married woman is not one of the 66 percent who must work because of economic necessity, there is some danger in turning over to another the complete responsibility for economic support. For some women, such dilemmas are academic. They have been full-time wives and mothers for years. If a woman has made a total lifetime commitment to marriage and family, only a crisis propels her to seek a career. If she is divorced or widowed at forty or fifty, she hasn't been trained as well to cope in today's world.

And it is still true that some women, especially older women, come back to work for enrichment and a little extra money. They are ambivalent about "going for it" when family needs intervene. Sometimes their ambivalence translates—in the eye of the beholder—as lack of commitment.

As Kevin Starr wrote in the *San Francisco Chronicle-Examiner,* "Such a woman" finds herself traumatized by all those steely-eyed, perfectly groomed, 25-year-old MBAs in slit skirts about whom she reads in the newspapers when they receive promotions to vice presidencies. These women seem to be positively untouched by the pieties and sentiments that dominated her at a comparable age."

In truth, these twenty-five-year-old women are a minority in a sea of young women struggling with the newfound image of female success. Many of them are raising children alone without support or alimony, going to school, and holding a job at or near the poverty level. Juggling career and family is a necessity. They may take two steps forward but step back at those crucial decision-making times, such as seeking more education or choosing lucrative career fields with more responsibility. Many women begin well, getting the "right degree" and a good job. But research shows that by mid-management time, women start lagging and rarely make it to the top. According to some, these women still have a way to go! According to others, they have made the wiser, more enlightened choice!

But Caryl Rivers of Boston University is optimistic about the future of liberated marriage, which she defines as one in which there is rough parity between "the dirt work and the glory."[14] Each woman—each couple—who intends to change from the traditional lifestyle will have to make adjustments. Some men have been strongly socialized to see housework as very unmasculine. But many people value a reasonably clean house and occasional home-cooked meals. The business of living, of maintaining self and home, is necessary, it is hard work, and it is not often perceived as stimulating. These facts can become friction.

Add babies—add more of the above. Who's to take care of it all if both parents work? If a woman tries to be the perfect housewife/mother in a Super-mom tee shirt, she may experience a physically and emotionally exhausting way of life.[15] Hilary Cosell asks, "Can we really do everything our mothers did, and everything our fathers did as well?"[16]

Child Care.   Along with household management, working parents must be concerned with finding effective child care where there is supervised play, learning, and social life. Many parents are concerned over some negative reports about the effects of full-time day care on children. Day care, which was widespread as well as federally and industrially funded during World War II, is now available only in private centers. Not many companies provide child care for their employees. In 1986, there were only 150 on-site day care centers in all of corporate America and little likelihood of much increase.[17] Some employers will agree to a part-time or flexible work schedule that enables a parent to be at home when the children come home from school. Sometimes a close friend or relative is willing to care for the children, or a live-in babysitter will exchange services in return for room and board. Some parents arrange for child care through help-wanted ads in company, school, or church newsletters. It must be noted that a stop at a distant sitter adds yet another chore in the work race for working parents. We have a way to go as a nation in committing ourselves to the care of our children as a resource worth cherishing.

Before enrolling a child at a day-care facility, it is important to be sure that the place provides clean and safe facilities, nutritious meals, growth-promoting activities, and a loving/caring environment. Generally speaking, good child care is expensive and subsidized day care is hard to find. Some parents have found that joining or setting up a co-op where members take turns solves the problem for them at little or no cost, often close to home or work.

Child care must be reliable, especially if a mother is competing with men at work. Panic over babysitters is no help to the serious pursuit of a career, nor is worry over a sick or distressed child. Parents' needs for leisure on weekends and holidays should also be considered. Many men, long socialized to see responsibility for children as someone else's problem, do not "see" what needs to be done, but leave it entirely up to Mother.

It would seem wise, then, to look at male/female roles as they relate to child care versus career. Should women feel free to choose either full-time work or full-time motherhood, or whatever combination meets their needs, without being pressured by the expectations of others? If so, then society should value their contributions as important on every level.

The Single Woman.   The single woman is uniquely under pressure as she struggles to succeed in what is still largely a man's world. Women who choose careers over family life have been viewed with a wide range of feelings from disapproval to awe. For the unmarried working woman, ambivalence over career versus family can last for years and undermine a serious commitment to a career. A Yale-Harvard study shows that white college-educated women have a 20 percent chance of marrying if they are single at age thirty. By age thirty-five, the odds drop to 5.4 percent; by age forty, to 1.3 percent.[18] Equally, the high divorce rate can make marriage and children seem like great risks.

Fortunately, old attitudes are changing. Society views the working woman of the 1980s with less disapproval, more awe, and great interest. But the path is not without obstacles. Some women are experiencing discrimination; others, excessive demands and expectations.

Since a career change is not viewed as problematic by society, the individual woman struggles alone to make such decisions while often working at a low-paying and unsatisfactory job. Society provides few support systems to assist her with career advancement or change. Many working women have begun to form support groups or "new girl networks" to help each other—a step in the right direction.

Teenagers and Young Adults

Teenagers who have done well in high school are usually confident and collegebound—but they are not the majority. Many of their peers have not yet learned necessary survival skills or experienced any feelings of achievement. They lack both the job skills and the sophistication needed to find work in a tight job market. Their sagging self-image is not improved when they are rejected by prospective employers who have neither the time nor the budget to train raw recruits.

Today, business and industry are engaged in myriad mysterious machinations that challenge the understanding of even the brightest adult. No wonder young people, fresh out of senior government class, are lost! Some high schools acknowledge students' needs by offering work experience and career observation and exploration programs, but often the shyest, least successful students will not even apply.

Some people feel that working while in school can be a valuable as well as profitable experience as long as grades don't suffer. Teens also need some time for social life and relaxation, time to explore and become involved in a variety of activities, if their financial situation will allow it.

For many, approaching the first rung of the ladder is the most difficult step in the entire lifetime career process. Statistics show that the unemployment rate for young adults is two to three times higher than the rate for the remainder of the population, but as the number of teens going into high school decreases that figure should begin to change. Walter Williams, who teaches at Temple

University, favors a lower minimum age and wage for teenagers. He maintains such changes would increase employment for the young, especially minorities, allowing them to step up onto the first rung of the career ladder and gain badly needed work experience. Such services as movie usher and car hop might be reinstated without taking jobs away from older people.[19] But many people are concerned that such legislation would put older people out of work or into jobs with lower pay.

Various programs for helping young people enter the job market have been suggested and many have been tried successfully. A National Job Corps could be modeled after the very successful California Conservation Corps. Such work helps the environment, develops skills, and earns money.

Nontraditional careers have little appeal for young people. The young, inexperienced, untried job seeker is reluctant to strike out into those uncharted waters and few do, especially among those who do not have a chance to mature and explore their potential in college. In truth, the young are rushing at a snail's pace in this direction. When young adults have personal and financial responsibilities, very few will take time out to completely retool for a nontraditional career.

Other young people, overeducated and underemployed, perhaps still living at home in delayed adulthood, will have much less chance of finding affordable housing and achieving their parents' standard of living. Often idealistic, they are ambivalent about putting all their energies into a career.

But despite the obstacles in launching a satisfying career, taking that first step, however small, can be a rewarding experience at any age.

The Aging

Opportunities for rewarding work become fewer for both men and women as they grow older. After age forty, job hunting becomes even more difficult. Many workers stay at jobs they've outgrown rather than face possible rejection. It seems that our youth-oriented, throw-away culture sees little value in older people. In playwright Lillian Hellman's words, they have "the wisdom that comes with age that we can't make use of."[20] But one study by Daniel Yankelovich for the Association of Retired Persons shows that conflict between the young and the elderly is largely a myth. Harmony and mutual respect is more the rule than the exception. One conclusion is that societal support is needed for both the aging and the young.[21]

Unemployment and economic need for work is higher among older women, especially minorities, than among younger white women. A national council reports that although they remain unemployed longer when seeking work, older women job hunt harder, hold a job longer with less absenteeism, perform as well or better, are more reliable, and are more willing to learn than men or younger women. Yet many older women earn inadequate pay and face a future of poverty in their retirement years.[22] One out of every six elderly women lives in poverty with an annual income less than $5,600. Only one in five has a pension and many have no health insurance. Fewer than half of all women over sixty-five are married. When "sexism meets ageism, poverty is no longer on the doorstep—it moves in," according to Tish Sommers, coordinator of a task force on older women for the National Organization for Women.[23] The number of men over sixty-five who have retired has increased dramatically, whereas the increase in older women's retirement has dropped very slightly.[24] Supporting two households is very costly, so no-fault divorce has hit older women harder, especially those who were married to men with moderate to low income.

Yet a 1981 report by the White House Conference on Aging shows that as a group, older Americans are the "wealthiest, best fed, best housed, healthiest, most self-reliant older population in our history."[25] This statement is small comfort to those living below the poverty line on meager fixed incomes, but it does explode some of the myths and fears that lurk in the aging psyche. Opportunities for moving in and up in a large company may shrink, but many older people begin successful small businesses, volunteer in satisfying activities, and stay active for many years. They have few role models because life expectancy was much shorter and expectations of life were fewer in previous generations. Today's older people are, in effect, plowing new ground.

Employers are beginning to recognize that the mature person can bring a great deal of experience, stability, and responsibility to a position. People don't lose ability and experience on the eve of their sixty-fifth or seventieth birthday any more than they grow up instantly at age twenty-one.

Minorities

Minorities, particularly blacks and Hispanics, are also caught in the stereotype bind. If they cluster in ghettos, they struggle just to break even. Unemployment for minorities, especially black men, is dramatically higher, while wages are noticeable lower. Among minority youth in cities, the unemployment rate can reach 50 percent. Many are unable to begin careers because opportunities are limited or withheld or because their basic skills are often weak. Their expectations are low because, among the poor, young people rarely get a chance to observe adult role models in successful positions. When minority people move up, many also move away from those they might have helped. The young are left to find themselves, often in a hostile environment and cut off from the mainstream. As they watch others making decisions that affect them and getting the lion's share of affluence, their future may seem hopeless. Minorities in decision-making roles are barely visible. Many of those who have moved into middle management positions find their careers blocked. Discrimination still exists, however subtle. Although the number of black businesses rose 47 percent between 1977 and 1982,[26] they are still relatively few. Inflation, recession, and unemployment have jeopardized their positions.

The picture for black men is especially difficult. Black men are falling behind black women and now have the highest unemployment rate as traditional women's jobs, but not men's, are growing.[27] They have higher unemployment than any minority group and earn less when they do work. But employed black men hold higher-paying jobs than black females.

Black women, on the other hand, earn 1 percent more than white women in hourly earnings. Because they work longer hours, they earn 7 percent more overall. But 52 percent of black women who head families live below the poverty line.[28] Though black women have moved into many clerical and other administrative support jobs, along with professional and managerial positions in recent years, automation threatens many of these gains in the clerical area.[29] Some black women are using military service as a way out of the poverty bind. About 29 percent of all enlisted women in 1984 were black.[30] The overall picture is mixed, but there is vast room for improvement.

Unemployment, 1984[31]

| White men | 5.3% | Black men | 12.2% |
| White women | 5.1% | Black women | 12.8% |

Refugees / Immigrants

Never before in history have so many people migrated in fear and suffering during such a short period of time as in this past decade. This migration has been due in part, according to former President Jimmy Carter, "to the failure on the part of the world to live by principles of peace and human rights."[32] If the career search is demanding for everyone, imagine the added stress of coping with a new language in a new culture—and worrying about family and friends left behind. Many immigrants feel caught in a bewildering whirl of low-status jobs, a mismatched work ethic, an ambiguous dress-for-success code, and a U.S. brand of go-for-it assertiveness.

The immigrant's first and most important task is to learn the language of the host country. People who feel unable to communicate are tempted to withdraw, isolating themselves from the larger society. In the long run, this isolation is usually self-defeating. Americans meet newcomers with emotions ranging from compassion to resentment over possible competition for jobs, as we sometimes tend to forget that all our ancestors were either Native American or "boat people."

• •

Origin of U.S. Immigrants[33]

	1931–59:	1960–69	1980–84
Asia	5%	12%	48%
Europe	58%	39%	12%
Latin America	15%	37%	35%
North America	21%	10%	2%
Other	1%	2%	3%

Note: Immigrants from Africa are almost nonexistent!

Persons with Handicaps

Society has also been less then successful at dealing with people who are noticeably disabled. A silent minority, too, they were expected to stay in their place, one of low expectations. They have often struggled with a poor self-image and feelings of hopelessness about making even a living, much less a contribution to society.

But now, people with limitations are asking for rightful recognition of the skills they possess. They are demanding more access to government, business, industry, education, and all phases of life. Society is forced to take note that here are "handi-capable" people able to make a living and to make valuable contributions.

The Economic Perspective

Counselor Veronese Anderson sees the white, affluent, successful male at the top of our society—and, by association, his family. At the lower levels of those earning modest to poor incomes, we find minorities in percentages far out of proportion to their numbers. Figure 2–2 shows this disparity pictured as a socioeconomic tower.

In 1984, nearly 33.7 million Americans were living in poverty. In the 1990s, the shift may be toward less overall poverty but a frightening increase in impoverished women, children, and minorities. Growth in the private sector does not "trickle down" to these segments of the population. If this shift continues, by the year 2000 the poverty population will consist almost solely of children and women, many of the latter alone and over sixty-five. Recessions and

● ●

FIGURE 2-2 Income Distribution of All U.S. Families, 1984

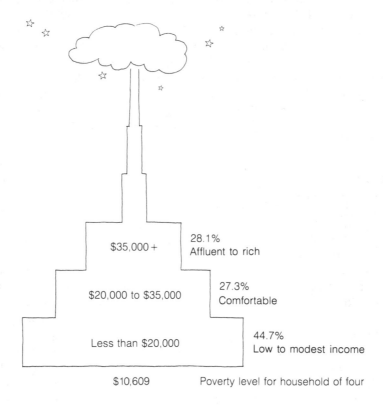

● ●

Source: *Statistical Abstract of the United States, 1985–1986* (Washington, D.C.: Bureau of the Census, 1983), p. 430.

job layoffs make the problem worse. And the U.S. Census Bureau shows that weekly spendable earnings dropped between 1970 and 1980, with an even sharper drop in 1981.[34]

Some people see discrimination against women and other groups as part of capitalistic planning. As economist Marilyn Power Goldberg points out, we need a "marginal workforce to smooth over cycles in the economy and to perform vital but menial and poorly paid jobs. We need to keep reinforcing their image of inferiority."[35]

John Kenneth Galbraith also sees society using the concept of the "convenient social virtue" to keep women and various minorities in a position of free service. Galbraith says, "The convenient social virtue ascribes merit to any pattern of behavior, however uncomfortable or unnatural for the individual involved, that serves the comfort or well-being of the more powerful members of the community." The nurse, the teacher, the nun, the community volunteer, the "cheerful, dutiful draftee," all have accepted social approval instead of pay. The economy benefits from free service. Galbraith sees the cheerful housewife of the nuclear family, who takes pride in her virtue as provider of goods, as the "consumer *par excellence,*" another advantage to the economy.[36] But the cheerful drudge and the dutiful draftee are both fading into the past.

NEW THEMES, CHANGING ATTITUDES

Today, after more than two decades of consciousness raising, everyone wants access to an enriched life. Perhaps most Americans agree, in theory if not in practice, that no one should be denied self-fulfillment because of sex, creed, color, nationality, disability, or age. But sweeping innovations in traditional roles require a willingness to take risks and change attitudes—beginning with our own. Men and women who want others to change are often surprised to learn that they must change themselves first. The result may be alienation or—with effort—a more rewarding closeness. One of the keys is good communication. Communicating effectively to improve human relations is a skill we can all learn and improve upon. Guidelines for improving relationships through good communication focus on solving problems instead of getting caught in an emotional vortex. Two key elements: *Take responsibility for your feelings. Change yourself, not others.*

Changing Lifestyles

Changes are in the air everywhere as people try new styles of living and then evaluate and adjust. Now that we've examined the inequities, let's look at some positive trends. Though the surge of "liberation" of the 1960s and 1970s has slowed down, women are easing into many areas, including sports, advertising, finance, medicine, and law. Secretaries, often quite knowledgable about management, become administrative assistants, and part of the management decision-making team. Women are more willing to accept power and responsibility in the workplace. The 1980s and 1990s see women striving to come into their own in a unique way.

Men are learning to provide nurturance for children. In *The Second Stage,* Betty Friedan admits that one failure of the women's movement was a blind spot about the family and she urges a revitalization and sharing of the traditional role of nurturer.[37] We see more "traditional marriages and more parents opting to stay at home to care for children. Many more men are taking parenting more seriously as male roles are reevaluated. And now these men as well as women are experiencing first hand that, though difficult, raising children *does* have its rewards.

Many writers, like Marilyn Ferguson, applaud the emergence of what is called the "feminine principle" in society. Men are beginning to see that operating behind a shield of power is sometimes cowardly. Men need liberation, too. Author Mark Gerzon says that men need new heroes.[38] Some men are refusing to relocate, take promotions, or travel it if means more time away from their families. Some say that changes from dominance to nurturance will make possible our survival as a race and as a planet.

Many women have achieved glamorous and rewarding positions, but they are now learning—as men have to learn—how to cope with job burnout. The frustration and weariness of sustaining success has taken its toll on some women, just as it has on some men. Women, too, will have to learn to balance the need for career achievement with enrichment in other areas of life.

Aging people are returning to school not only for enrichment but to learn new skills. It's a memorable experience to see a seventy-two year old grandmother receive a degree cheered on by a group of balloon-waving grandchildren. A sixty-five year old who received her MA in psychonutrition now supports herself by giving seminars and workshops.

Minorities also are moving up, becoming more visible in every area of life. The disabled are wheeling and whizzing out of isolation and assertively speaking up about their needs. Like the elderly, they are starting to feel a sense of energy and ability to change their lot in life.

Marilyn Ferguson speaks of a conspiracy of people beginning to "take charge of their lives," to make changes that deal with the transformation of the person and that could ultimately change society. Some of the changes she predicts could be described within our two frameworks as balancing the Timid/Tough Spectrum or becoming a self-actualized person.[39]

Jean Houston's exciting brain/mind research asks, "What is the possible human?" and shows us on the verge of a giant step forward toward new forms of consciousness and fulfillment. She affirms that our human systems are vastly superior to anything technology could invent; we have only begun to plumb the depths of our inner selves. We may be reaching a "golden age of body/mind control that challenges us to a new humanity."[40] It's a time, then, for all of us to make "thought-full" decisions about what we wish to be and what roles we want to play. Growing as a person means changing, adjusting to both inner and outer reality. It means expanding into new and exciting areas of life. Stereotypes about how we should be hold us back from becoming what we could be.

It seems that in our society we have come to a time of decision about how we want to be. More aware of our fragile environment, our energy shortage, our waste of resources, we know that we can't "have it all." But a further look at our needs, wants, and values might show us that we can have more than enough. It can be a good time for us if we act wisely, giving all of us a chance to develop more balanced lives and to free ourselves from stereotypes. To paraphrase Elizabeth Cady Stanton, "the true person is as yet a dream of the future." Let's hope that that future is not too distant.

· · · · · · ▼ · · · · · · **Self-Assessment Exercises**

The following exercises are designed to start you thinking about roles and considering their effects on your life and work.

1. Thinking About Stereotypes

a. List five roles that you play in life and tell how each affects you.

_____

_____

_____

_____

_____

b. What is expected of you in each of these roles?

_____

_____

_____

_____

_____

c. Do you live your roles as you choose or as others expect you to? Explain.

_____

_____

2. The Timid/Tough Spectrum

a. List words from Figure 2-1, the Timid/Tough Spectrum, that describe you:

_____

b. Check (√) where you stand on the Timid/Tough Spectrum:

_____ Timid   _____ Balanced   _____ Tough

c. Discuss how your gender limits or liberates you.

_____

_____

3. Identifying Major Components of Your Life

a. Rank the components of your life structure in order of importance to you.
Think of how you would list them if you were starting with none of them.

_____ Career   _____ Ethnic/national ties

_____ Marriage   _____ Religion/spiritual development

_____ Family   _____ Leisure

_____ Education   _____ What else?

b. Do the significant people in your life agree with your ranking?

Yes _____   No _____

c. What problems do you see in fitting each of these components into your
life? Into the life structure of those around you?

_____

_____

_____

4. Planning for the Future

a. What practical steps can you take to balance your role behavior and lib-
erate yourself from stereotypes?

_____

_____

_____

b. Is the American Dream for you? For everyone? Explain.

_____

_____

_____

Group Discussion Questions

1. Talking About Stereotypes

Pair with someone of different age, sex, or ethnic background (or all three). Finish the following statements:

Men/women are   Young/old people should

Men/women should   Minorities are

Young/old people are   Minorities should

2. Deciding Specific Cases

a. The Institute of Occupational Health and Safety states that women hold a disproportionate share of the ten most stressful jobs. Secretary is second on the list of most stressful jobs. Do you agree? Why or why not?

b. In Santa Clara County, California, 75 highly skilled secretaries employed by the state demonstrated because the state paid a car washer $300 more per month than a secretary. Were the secretaries justified in demonstrating? Do you believe in equal pay for comparable worth?

3. Ordering Priorities

William Brodhead (D-Mich.) resigned from Congress "to spend more time with family" and because of ethical concerns about increasing pressure to take money in exchange for votes.

a. List in order of importance Representative Brodhead's life components as demonstrated by that decision.

b. What values did he have to give up in resigning from Congress?

c. What values did he affirm?

4. Summing It Up

Discuss in class or write your answers on a separate sheet of paper:

a. What have you learned from this chapter?

b. What stereotypes and prejudices would you like to change in yourself and in society?

PERSONALITY AND PERFORMANCE: PIECES OF THE PUZZLE

FOCUS

Assess your personality.

Identify your skills.

Pinpoint your relationship to Data, People, and Things.

• • • • • •

Y ou are gathering information to match a special person—you and your needs, wants, and values—with satisfying positions in the world of work. When you finally enter the workplace, you may have to make some compromises, but the ideal is to minimize the compromises and maximize the match.

A major decision point is interest area. Where do you, with all the unique facets of your personality, feel most comfortable? The human personality is like a stained glass window—a mosaic of light and color. A stained glass window is an enduring object of carefully chosen colors, yet it changes with the changing sun. In darkness it seems to disappear, but in the light it comes alive with color.

> It takes
>   its life from light
>   it sleeps at night
>   and comes ablaze at dawn
>   it holds the day
>   'til shadows fade
>   its brilliance strangely gone.

Analogously, the human personality can be seen as a mosaic of six major themes.

AREAS OF INTEREST: THE PERSONALITY MOSAIC

Psychologist and vocational counselor John Holland says that one of six major personality types—or perhaps a combination of two or more types—plays a highly important role in an individual's career choice.

Most of us probably cannot deal with many areas of interest. We become preoccupied with a certain field or activity early in life. This area becomes our focal point, largely because of choices that stem from our needs, wants, and values.[1]

You can observe how others focus on certain interests. When friends or relatives arrive for the weekend, they generally scatter in the directions of their wants and values. The refrigerator, the stereo, the football game on TV, the garden, the new drapes, the video game, the grandparents, the children, the antique car, a good discussion, a crossword puzzle—each will be a magnet for someone's attention. Since each person notices and experiences things differently, you are unique in the combination of things that interest you. Generally, the interests that predominate in a personality mosaic are among the most important keys to career satisfaction.

Becoming aware of your "lesser lights" can also provide illumination and enrichment. We are all born with innumerable possibilities. Some talents remain undeveloped for half a lifetime; then new abilities surface in time to bring joy to those middle and senior years. Personal growth leads to the discovery of new dimensions in ourselves.

Perhaps, too, you can see as an ideal the "universal person" of the Renaissance: able to be all things with apparently equal ease, at home in all settings and with all people, truly self-actualized.

In this chapter, you can identify the predominant orientation of your personality in an inventory called the Personality Mosaic. It's important to take this inventory before reading the interpretations that follow. Then you can analyze the kinds of activities you've been enjoying all your life. Having reminded yourself of your interests, you will be ready to tie this data into the Job Group Chart in Chapter 4.

Personality Mosaic

Circle the numbers of statements that clearly sound like something you might say or do or think—something that feels like *you*. Put question marks (?) in front of any items that you aren't sure of to see how they change your score. Put the letter X on the numbers of statements that feel very unlike you, to obtain a *"not you"* score.

1. It's important for me to have a strong, agile body.

2. I need to understand things thoroughly.

3. Music, color, writing, beauty of any kind can really affect my moods.

4. Relationships with people enrich my life and give it meaning.

5. I am confident that I'll be successful.

6. I need clear directions so I know exactly what to do.

7. I can usually carry/build/fix things myself.

8. I can get absorbed for hours in thinking something out.

9. I appreciate beautiful surroundings: color and design mean a lot to me.

10. I'll spend time finding ways to help people through personal crisis.

11. I enjoy competing.

12. I'll spend time getting carefully organized before I start a project.

13. I enjoy making things with my hands.

14. It's satisfying to explore new ideas.

15. I always seem to be looking for new ways to express my creativity.

16. I value being able to share personal concerns with people.

17. Being a key person in a group is very stimulating to me.

18. I take pride in being very careful about all the details of my work.

19. I don't mind getting my hands dirty.

20. I see education as a lifelong process of developing and sharpening my mind.

21. I like to dress in unusual ways, try new colors and styles.

22. I can often sense when a person needs to talk to someone.

23. I enjoy getting people organized and on the move.

24. I'd rather be safe than adventurous in making decisions.

25. I like to buy sensible things I can make or work on myself.

26. Sometimes I can sit for long periods of time and work on puzzles or read or just think about life.

27. I have a great imagination.

28. I like to help people develop their talents and abilities.

29. I like to be in charge of getting the job done.

30. I usually prepare carefully ahead of time if I have to handle a new situation.

31. I'd rather be on my own doing practical, hands-on activities.

32. I'm eager to read or think about any subject that arouses my curiosity.

33. I love to try creative new ideas.

34. If I have a problem with someone, I'll keep trying to resolve it peacefully.

35. To be successful, it's important to aim high.

36. I don't like to have responsibility for big decisions.

37. I say what's on my mind and don't beat around the bush.

38. I need to analyze a problem pretty thoroughly before I act on it.

39. I like to rearrange my surroundings to make them unique and different.

40. I often solve my personal problems by talking them out with someone.

41. I get projects started and let others take care of details.

42. Being on time is very important to me.

43. It's invigorating to do things outdoors.

44. I keep asking, "Why?"

45. I like my work to be an expression of my moods and feelings.

46. I like to help people find ways to care more for each other.

47. It's exciting to take part in important decisions.

48. I am usually neat and orderly.

49. I like my surroundings to be plain and practical.

50. I need to stay with a problem until I figure out an answer.

51. The beauty of nature touches something deep inside me.

52. Close personal relationships are important to me.

53. Promotion and advancement are important to me.

54. I feel more secure when my day is well planned.

55. I'm not afraid of heavy work and usually know what needs to be done.

56. I enjoy books that make me think and give me new ideas.

57. I look forward to seeing art shows, plays, and good films.

58. I am very sensitive to people who are experiencing emotional upsets.

59. It's exciting for me to influence people.

60. When I say I'll do it, I do my best to follow through on every detail.

61. Good, hard physical work never hurt anyone.

62. I'd like to learn all there is to know about subjects that interest me.

63. I don't want to be like everyone else; I like to do things differently.

64. I go out of my way to be caring to people with problems.

65. I'm willing to take some risks to get ahead.

66. I feel more secure when I follow rules.

67. The first thing I look for in a car is a well-built engine.

68. I like a conversation to be intellectually stimulating.

69. When I'm creating, I tend to let everything else go.

70. I feel concerned that so many people in our society need help.

71. It's fun to persuade people to follow a plan.

72. I'm very good about checking details.

73. I usually know how to take care of things in an emergency.

74. Reading about new discoveries is exciting.

75. I appreciate beautiful and unusual things.

76. I often go out of my way to pay attention to people who seem lonely and friendless.

77. I love to bargain.

78. I like to be very careful about spending money.

79. Sports are important to me in building a strong body.

80. I've always been curious about the way nature works.

81. It's fun to be in a mood to try something unusual.

82. I am a good listener when people talk about personal problems.
83. If I don't make it the first time, I usually bounce back with energy and enthusiasm.
84. I need to know exactly what people expect me to do.
85. I like to take things apart to see if I can fix them.
86. I like to study all the facts and decide logically.
87. It would be hard to imagine my life without beauty around me.
88. People often seem to tell me their problems.
89. I can usually connect with people who get me in touch with a network of resources.
90. It's very satisfying to do a task carefully and completely.

Scoring Your Answers:

To score, circle the same numbers that you circled on the Personality Mosaic.

R	I	A	S	E	C
1	2	3	4	5	6
7	8	9	10	11	12
13	14	15	16	17	18
19	20	21	22	23	24
25	26	27	28	29	30
31	32	33	34	35	36
37	38	39	40	41	42
43	44	45	46	47	48
49	50	51	52	53	54
55	56	57	58	59	60
61	62	63	64	65	66
67	68	69	70	71	72
73	74	75	76	77	78
79	80	81	82	83	84
85	86	87	88	89	90

Count the number of circles in each column and write the totals in the spaces:

R__4__   I__12__   A__9__   S__15__   E__8__   C__11__

List the letters R, I, A, S, E, and C, according to your scores, from highest to lowest:

1st__S__   2nd__I__   3rd__C__   4th__A__   5th__E__   6th__R__

Does adding in the items you're unsure of (?) change the order?_____

How?_____

In which areas do you have the most negatives (X)?_____
_____*R*_____

Do you have a tie score in two or more columns? If so, the remainder of this chapter will help you to decide which column represents the "real you."

To get more in touch with yourself, read aloud some of the statements for each orientation from the Personality Mosaic. *Be* that kind of person. Embellish and dramatize the statements to see how that kind of behavior feels. You may want to role-play this activity in a group.

INTERPRETING THE PERSONALITY MOSAIC

The inventory you have just taken is based on the six personality orientations identified by John Holland. As you can see from your score, you are not just one personality type—that is, you are not a person with fifteen circles in one area and no circles in any of the others. In most people one or two characteristics are dominant, two or three are of medium intensity, and one or two may be of low intensity. A few people score high in each category because they have many interests. Others, who don't have many strong interests, score rather low in all areas.

Here is an overview of the six personality types, followed by a discussion of each orientation and its relationship to the others. Try to find yourself in the following descriptions.

• **Realistic Personality**

Hands-on people who enjoy exploring things, fixing things, making things with their hands

Express themselves and achieve primarily through their bodies rather than through words, thoughts, feelings

Usually independent, practical minded, strong, well coordinated, aggressive, conservative—the rugged individualist

Like the challenge of physical risk, being outdoors, using tools and machinery

Prefer concrete rather than abstract problems

Solve problems by doing something physical

- **Investigative Personality**

  Persons who "live" very much in their minds

  Unconventional and independent thinkers, intellectually curious, very insightful, logical, persistent

  Express themselves and achieve primarily through their minds rather than through association with people or involvement with things

  Like to explore ideas through reading, discussing

  Enjoy complex and abstract mental challenges

  Solve problems by thinking and analyzing

- **Artistic Personality**

  Persons who are creative, sensitive, aesthetic, introspective, intuitive, visionary

  See new possibilities and want to express them in creative ways

  Especially attuned to perception of color, form, sound, feeling

  Prefer to work alone and independently rather than with others

  Enjoy beauty, variety, the unusual in sight, sound, texture, people

  Need fairly unstructured environment to provide opportunities for creative expression

  Solve problems by creating something new

- **Social Personality**

  People persons who "live" primarily in their feelings

  Sensitive to others, genuine, humanistic, supportive, responsible, tactful, perceptive

  Focus on people and their concerns rather than on things or deep intellectual activity

  Enjoy closeness with others, sharing feelings, being in groups, unstructured settings that allow for flexibility and caring

  Solve problems primarily by feeling and intuition, by helping others

- **Enterprising Personality**

  Project persons who are thoroughly absorbed in their involvements

Energetic, enthusiastic, confident, dominant, political, verbal, assertive, quick decision makers

Leaders who are talented at organizing, persuading, managing

Achieve primarily by using these skills in dealing with people and projects

Enjoy money, power, status, being in charge

Solve problems by taking risks

- **Conventional Personality**

Persons who "live" primarily in their orderliness

Quiet, careful, accurate, responsible, practical, persevering, well organized, task oriented

Have strong need to feel secure and certain, get things finished, attend to every detail, follow a routine

Prefer to work for someone of power and status rather than be in such a position themselves

Solve problems by appealing to and following rules

• • • • • • • • • •

FOR THE MOST PART
I do the thing which my
own nature drives
me to do.
—ALBERT EINSTEIN

• • • • • • • • • •

Realistic Personality

Realistic individuals are capable and confident when using their bodies to relate to the physical world. They focus on *things,* learn through their hands, and have little need for conversation. Because of their facility with physical objects, they are often good in emergencies. Their ability to deal with the physical world often makes them very independent. Since these characteristics describe the stereotypical male, many women shrink from displaying any capability in this area, and often women are discouraged from doing so. Realistic people sometimes get so absorbed in putting *things* right that they can forget about everything else.

Investigative Personality

The investigative type deals with the "real world" of things but at a distance. These individuals prefer to read, study, use books, charts, and other data instead of getting their hands on *things*. When involved with people, they tend to focus on ideas. Wherever they are, they collect information and analyze the situation before making a decision. If they enjoy the outdoors, it's because they are curious, not because they enjoy rugged, heavy, physical work. Their curiosity sometimes leads them to explore their ideas to the exclusion of all else.

Artistic Personality

The artistic type is creative, but not necessarily with paint and canvas. These individuals express creativity not only with material objects but with data and systems as well. The weaver designs and makes fabric; the poet creates with words; the choreographer arranges dancers in flowing patterns. The industrialist creates new systems for the flow of goods; the program planner creates better delivery of services in a variety of settings. Creative people see possibilities beyond the usual. They would rather create ideas than study them. They like variety and are not afraid to experiment, often disregarding rules. Their ideas don't always please others, but opposition doesn't discourage them for long.

Artistic types focus on whatever strikes their creative fancies. Sensitivity to sight, sound, and touch will draw some of them to the fine arts such as drama, music, and literature. Others will be content just to enjoy aesthetic experience, whereas still others will create new ways of doing things—new systems. If they like the outdoors, it is from an aesthetic standpoint. They love its beauty and its power to inspire their creativity—but not its ability to make them perspire with heavy work. Their irrepressible spirits and enthusiasm can often keep them focused on a creative project to the exclusion of all else. Not producing up to standard (their own) can plunge them to the depths.

Social Personality

The social personality focuses on people and their concerns. Sensitive to people's moods and feelings, these individuals enjoy company and make friends easily. Their level of caring may range from one person to the entire human race. Their relationships with people depend on their ability to communicate both verbally and nonverbally, listening as well as speaking. Their empathy and ability to intuit emotional cues help them to solve people problems sometimes even before others are aware of them. They can pull people together and generate positive energy for a good cause. Since the social orientation seems to describe the "typical female," many men shrink from expressing or dealing with deep feelings. The social personality types sometimes focus on people concerns to the exclusion of all else. They sometimes appear "impractical," especially to the realistic types.

Enterprising Personality

The enterprising person is a leader who initiates projects but often gets others to carry them out. Instead of doing research, these people rely on intuition about what will work. They may strike an observer as restless and irresponsible since they often drop these projects after the job is underway. But many activities would never get off the ground without their energizing influence. They need to be part of the "in crowd," but since their relationships center around tasks, they may focus so dynamically on the project that the personal concerns of others (and even their own) go unnoticed.

Conventional Personality

The conventional person also is task oriented but prefers to carry out tasks initiated by others. Since they are careful of detail, these individuals keep the world's records and transmit its messages. They obey rules and they value order in the world of data. Their sense of responsibility keeps the world going as they focus on the tasks at hand to the exclusion of all else.

The Personality Hexagon

The six personality orientations can be arranged in a hexagon. In Figure 3-1, the types next to one another are most similar. The words linking them indicate their shared traits or interests. For example, realistic and investigative people focus on things. The R person does something to the thing; the I person analyzes it. Investigative and artistic types are both idea people. The I explores and sometimes develops ideas logically; the A invents them intuitively. Artistic and social people need to be in tune with their feelings. Social and enterprising people are people leaders; the S person is concerned about people, the E person wants to get people motivated to undertake a task. The conventional person will carry out the details of the task to the last detail. Thus the E and C are both task oriented in different ways, the E person initiating and leading and the C type carrying through to completion with the utmost responsibility. Both C and R types value order: the C values data/paper order; the R values physical order.

People seek out work activities that enable them to be with others of like personality. Workplaces, too, tend to gather similar types and reflect the style of these workers.

· ·

FIGURE 3-1 Personality Types: Similarities and Differences

· ·

Source: Adapted from John Holland, *Making Vocational Choices: A Theory of Careers* (Englewood Cliffs, N.J.: Prentice-Hall, 1973), copyright © 1970, by special permission of John Holland and Prentice-Hall, Inc. See also John Holland, *Self-Directed Search* (Palo Alto, Calif.: Consulting Psychologists Press), copyright © 1970.

The types opposite each other on the hexagon are most dissimilar. For example, the artistic personality is independent, doesn't mind disorder, and likes to try new things. The conventional person depends more on other people, likes order, and would prefer things to stay the same.

Two people who are strongly opposite in personality can improve their relationship by understanding the differences between them. A realistic person doesn't deal much with people's feelings, while a social person sees much of life through feelings. That's just the way they are. The introspective I person is amazed at the outgoing E person's ability to act without doing much research. Since opposites complement each other, it can be advantageous to see a radically different personality as a potential source of support and enrichment. Wise employers will hire those whose personality orientation is appropriate for the work to be done.

Imagine six people sitting around the hexagon. Each person is a strong representative of a personality type. Give the group an issue to discuss (such as lower taxes, in Figure 3-2) and each person will look at it in a different way.

• •

FIGURE 3-2 Personality Types: Typical Talk

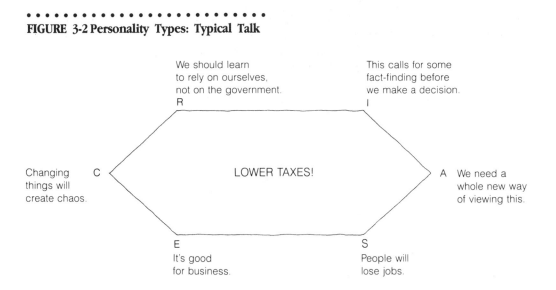

Sometimes we have personality conflicts within us. We'd like to be creative and try something different, but our conventional nature tells us that's a
"no-no." We'd like to take an enterprising risk, but our investigative side wants
to gather all the facts before deciding. Realistic folks who like to be alone dealing with physical objects still need some people interaction, too. Each personality type is surprised to find out that the characteristics of an opposite type can
work in their own lives. The social personality often neglects to allow for
needed time alone; the enterprising, to find out facts before acting; the artistic,
to be careful of detail; the realistic person, to stay in touch with other people;
the investigative person, to take a risk; and the conventional person, to try
something new!

A manager and electrical engineer is orienting a group of older women to
his company. The conversation turns to personal matters and he shares his early
difficulties in communicating with his wife. He found it hard to understand her
continued wish that he would *talk* to her. When a divorce threatened, he went
off for some communications training and struggled with this strange new activity: sharing feelings he never knew he had. The women related well to this
story. After a tour of the plant, they agreed that working with electronic circuits
wasn't for them. The engineer replied that it would be as hard for them to work
in his more realistic/investigative area as it was for him to learn the social skills
of dealing with people and their feelings!

It is likely that you will find a job difficult if it lies in an area very different
from the interests of your personality type. Even people who have a strong
orientation in one direction will be most comfortable the closer they are to a

career in that area. An engineer with thirteen years' experience in the field admitted that he had thought engineering would involve his hands, and he now wished to become a technician. An industrial arts teacher wished that his job didn't involve motivating people all the time, but his industrial specialty was "too clerical" because it dealt with safety and time studies. Both these people would have been more content with work that let them use machines and tools in some way.

One realistic/artistic woman illustrates what it feels like to be doing "what you are fitted for," as Maslow says. She says, "Each time I touch a piece of fabric, magic occurs. I don't see corduroy or cotton but a dress, a shirt, priscilla curtains with tiebacks. Each time I sit on my chair facing the sewing machine, I disappear. I've gone into my hands. . . . fabric, foot, and needle join hands to perform one function. In the process, they become one, and as in a chemical reaction, a totally different thing emerges. Not just a dress or curtain, but a new me.[2]

At first the results of the Personality Mosaic may not seem like you. One woman told a group that she was certain she was not investigative. Her next thought was, "I wonder *why* it turned out that way?" Take time to study and understand each personality type and only then accept the data that really seem to fit you well.

Understanding your personality can facilitate a good career decision. Understanding the personality of others can improve human relationships and ease your acceptance of the choices that others make. But every day we all act in these six modes to some extent:

Realistic: Physical Needs

Running on the beach

Eating meals

Fixing the sink

Artistic: Aesthetic Needs

Enjoying a sunset

Wearing complementary colors

Decorating a cake

Investigative: Mind Needs

Discussing politics

Reading *War and Peace*

Planning a trip to Europe

Social: People Needs

Laughing with a friend

Hugging the baby

Going to a party

Enterprising: Accomplishment Needs

Organizing a party

Saying "Hello" first

Applying for a job

Conventional: Structure Needs

Straightening your closet

Finishing a paper on time

Stopping at a stop sign

. . . .
Courtesy of Mal Hancock

Does growth mean allowing all these dimensions to surface and to actualize to the best of your ability? As you grow, will you feel comfortable in all these areas? Your career decision may fall within the area of your dominant personality type or a blend of several, or in an area that is difficult for you. You will need extra energy if you veer away from your dominant orientations. Discuss your dominant personality characteristics with someone and explain why they feel right to you.

Now we'll begin to analyze these interests and activities you've been involved with all your life and relate them to skills.

ACTIVITY ANALYSIS

Your personality expresses itself by means of your actions. In Chapter 1's "Candid Camera—3-D" exercise, you listed just about every activity you could think of that you've done in your life: jobs, community and extracurricular activities, education, and other projects. Then you listed all the things you had to do to accomplish each activity. This analysis produced your expanded activity list— data that will help you choose satisfying life activities.

Sometimes a person will not analyze activities in enough detail. A woman says that she is a realistic person because she likes to garden. Her notebook shows a list of seeds, a planting schedule, a layout of her garden. Asked how her garden was doing, she said, "Not too well." She obviously loved collecting, organizing, and analyzing data but didn't get out to the garden very much! Her activity analysis finally showed that she was much more investigative than realistic. So study your lists to be sure that you have broken down each activity into as many specific component activities as possible. They will be important for the exercises that follow.

Skills

As you can see, if you actually listed all the activities you've ever done your list would be enormous. Now here is one of the most important connections for you to make. When you've *done* any activity, that means you *can* do it! You've shown you have the ability and that ability is a skill! Many people think they have no skills because they can't play the oboe or type 100 words per minute. But in reality they have been accomplishing things successfully for many years and have the capacity to accomplish much more. One huge factor is confidence. If you *think* you can, then you are well on the way to accomplishment. At least you can probably do something closely related to your dream job.

For example, a teacher completed an interest inventory that suggested a career in the performing arts. Acting seemed intriguing but not likely to provide much income for a beginner. It suddenly dawned on the teacher how much she loved "appearing" in a class or workshop, making people laugh and appreciate her. She loved to perform well for her students! She remembered that when she first became a teacher, she had had little confidence and either over- or under-disciplined her classes as a result. Confidence grew with the realization that she could teach and have fun doing it. Now she rarely misses a chance to talk with a group.

All your activities flow from ten basic aptitudes. With these ten aptitudes or basic skills a person can do *everything*. That person is *skilled!* Though most people can operate in all of these areas reasonably well, they will be more comfortable in some than in others. We will group these aptitudes and their related skills according to their interaction with Data, People, and Things.

Data Skills[3]

1. **Logical Intelligence:** Think, observe, plan, analyze, evaluate, understand, problem solve. Put ideas and information together to deal with complex operations, to plan, organize work. Keep track of verbal and numerical information in an orderly way, make decisions using common sense based on "practical" experience.

2. **Intuitive Intelligence:** Imagine, compare, see things "holistically," decide based on best guesses and "intuitive" common sense rather than rules or measurements. Use words, numbers, or symbols creatively, develop new ideas, new processes, new combinations.

3. **Verbal Ability:** Use words to read, research, write, listen, record, discuss, direct, instruct, communicate, motivate.

4. **Numerical Ability:** Use numbers and symbols to figure, calculate, estimate, keep books, budget, analyze.

5. **Precise Detail:** Follow directions exactly, make decisions based on set rules or measurements; attend to small details in proofreading words or numbers or examining lines and shapes of products.

6. **Multidimensional Awareness:** Understand, visualize, relate two- or three-dimensional lines or shapes, spaces, shading—sometimes in color.

People Skills

7. **Businesslike Contact with People:** Manage, supervise, organize, motivate, entertain, train, serve, negotiate with, cooperate with people.

8. **Influencing People:** Persuade/inspire others to think or behave in certain ways. Teach, exchange, interpret ideas/facts/feelings, help solve personal problems.

Thing Skills

9. **Finger/Hand Agility:** Use fingers/hands to make, repair, process, test, assemble, operate various products/machines/tools using special techniques, sometimes highly complex.

10. **Whole Body Agility:** Use the whole body to handle, carry, lift, move, balance, or coordinate itself or things.

These ten skill areas range from almost invisible activities of the mind to highly visible activities of the body. The interests you have been listing are usually a good clue to your skills. Most people acquire skills in areas they enjoy and tend to neglect other areas. If you like something, you spend time doing it . . . get better at it and like it more . . . and spend more time . . . And it's comforting to note that most jobs, by definition, require only average skills.

We came into this world already well equipped for action. Unless a serious defect exists, our growth and potential for growth are phenomenal. Look at a six-month-old and be amazed at the complexity of skills compared with those of a newborn infant. Compare with a six-year-old and be further astounded!

But somewhere along the line confidence and energy may begin to lag. Jean Houston, brain researcher, says that by age seventeen we are using only 17 percent of our body's potential for flexible movement compared to our use at age three. And she says that as the body goes, so does the mind. Houston finds that even the very elderly, with correct exercise, can "remake" their bodies in six months. Their mental and emotional powers are greatly enhanced.[4] "The true person is as yet a dream of the future."

We try to divide the human person into mind, body, and emotions, but that's only a mental exercise. Philosophers have struggled for centuries to define these quite ordinary terms. Since our educational system stresses mental activities, we sometimes infer that men and women who work with their hands are not "using their heads." In reality, the two cannot be separated; they can only be examined separately as two different modes of living and learning.

The Skills Trio

There are three kinds of skills: transferable, work-specific, and personal responsibility skills.[5] The ten basic aptitudes and their related skills are called *transferable* skills because they can be used in many kinds of activities and transferred from one job to another. For example, planning, which draws upon logical intelligence can involve the following steps: (1) determine/establish objectives, (2) set policies, procedures, (3) do long/short range forecasts, (4) schedule strategies, (5) evaluate/revise the program.

Perhaps 80 to 90 percent of the content of most jobs requires transferable skills—those you already have. The other 10 to 20 percent may require on-the-job training (OJT), further formal education, or both. A salesperson, for example, depends largely on transferable skills and can learn the needed *work-specific skills* quickly. Some jobs require quite a bit of special training, especially in science, technical fields, and the arts. This special training gives us work-specific skills such as those used by electronics technicians, business managers, doctors, and ballerinas. But all these people need transferable skills, too. Managers include, for example, teachers and housewives since both manage complex organizations. Even though they may have limited business experience, they have been using management skills. They have supervised *people;* organized data, people, and things; managed records and budgets; made decisions; resolved conflicts; ensured the smooth flow of goods, services, and transportation; and worked in community relations. As Ray Killian says, "Much of this experience can be transferred . . . to supervisory skills."[6]

If you are enthusiastic, committed, careful, prompt, cheerful, and able to use your common sense, you have *personal responsibility skills.* Such skills sometimes develop at an early age, often independent of formal education. They reflect how well you manage *yourself* in relation to data, people, and things. Do you manage yourself responsibly, creatively, and with initiative? Do you use common sense? Common sense, energy, dedication, responsibility, intuition, creativity: all are traits that can be learned, that develop with the help of both achievement and disappointment. No one really knows how! You have survived modern life so far. Your physical, mental, emotional, social, and financial well-being have depended upon your abilities. You *must* possess a good measure of skills in all areas.

Work Qualities

The ways in which you use your skills to perform various activities involve four basic work qualities: repetition, variety, physical risk, and status.

Work Qualities

- **Repetition:** Duties involve a set way of doing things, sometimes over and over again.
- **Variety:** Duties change frequently requiring a flexible response, different knowledge and skills.
- **Physical Risk:** Duties involve pressure in stressful, dangerous situations but sometimes provide adventure and excitement.
- **Status:** Duties involve recognition that you are someone important or in authority.

Dealing with Data, People, and Things. Skills give your mind and body the power to act on the world around you. You can use the ten basic skills in a multitude of combinations. But that world around you has only three areas you can relate to: ideas and information (data), people, and things.

Data: A human mind can take in and give out great quantities of information, or data, in the form of words, numbers, and symbols. All day long the mind clicks away expressing complex thoughts and ideas, often creatively, and always in a way unique to the individual. When you notice you are out of milk and jot it down on the grocery list, you've just processed some data. Reading, writing, speaking, and listening all deal with data (ideas and information). Every activity deals with data from simple to complex. The cry of the newborn gives us data about how the baby feels. Lights blinking on a machine can give us data about what to do next and when. Some people think of data as complex numbers and

Go away! I'm peopled out.

computer printouts. But data includes all kinds of ideas and information: the words you speak, read, listen to; the music you enjoy; the smiles of your friends; the colors of the sunset. Anything that is not a person or a concrete object is called data and we deal with it on various levels of complexity from just noticing it to copying it to developing it.

People: Another kind of activity depends upon interaction with people, ranging from saying hello to helping someone solve a personal problem, simple or serious. *We use a great deal of data to deal with other humans.* We involve all sorts of body/mind perceptions and linguistic skills. The emotions, which are physical responses to sensory information, permeate our mental processes and influence our behavior and relationships with others. We deal with people at various levels of complexity from saying "Hello" and waiting on them to dealing with their long-term personal growth. A rent-a-car clerk in an airport noticed that she liked working with people, but not the public! And, conversely, a person who thought she wanted to be a counselor found the people contact she experienced as a bank teller to be just right.

Who would think that the ability to use love and affection would make a manager more effective? Harold Leavitt, professor of organization behavior at the Stanford University Graduate School of Business, says, "Worker expectations and job values are changing, and being in management is going to require a lot more love and affection—more emphasis on vicarious and helpful behavior . . . less on control and competition. . . . Managing software programs is less disciplined, more artsy than managing hardware programs . . . harder to control except by building good will.[7] So the balanced manager can draw on many types of skills and behaviors along the Timid/Tough Spectrum.

Things: We relate to physical objects in any number of ways: building, repairing, carrying, making things, running machines; tinkering with gadgets from food processors to power saws. The physical object that we use may be ourselves as in such activities as sports and dance. The involvement can be from simple (putting up a picture) to complex (repairing a satellite). The body skills used require various degrees of strength, agility, and coordination in relating to other physical objects. The way the body fixes and builds things often requires creative ability. And of course you need the data required to deal with those things.

You learned to deal with data, people, and things at all levels early in life. Look again at your "Candid Camera—3-D" lists from Chapter 1. How many times have you planned events, organized people, or repaired objects in your lifetime? Your skills with data, people, and things work together in a blend of mental and physical abilities, emotionally expressed in creating music, art, literature, and in scientific and technical works. But stop and think: Every day— using your mind, body, and emotions—*you* create your life.

Instead of groaning at your "lack of talent," think of all the talents you've used effectively in a life filled with data, people, and things. And since the majority of workers have only average skills, most people can do most jobs. And that includes you! The question is, then: Of all the skills you possess, which do you enjoy using? And more important, which would you like to use in a work setting? Do you prefer to work primarily with data, people, or things? And of all the jobs you *can* do, which would you *like* to do?

Observe yourself. What skills are you motivated to acquire and develop to get where you would like to be? In what ways would you like to focus your transferable skills to work-specific skills? If you have good finger dexterity, for example, would you prefer to become adept at the guitar, the typewriter, brain surgery, or all three? Are you willing to devote some time to further training and education to acquire work-specific skills? Which personal responsibility skills are your strengths? Which will you work to improve? These are important decision points.

People often underestimate what they have done in life. When a high school graduate was asked to make a list of her job activities in a drive-in, she replied that she had done nothing of importance. "All I did was make hamburgers." But speaking informally, she was able to describe what she did in more detail. That became her list. She then coded each activity with a P, T, or D (P means dealing directly with people; T dealing directly with things (material objects); D ideas and information alone, or data): She noticed when supplies were running low and ordered (D) and put them away (T). She took charge when the owners were away (D). She showed new clerks what to do (P). Sometimes she did minor repairs on kitchen equipment (T). She made all the sauces (T). She settled arguments between kids and clerks about orders (P). She could always tell when a new clerk wasn't going to work out (D).

After a great deal of work, her list was polished to read:

Human Relations (People, Data)

Worked well with customers/employers, coworkers (good teamwork)

Oriented, trained, evaluated employees

Settled customer/employee arguments

Materials Maintenance (Things, Data)

Inventoried, ordered, stored, prepared materials

Did maintenance/repair

Opened and closed business

Handled cash/cash register

Data Without People or Things

Organized/scheduled work

Her job activities drew on several of the ten basic skills to a modest degree, especially logical intelligence, verbal ability, businesslike contact with people, finger/hand agility and, occasionally, intuitive intelligence, numerical ability, and precise detail. Her work also had a great deal of the work quality *variety.*

A section of her résumé, developed for a management trainee position in a small restaurant, summarized her experience as a supervisor/cook as follows:

Inventoried, ordered, prepared, and stocked food supplies. Settled employee and customer problems and complaints. Oriented/trained new employees, informally evaluated performance. Did minor repairs/maintenance. As occasional acting manager, opened and closed shop, handled cash/cash register.

A personal paragraph included: good teamwork with customers, employees, and coworkers, notice and take care of details, reliable.

. . . .

FIGURE 3-3 Connections

The Six Personality Types: Realistic, Investigative, Artistic, Social, Enterprising, Conventional

Express themselves through	The Ten Basic Attitudes or Skills

Logical Intelligence   Multidimensional Awareness
Intuitive Intelligence   Businesslike Contact with People
Verbal Ability   Influencing People
Numerical Ability   Finger/Hand Agility
Precise Detail   Whole Body Agility

And act on the whole world	Data: Words Numbers Behaviors Symbols People: Infants Children Adults Senior Citizens Things: Tools Gadgets Materials Equipment	using just four	Work Qualities

Repetition
Variety
Physical Risk
Status

. . . .

If you think you can't
You won't!
If you think you can,
You will!

. . . .

In this chapter, then, you've discovered your very own Personality Mosaic. You have identified skills that have motivated you to act successfully in the past and will carry you into the future. And you are putting together some extremely valuable pieces of the career decision puzzle. In short, you have been gathering important words to describe the one and only YOU!

. . . .

▼ **Self-Assessment Exercises**

1. Six Personality Types

Circle the personality types that describe you best: realistic, investigative, artistic, social, enterprising, conventional.

2. Data, People, Things Indicator

Use the Activity Lists you have been working on from Chapter 1, Candid Camera—3-D. If they are now as long as you can make them and you have broken down your activities into specific component activities, code all these activities with a P, T, or D as follows:

P = interacting directly with people
T = interacting directly with things
D = using ideas and information (called Data) without interacting
    with people or things

Then decide your most important orientations by checking the following:

Data: I want to get involved with Data on my job:

_____ At a modest level with data that is easy to learn or that I simply keep track of while others direct my work.

_____ At a high level by putting ideas and information together to plan/organize work and perhaps develop new ideas and way to do things.

People: I want to get involved with People on my job:

_____ At a modest level by being friendly and cooperative, greeting and serving them, discussing simple problems with them.

_____ At a high level by leading/influencing/organizing/motivating them, teaching/entertaining them, negotiating, or exchanging ideas with them, counseling them.

Things: I want to get involved with Things on my job:

_____ At a modest level by following simple procedures set up by others.

_____ At a high level by working with more complex procedures/equipment that allow my own input.

3. Identifying Favorite Activities

From your expanded activity list, star and then write your favorite activities in the Favorite Activities Chart. Be sure to state what you *did* as specifically as possible. Then check (√) the numbers of the ten basic skills you used to perform each favorite activity. For example, if you ordered supplies by phone, you would check 4, 5, and 7. If you arranged food attractively on a plate, you would check 6 and 9.

Favorite Activities Chart

Activity	1. Logical intelligence	2. Intuitive intelligence	3. Verbal ability	4. Numerical ability	5. Precise detail	6. Multidimensional awareness	7. Businesslike contact with people	8. Influencing people	9. Finger/hand agility	10. Whole body agility

Which of the basic ten activities do you like to use the most? _____

4. The Ten Basic Skills

Circle the numbers of the ten basic skills that you prefer to use:

1. Logical intelligence	6. Multidimensional awareness
2. Intuitive intelligence	7. Businesslike contact with people
3. Verbal ability	8. Influencing people
4. Numerical ability	9. Finger/hand agility
5. Precise detail	10. Whole body agility

5. Proud Accomplishment Articulator

Collect words that describe you using the following checklist.

Action Verb Checklist

Check off the action verbs that apply to you. Doublecheck the actions you enjoy and wouldn't mind repeating.

In the past when using DATA I have:	Interacting with PEOPLE I have:	Dealing with THINGS I have:
_____ Administered	_____ Assigned	_____ Adjusted
_____ Analyzed	_____ Assisted	_____ Altered
_____ Budgeted	_____ Cared for	_____ Arranged
_____ Compared	_____ Communicated	_____ Assembled
_____ Computed	_____ Coordinated	_____ Balanced
_____ Compiled	_____ Consulted	_____ Built
_____ Coordinated	_____ Counseled	_____ Cleaned
_____ Decided	_____ Delegated	_____ Cut
_____ Designed	_____ Developed	_____ Decorated
_____ Developed	_____ Directed	_____ Demonstrated
_____ Evaluated	_____ Encouraged	_____ Driven
_____ Illustrated	_____ Entertained	_____ Fabricated
_____ Formulated	_____ Evaluated	_____ Fitted
_____ Implemented	_____ Hired	_____ Guarded

In the past when using DATA I have:	Interacting with PEOPLE I have:	Dealing with THINGS I have:
_____ Innovated	_____ Instructed	_____ Guided
_____ Interpreted	_____ Interviewed	_____ Handled
_____ Learned	_____ Led	_____ Improved
_____ Marketed	_____ Listened	_____ Inspected
_____ Organized	_____ Managed	_____ Installed
_____ Planned	_____ Motivated	_____ Lifted
_____ Promoted	_____ Negotiated	_____ Made
_____ Publicized	_____ Organized	_____ Measured
_____ Read	_____ Persuaded	_____ Mixed
_____ Recorded	_____ Protected	_____ Moved
_____ Reported	_____ Referred	_____ Operated
_____ Researched	_____ Represented	_____ Processed
_____ Scheduled	_____ Served	_____ Repaired
_____ Synthesized	_____ Shared	_____ Set up
_____ Theorized	_____ Sold	_____ Shaped
_____ Visualized	_____ Supervised	_____ Tended
_____ Written	_____ Trained	_____ Tested

Adjective Checklist

Check off the personal responsibility adjectives that apply to you and describe your method of work.

I am:

_____ Articulate	_____ Loyal
_____ Conscientious	_____ Persistent
_____ Committed	_____ Persuasive
_____ Competent	_____ Positive
_____ Confident	_____ Productive
_____ Consistent	_____ Qualified

_____ Decisive	_____ Reliable
_____ Dependable	_____ Resourceful
_____ Effective	_____ Responsible
_____ Efficient	_____ Sensitive
_____ Energetic	_____ Self-motivated
_____ Enthusiastic	_____ Stable
_____ Experienced	_____ Successful
_____ Flexible	_____ Thorough
_____ Knowledgeable	_____ Well organized

6. Personal Responsibility Skills Checklist

Evaluate yourself and your ability to handle data, people, and things. After each statement put a check ($\sqrt{}$) for "Good" and (+) for "Could Improve."

	Good	Could improve
a. Evaluate YOURSELF		
Dress appropriately for work	$\sqrt{}$	_____
Manage needs and wants without interfering with the rights of others	$\sqrt{}$	_____
Control and channel impulses and feelings in an effective way	_____	$\sqrt{}$
Display common sense, enthusiasm, a sense of humor	_____	$\sqrt{}$
b. Evaluate your interaction with PEOPLE		
Respond with tact and courtesy	$\sqrt{}$	_____
Accept criticism without anger and learn from others	_____	$\sqrt{}$
Respect and compliment the ideas and good work of others	$\sqrt{}$	_____
Share with and assist others; enjoy teamwork; admit mistakes; know when to apologize, communicate assertively without attacking or blaming others	_____	$\sqrt{}$

c. Evaluate your interaction with DATA and
   THINGS

	Good	Could improve
I usually:		
Follow rules and help make them more reasonable	✓	
Work independently without many questions or much outside help		✓
Am flexible and willing to learn and to try new and unfamiliar tasks	✓	
Carry through on difficult or pressured work on time, without excuses		✓
Take care of property, equipment	✓	

7. Work-Specific Skills

List your work-specific skills—those acquired by education or training to do a particular job:

_____   _____

_____   _____

_____   _____

_____   _____

8. Sharing Your Discoveries

In the space that follows (or on a separate sheet of paper), write an enthusiastic paragraph or letter about yourself and your abilities to a potential employer (or friend). Use as many of the skill words from this chapter as possible to describe yourself and show that you would be an effective worker.

THE CAREER CONNECTION: FINDING YOUR JOB SATISFIERS

F O C U S

Identify your key qualities.

Find your key qualities on the Job Group Chart.

Survey the job market for your interest areas.

· · · · · ·

W hen you have surveyed your life activities, skills, and interests, you are ready to summarize all of this information in the Key Qualities Indicator. You will then connect this data with the whole U.S. job market. About 20,000 different occupations have been identified and defined by the U.S. Department of Labor. The results of this investigation are contained in a monumental work called the *Dictionary of Occupational Titles* (DOT).[1] The book is a gold mine of information—if you know how to dig for the gold. Because of alternate titles for the same job, the 20,000 occupations result in about 40,000 listings. Job titles are listed both alphabetically and by industry. The alphabetical listings give the code number needed to find a short description of each job, which is located among descriptions grouped by occupational area. These clusters of similar jobs make the search much easier.

The DOT supplement, *Guide for Occupational Exploration,*[2] provides additional help by classifying jobs into sixty-six groups. A *job group* is a cluster of occupations that call for similar worker characteristics, called *key qualities.* In this chapter you will rate yourself on these key qualities. From this self-rating you will be able to see which groups of jobs are most in harmony with your interests and skills. Sixty-six job groups with 20,000 jobs—there must be a job for you!

· · · · · · · · · · · · ·

Key Qualities Indicator

- Circle the *numbers* of those qualities that are important for you in your career. It is not necessary for the entire description of each quality to apply to you.

- Now go back and place an **M** in front of the numbers of those skills you want to use at a modest level of ability. Place an **H** in front of the numbers of those skills you want to use at a high level of ability.

Data Skills

_____ **1. Logical Intelligence:** Think, observe, plan, analyze, evaluate, understand, problem solve. Put ideas and information together to deal with complex operations, to plan, organize work. Keep track of verbal and numerical information in an orderly way, make decisions using common sense based on "practical" experience.

_____ **2. Intuitive Intelligence:** Imagine, compare, see things "holistically," decide based on best guesses and "intuitive" common sense rather than rules or measurements. Use words, numbers, or symbols creatively, develop new ideas, new processes, new combinations.

_____ 3. **Verbal Ability:** Use words to read, research, write, listen, record, discuss, direct, instruct, communicate, motivate.

_____ 4. **Numerical Ability:** Use numbers and symbols to figure, calculate, estimate, keep books, budget, analyze.

_____ 5. **Precise Detail:** Follow directions exactly, make decisions based on set rules or measurements; attend to small details in proofreading words or numbers or examining lines and shapes of products.

_____ 6. **Multidimensional Awareness:** Understand, visualize, relate two- or three-dimensional lines or shapes, spaces, shading—sometimes in color.

People Skills

_____ 7. **Businesslike Contact with People:** Manage, supervise, organize, motivate, entertain, train, serve, negotiate with, cooperate with people.

_____ 8. **Influencing People:** Persuade/inspire others to think or behave in certain ways; teach, exchange, interpret ideas/facts/feelings, help solve personal problems.

Thing Skills

_____ 9. **Finger/Hand Agility:** Use fingers/hands to make, repair, process, test, assemble, operate various products/machines/tools using special techniques, sometimes very complex.

_____ 10. **Whole Body Agility:** Use the whole body to handle, carry, lift, move, balance, or coordinate itself or things.

Work Qualities

11. **Repetition:** Duties involve a set way of doing things, sometimes over and over again.

12. **Variety:** Duties change frequently, requiring a flexible response, different knowledge and skills.

13. **Physical Risk:** Duties involve pressure in stressful, dangerous situations but sometimes provide adventure and excitement.

14. **Status:** Recognition that you are someone important or in authority.

THE JOB GROUP CHART

Now comes the moment you've been waiting for—time to identify all the groups of jobs that have your satisfiers. Your future career will turn up somewhere on the Job Group Chart.[3] The chart is subdivided as follows:

Personality Types: Jobs that are compatible with the six personality types are grouped together—realistic, investigative, artistic, social, enterprising, and convention—as you identified in the Personality Mosaic. The chart then makes an even finer distinction, however, by subdividing the personality types into twelve interest areas. Realistic, for example, is subdivided into mechanical, industrial, nature, protective, and physical performing areas. Realistic persons will find appealing jobs by studying these categories. They will discover that people with similar personalities work in them..

Job Groups: The numbers 1–66 in the lefthand column refer to the sixty-six job groups identified by the Department of Labor. All jobs in a group have similar characteristics, with some slight exceptions. They call for similar preferences regarding involvement with data, people, and things; they have the same key qualities; and they call for the same skills. For example, one job group is "engineering." There are many kinds of engineering—civil, electrical, mechanical, to name a few—but all engineers and engineering jobs have many characteristics in common, even though the job titles are not identical.

Decimal Code: Decimal numbers such as 05.01 refer to the numbered items in the Department of Labor's *Guide for Occupational Exploration,* available in many libraries and state employment offices. The first two digits, 01 through 12, designate the twelve interest areas.

Key Qualities: Each of the fourteen columns following in the job group has a symbol in it. The symbol M means an average need for the key qualities in that particular group of jobs; the symbol H means higher than average need. The symbol ● means that the quality is needed without indicating any degree of need.

Job Group Chart Directions: Finding Your Satisfiers

1. Read the description of each job group found in the left margin of the Job Group Chart. Circle any of the numbers, 1 through 66, of groups that interest you.

2. Using a colored pencil, locate the key qualities at the top of each column that match those you circled on the Key Qualities Indicator. Then go down the columns you have marked and put circles around each symbol indicating your satisfiers. *Do the whole chart.* When you finish, you will discover which job groups have most of your satisfiers.

3. Notice that the twelve interest areas are grouped by personality type. Find your personality types but also look in other areas for satisfiers.

R—REALISTIC JOB GROUPS

Column headers:
1. Logical Intelligence
2. Intuitive Intelligence
3. Verbal Ability
4. Numerical Ability
5. Precise Detail
6. Multidimensional Awareness
7. Businesslike Contact with People
8. Influencing People
9. Finger/Hand Agility
10. Whole Body Agility
11. Repetition
12. Variety
13. Physical Risk
14. Status

MECHANICAL

#	Code	Description	1	2	3	4	5	6	7	8	9	10	11	12	13	14
1.	05.01	Engineering: Applying research of science and math to design of new products and systems.	H	H	H	H	M	H	M	M	M			•		
2.	05.02	Managerial Work–Mechanical: Managing technical plants or systems.	H	H	H	H	M	H	H	M	M			•		•
3.	05.03	Engineering Technology: Collecting, recording, coordinating technical information.	H	H	M	H	H	H			H					
4.	05.04	Air and Water Vehicle Operations: Operating planes/ships to carry freight/passengers.	H	H	H	H	H	H	H		M	M			•	•
5.	05.05	Craft Technology: Doing highly skilled hand/machine custom work.	M	M		M	H	H			H	M		•		
6.	05.06	Systems Operation: Caring for large, complicated mechanical systems like heating/power.	M		M	M	H	M	M		M			•		
7.	05.07	Quality Control: Checking/testing materials/products in nonfactory situations.	M	M		M	H	M			M		•			
8.	05.08	Land Vehicle Operation: Operating/driving vehicles that haul freight.	M			M	M				M	M	•			
9.	05.09	Materials Control: Keeping records of flow/storage of materials and products.	M		M	M	H		M		M		•			
10.	05.10	Skilled Hand and Machine Work: Doing moderately skilled hand/machine work.				M	H	M			M		•			
11.	05.11	Equipment Operation: Operating/driving heavy equipment such as in construction, mining.	M				H	M			M	M	•			
12.	05.12	Manual Labor–Mechanical: Doing nonfactory manual labor with machines, tools.					H	M			M	M	•			

INDUSTRIAL

#	Code	Description	1	2	3	4	5	6	7	8	9	10	11	12	13	14
13.	06.01	Production Technology: Setting up/operating machines to produce goods in specific ways.	M			M	H	M	H		M					
14.	06.02	Production Work: Doing hand/machine work to make a product: supervising/inspecting.	M			M	H	M	H		M		•			
15.	06.03	Quality Control: Testing, weighing, inspecting, measuring products to meet standards.	M				H	M			M		•			
16.	06.04	Manual Labor–Industrial: Basic manual labor in production requiring little training.						M			M	M	•			

NATURE

#	Code	Description	1	2	3	4	5	6	7	8	9	10	11	12	13	14
17.	03.01	Managerial Work–Nature: Planning work for farming, fisheries, logging, horticulture.	H	H	M	M	M	M	M		M			•		
18.	03.02	General Supervision–Nature: Supervising on farms, in forests, fisheries, nurseries, parks.	M	M	M	M	M	M	H		M			•		•
19.	03.03	Animal Training/Care: Training, breeding, raising, showing, caring for nonfarm animals.	M	M	M		M	M			M	M	•	•		
20.	03.04	Manual Labor–Nature: Doing basic physical labor related to farming, fishing, gardening.						M			M	M	•			

PROTECTIVE

#	Code	Description	1	2	3	4	5	6	7	8	9	10	11	12	13	14
21.	04.01	Safety/Law Enforcement: Administration, enforcement of laws/regulations.	H	H	H		M	M	H	H	M			•	•	•
22.	04.02	Security Services: Protecting people and property from crime, fire, other hazards.	M	M	M			M	M		M	M	•		•	

PHYSICAL PERFORMANCE

#	Code	Description	1	2	3	4	5	6	7	8	9	10	11	12	13	14
23.	12.01	Sports: Of all sorts; playing, training, coaching, and officiating.	M	M	M		M	M	M	M	H	H			•	•
24.	12.02	Physical Feats: Amusing/entertaining people with special physical skills/strengths.	M	M	M		M	H	M		H	H			•	•

I—INVESTIGATIVE JOB GROUPS

SCIENTIFIC/ANALYTIC

	1. Logical Intelligence	2. Intuitive Intelligence	3. Verbal Ability	4. Numerical Ability	5. Precise Detail	6. Multidimensional Awareness	7. Businesslike Contact with People	8. Influencing People	9. Finger/Hand Agility	10. Whole Body Agility	11. Repetition	12. Variety	13. Physical Risk	14. Status
25. 02.01 Physical Sciences: Research/development in physics, chemistry, geology, computer science.	H	H	H	H	M	H		M	M					
26. 02.02 Life Sciences: Studying functions of living things/ways they relate to environments.	H	H	H	H	M	H		M	H					
27. 02.03 Medical Sciences: Practicing medicine to prevent, diagnose, cure illnesses of people or animals.	H	H	H	H	M	H	M	H	H			•		•
(1) 05.01 Engineering: Applying research of science and math to design of new products and systems.	H	H	H	H	M	H	M	M	M			•		
28. 02.04 Laboratory Technology: Doing laboratory work to carry out studies of various researchers.	H			H	M	H		M						
29. 11.01 Mathematics/Statistics: Using numbers and computers to analyze and solve problems.	H	M	H	H	H	H	M	M	M					

A—ARTISTIC JOB GROUPS

ARTISTIC/CREATIVE

	1.	2.	3.	4.	5.	6.	7.	8.	9.	10.	11.	12.	13.	14.
30. 01.01 Literary Arts: Producing creative pieces from writing to publishing for print, TV, films.	H	H	H					M	M					•
31. 01.02 Visual Arts: Doing artistic work (paintings, designs, photographs) for sale or for media.	H	H					H	M	M	H				
32. 01.03 Performing Arts–Drama: Performing, directing, teaching for stage, radio, TV, film.	H	H	H				H	M		M				•
33. 01.04 Performing Arts–Music: Playing an instrument, singing, arranging, composing, conducting music.	H	H	H		H	H	H	M	H	H				•
34. 01.05 Performing Arts–Dance: Performing, teaching, choreographing dance routines.	H	H	M		M	H	H	M	H	H				•
35. 01.06 Craft Arts: Producing handcrafts, graphics, decorative products.	M	M			H	H			H					
36. 01.07 Amusement Arts: Entertaining/doing novel routines at carnivals, circuses, fairs.	M	M	M			M	H	M		M	•			
37. 01.08 Modeling: Posing for artists; displaying clothing, accessories, other products.	M							M		M	•			•

S—SOCIAL JOB GROUPS

HUMAN SERVICES

	1.	2.	3.	4.	5.	6.	7.	8.	9.	10.	11.	12.	13.	14.
38. 10.01 Social Services: Helping people deal with personal, vocational, educational, religious concerns.	H	H	H	M			H	H				•		•
39. 10.02 Nursing/Therapy Services: Providing diagnosis and therapy to help people get well.	H	H	H	H	H	M	H	H	M	M		•		
40. 10.03 Child/Adult Care: Assisting with medical/physical care/services.	M	M	M		H		M	M	M	M	•	•		

ACCOMMODATING

	1.	2.	3.	4.	5.	6.	7.	8.	9.	10.	11.	12.	13.	14.
41. 09.01 Hospitality Services: Touring, guiding, greeting serving people to help them feel comfortable.	M	M	M		M		H	M	M			•		•
42. 09.02 Barber/Beauty Services: Hair/skin care to help people with personal appearances.	M	M	M		M	H	M	M	H			•		
43. 09.03 Passenger Services: Transporting people by vehicle; also instructing/supervising.	M	M		M	M	M	M		M	M	•			
44. 09.04 Customer Services: Waiting on people in a routine way in business settings.	M		M	M	M		M		M		•			
45. 09.05 Attendant Services: Providing personal services to people at home or when traveling.	M		M				M		M	M	•			

S/E—SOCIAL/ENTERPRISING JOB GROUPS

LEADING/INFLUENCING

		1. Logical Intelligence	2. Intuitive Intelligence	3. Verbal Ability	4. Numerical Ability	5. Precise Detail	6. Multidimensional Awareness	7. Businesslike Contact with People	8. Influencing People	9. Finger/Hand Agility	10. Whole Body Agility	11. Repetition	12. Variety	13. Physical Risk	14. Status
46. 11.02	Educational/Library Services: Teaching, providing library services.	H	H	H	M	H		H	H				•		•
47. 11.03	Social Research: Studying people of various backgrounds both past and present.	H	H	H	H	H			M				•		
48. 11.04	Law: Counseling, advising, representing people, businesses regarding legal matters.	H	H	H	H	M		H	H				•		•
49. 11.05	Business Administration: Designing procedures, solving problems, supervising people in business.	H	H	H	H	M		H	H				•		•
50. 11.06	Finance: Setting up financial systems; controlling, analyzing financial records.	H	H	H	H	H		H	M						•
51. 11.07	Services Administration: Designing procedures, solving problems, supervising people in business.	H	H	H	M	M		H	H				•		•
52. 11.08	Communications: Writing, editing, translating information for media—radio, print, and TV.	H	H	H	M	M		M	M				•		•
53. 11.09	Promotion: Advertising, fund raising, sales, and public relations.	H	H	H	H			H	H				•		•
54. 11.10	Regulations Enforcement: Checking/enforcing government regulations, company policies, procedures.	H	H	H	M	M	M	M	M				•		
55. 11.11	Business Management: Taking responsibility for operation and supervision of a business.	H	H	H	M	M	M	H					•		•
56. 11.12	Contracts and Claims: Negotiating contracts, investigating claims.	H	H	H	M	M		H	H				•		•

E—ENTERPRISING JOB GROUPS

PERSUADING

		1.	2.	3.	4.	5.	6.	7.	8.	9.	10.	11.	12.	13.	14.
57. 08.01	Sales Technology: Selling technical equipment or services including insurance. Also clerical work.	H	H	H	H	M	M	M	H	M					•
58. 08.02	General Sales: Selling goods and services, wholesale/retail to individuals, business, or industry.	M	M	M	M			H	M						
59. 08.03	Vending: Peddling, promoting items in public settings.				M			H	M	M		•			

C–CONVENTIONAL JOB GROUPS

BUSINESS DETAIL

		1.	2.	3.	4.	5.	6.	7.	8.	9.	10.	11.	12.	13.	14.
60. 07.01	Administrative Detail: Doing secretarial/technical clerical work.	H	H	H	M	H		H	M	M			•		
61. 07.02	Mathematical Detail: Keeping numerical records, doing basic figuring.	M		M	M	H		M		M		•			
62. 07.03	Financial Detail: Keeping track of money flow to and from the public.	M		M	M	H		M		M		•			
63. 07.04	Oral Communications: Giving information in person or by communication systems.	M		M	M	M		M	M	M		•	•		
64. 07.05	Records Processing: Putting records together and keeping them up to date.	M		M	M	H		M		M		•			
65. 07.06	Clerical Machine Operation: Using various machines to record, process, and compute data.	M				H		M		H		•			
66. 07.07	Clerical Handling: Keeping data in order by filing, copying, sorting, delivering.	M		M		M				M		•			

Job Group Chart Follow-up

Some lucky people find the job of their dreams just by observing where their circles line up opposite one job group on the Job Group Chart. Perhaps the assessment results supported goals they had already established. Many are surprised to find a good career choice they had never considered before. If you think you have already made your career choice, ask yourself these questions.

- Is this career clearly your own choice?
- Are you afraid to take a look at other alternatives?
- Are you willing to keep an open mind by considering important factors that may change your decision?
- Can you support your choice with facts about your skills, interests, and values?

Most people are dismayed to find themselves definitely at sea in an ocean of many choices. If you are wondering why YOU don't have a nice, neat job title in hand, you may be tempted to give up. But if you keep searching, you will have a great chance to learn more about yourself and the work world. You will be more willing to explore important supporting factors that go into a career choice, and you will have the joy of learning that many enjoyable careers would suit you equally well. All in all, the career search process is a confidence builder. Even those with a clearcut career choice need to learn about the job market and how to connect with it.

- Study the Job Group Chart line by line to find groups that look interesting. Some of your satisfiers may be more important than others. Try to be as flexible as possible. Maybe you have indicated that the physical activity related to whole body agility is an important quality for you, but in looking at the other qualities that are required in such jobs, you find that most of those jobs would not suit you.

- Double star (**) any job group that has all of your satisfiers. If you choose a job group that is not listed under any of your top three personality types, you may still be able to find ways to express your personality in some jobs in the group. Be aware that the Job Group Chart is only an imperfect summary of the qualities to be found in thousands of jobs. An individual company can change a job title, alter the job duties at will, and come up with something that no job chart could describe in one line! It's important not to force the data about yourself to make it fit the Job Group Chart. But it's important to be open to all sorts of possibilities that may be hidden there.

▼ Mini-Career Search: Four Worlds/Twelve Interest Areas

Now that you have looked over the whole job market, step back and identify those interest areas that are important to you by taking the "Four Worlds" Inventory. Circle the numbers of those statements that sound like you or something you might say. I enjoy myself and lose track of time when I'm:

1. Having a friendly conversation with someone
2. Organizing my papers, files, and notebooks
3. Thinking up new ideas
4. Fixing something
5. Talking someone into doing a project
6. Keeping assignments up to date
7. Doing a puzzle
8. Tinkering with some gadget
9. Helping someone
10. Taking responsibility for every detail of an assignment
11. Reading to explore new things
12. Being physically active
13. Sharing my feelings
14. Completing a job as carefully as possible
15. Creating something different
16. Using my hands in some project
17. Getting people organized
18. Keeping track of my accounts
19. Discussing or reading some complicated idea
20. Doing physically daring things

To find out which world you live in, circle on the following table the same numbers you circled on the Mini-Career Search. Then count the circles in each column to learn which is your world.

						Totals
People	1	5	9	13	17	3
Paper	2	6	10	14	18	2
Mind	3	7	11	15	19	1
Matter	4	8	12	16	20	0

CAREER FOCUS

With your unique personality, you tend to live in one or more of "four worlds": People, Paper, Mind, or Matter. By identifying which are important to you, you can zero in more closely on interest areas in the Job Group Chart of importance to you.

World of Matter: Things/Body

- Mechanical
- Industrial (Factory)
- Nature (Plants/ Animals
- Protective
- Physical Performing

Generally involved with things from simple to complex. Little involvement with people unless supervising or managing. Use of data depends on complexity of job. Skills required range from finger/hand to whole body agility, coordination, strength—along with moderate intelligence, some multidimensional awareness and, in many cases, ability with numbers.

World of Mind: Ideas/Intellect

- Scientific/Analytic
- Artistic/Intuitive

Usually involves high to medium use of data. Little involvement with people except in medicine. Often deals with things or thinking about things, problem solving. Skills required are generally above-average logical and intuitive intelligence, verbal and often numerical ability, and in some cases a well-developed sense of multidimensional awareness and color.

World of People: Helping/Motivating

- Human Services
- Accommodating
- Leading/Influencing
- Persuading/Selling

Generally an ongoing involvement with people. Level of involvement with data increases with complexity of work. Usually little or no involvement with things except in jobs requiring physical contact. Requires a range of "people skills": facility in dealing with people, solving people problems, and providing human services.

World of Paper: Words/Numbers/Symbols

- Business Detail

Consistent use of data: words, numbers, symbols. Usually little involvement with people beyond what is required to process business details. Deals with things in terms of office machines. Skills required are moderate intelligence in most cases, verbal and numerical ability, an eye for detail, and in some cases finger/hand agility.

The Twelve Interest Areas

Which are of interest to you at this time?

01 Artistic: An interest in creative expression of feelings/ideas.

02 Scientific: An interest in discovering, collecting, analyzing information about the natural world, and applying scientific research findings to problems in medicine, the life sciences, and the natural sciences.

03 Nature: Plants and Animals: An interest in working with plants and animals, usually outdoors.

04 Protective: An interest in applying mechanical principles to practical situations by use of machines or tools.

06 Industrial: An interest in repetitive, concrete, organized activities done in a factory setting.

07 Business Detail: An interest in organized, clearly defined activities requiring accuracy and attention to details, primarily in an office setting.

08 Persuading/Selling: An interest in bringing others to a particular point of view by personal persuasion, using sales promotion techniques.

09 Accommodating: An interest in catering to the wants and needs of others, usually on a one-to-one basis.

10 Human Services: An interest in helping others with their mental, spiritual, social, physical, or vocational needs.

11 Leading/Influencing: An interest in leading and influencing others by using high-level verbal or numerical abilities.

12 Physical Performing: An interest in physical activities performed before an audience.[4]

As noted, the twelve interest areas that represent the job market as a whole can be grouped into four "worlds": People, Paper, Mind, and Matter. Each world relates to one or more of the six personality types: realistic, investigative, artistic, social, enterprising, and conventional.

The world of matter (or things) involves the five interest areas—mechanical, industrial, nature, protective, and physical performance—associated on the

Job Group Chart with realistic jobs and personality. The realistic personality gravitates toward jobs that deal with mechanical systems; factory or production work; heavy outdoor work with nature; police, fire, or other protective work; and physical performing activities such as sports and acrobatics. Some jobs in the world of matter give the R person with a social bent the opportunity to have the best of two worlds—things and people—by doing some management and supervision.

Social persons who score high in some material categories may wish to work with things only if they are also realistic types. Social persons already in thing-oriented jobs might wish to try management, supervision, or even personnel, training, or selling. In such social/investigative areas as the health field, they would work with both people and things. Realistic personalities with few social characteristics often find that a promotion to management status brings headaches they'd rather be without.

The mind world is for the logical/rational, investigative personality with a strong realistic bent who enjoys the physical/biological sciences and engineering. Purely investigative persons with little interest in the physical world usually take their inquiring minds into areas such as theoretical math or research in social sciences or business—that is, any area that requires little interaction with things or people.

Artistic persons use their intuitive minds in painting, sculpture, or crafts, if they have a facility with things. The more investigative artistic types deal with music and writing. Some artistic persons with little specific "talent" give creative expression to their many ideas in a variety of other environments.

The world of people extends to four interest areas—human services, accommodating, leading/influencing, and persuading—associated with the social category of jobs and personality. Jobs in these areas involve helping or motivating people. For new career seekers who would love to work with people, opportunities range from waiter to psychiatrist, from manager to mortician! Such jobs involve being with people all day: greeting people, waiting on them, taking charge of a group, solving business or personal problems. These jobs often require leadership to organize a group, show people what to do, and direct a project.

If you wish to work with people at a high level, consider earning a degree in business or one of the behavioral sciences. You will need to have or develop creativity and intuition if you work with people on any but the lowest level. If you are a social type in a realistic, investigative, artistic, or conventional job, look around your workplace for a job that will give you more contact with people.

The world of paper (which now includes the videoscreen world) attracts conventional people who are careful about detail. If you have a realistic bent, you will enjoy paperwork related to machinery such as computers or calculators. If you have a social bent, you will like gathering information from people and passing it on. If you are working in any other category, look for some ways to handle the data of your work environment.

People are attracted to jobs for all sorts of reasons besides interest in the job itself. We want people to like us. We'd like to feel important. We want to avoid competition, to please our parents, to look like the stereotypical successful male or female, to earn more money. We are influenced by the convenience and availability of jobs. All of these reasons tap into our value system. But can you find satisfaction in a career field that doesn't interest you? This all-important question must be balanced out with your values. If you pay attention to your strong interests, you will have fewer conflicts with your value system.

Just a Job or a Career?

Another thing to keep in mind as you choose a career is the degree of commitment you are willing to make. Do you want a career or just a job? A job might be defined as something one does to earn money, requiring little involvement beyond one's physical and mental presence performing in a routine way. Many people at all levels of intelligence and creativity use work in this way: some because their job is the only work they want or can get; others to support hobbies and creative activities for which there seem to be no work opportunities.

A career, in contrast to a job, can be seen as a series of work experiences that represents progression in a field. It is work that captivates much of a person's total energy. A career is planned for, trained for, and involves dedication of time and talent beyond the minimum required.

When two people are doing identical work, one may view it as "just a job" and another as "my career." Sometimes a person trains and sacrifices to achieve a career only to face disillusionment for some unforeseen reason and ends up performing tasks mechanically, seeing no way out. Conversely, some people have been known to perform what society calls "menial" work with a level of dedication worthy of a professional.

Some work is almost impossible to perform without a great deal of personal involvement. In our society, for example, "moving up" generally is an all-consuming activity. How much are you willing to sacrifice? For some, "success" has meant loss of family, health, friendship, and leisure. One can get caught up in work only to find that other values have slipped away. Others can pursue a career with great dedication and yet manage to keep a balance.

How much involvement is enough for you? Sometimes your commitment to a career increases greatly when you become aware of your interests and skills and the way they relate to the world of work. Motivation and energy soar. Keep the question of commitment in mind as you consider your career choice.

Library Research

Library research enables you to survey the whole job market and eliminate those areas that would not work for you while you zero in on those that are important. Your most helpful guides will be the *Guide for Occupational Exploration* and the *Dictionary of Occupational Titles*. The McKnight *Worker Trait Group Guide* is another of the many helpful books about careers[5] and is easy to handle because it lists only nationally important job titles. You can find these books in career centers, library reference rooms, and state employment offices.

Before you go to the library, list all the job groups that you would like to explore. Use the decimal code number from the Job Group Chart for easy reference. At the library, look up those numbers in the *Guide for Occupational Exploration*. As you explore the job groups, make a list of all the job titles listed after each one that you would like to explore further. Eliminate areas that don't interest you, but keep groups and titles on your list until you have explored each one. This process enables you to survey the entire job market without looking up *every* job title or even every job group.

Suppose you are interested in Job Group 55, Business Management, code number 11.11. In the *Guide for Occupational Exploration* you will find this information:

> Workers in this group manage a business, such as a store or cemetery, a branch of a large company, such as a local office for a credit corporation, or a department within a company, such as a warehouse. They usually carry out operating policies and procedures determined by administration workers, such as presidents, vice-presidents, and directors. Some managers own their own businesses and are considered self-employed. Managers find employment in all kinds of businesses as well as government agencies.

This paragraph is followed by answers to some important questions: What kind of work would you do as a business manager? What skill and abilities do you need for this kind of work? How do you know if you would like or could learn to do this kind of work? How can you prepare for and enter this kind of work? What else should you consider about these jobs? This information is followed by a list of all the job categories in the Business Management group:

11.11.01 Lodging

11.11.02 Recreation and Amusement

11.11.03 Transportation

11.11.04 Services

11.11.05 Wholesale-Retail

Each of these listings is subdivided into specific job titles, each identified by a nine-digit number. Under Wholesale-Retail, for example, you will find: Manager, Retail Store 185.167.046. If this particular job interests you, you can find a description of it in the *Dictionary of Occupational Titles* just by looking up the nine digit number, 185.167.046. The section will include other similar job titles so that you can explore a variety of jobs.

Remember that titles for the same job differ from one company to another. But if you know what general functions you want to perform, and if you spend enough time with these books, you will have an overview of the whole job market and understand what you can do in it.

By now you should have your job chart well marked. You've noticed which of the twelve interest areas your circles tend to cluster in and which of the sixty-six job groups offer your most important satisfiers. Whenever many of your likes and skills point toward the same job group, you've hit the bullseye on the career target.

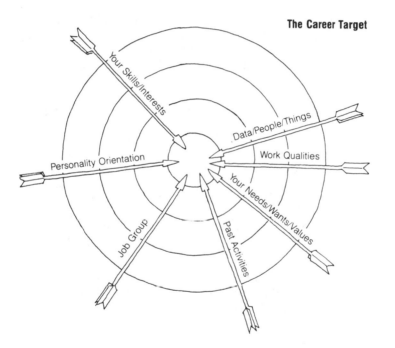

The Career Target

At this point you might be feeling a little scared/anxious/confused. These are all normal feelings for anyone on the verge of a *great discovery!* Keep going! Don't be overwhelmed if you find that several jobs look good to you. Some people are comfortable in a number of areas. Sometimes a person needs more experience with work before making a decision. Give yourself more time if you need it. Don't decide to decide without seeing clearly.

There are still other activities you can do to help your decision along. Finding out about projected job market trends for your areas of interest can be helpful here. But one of the best ways to decide is to get some "inside information" through work experience, group tours of workplaces, or interviewing people who work in your area of interest. The rest of this manual will give you some help with these concerns.

Making a good career decision is a growth process, and growth takes patience. You can't make a flower grow by pulling on it!

▼ Self-Assessment Exercises

1. Job Groups Expanded

A list of the sixty-six Job Groups and their subcategories follows. They are in a somewhat different order here than in the Job Group Chart. Circle those of interest to you at this time.

Summary List of Interest Areas, Job Groups, and Subgroups

01	ARTISTIC/CREATIVE

01.01   Literary Arts
01.01-01 Editing
01.01-02 Creative Writing
01.01-03 Critiquing

01.02   Visual Arts
01.02-01 Instructing and
          Appraising
01.02-02 Studio Art
01.02-03 Commercial Art

**01.03   Performing Arts:
          Drama**
01.03-01 Instructing and
          Directing
01.03-02 Performing
01.03-03 Narrating and
          Announcing

**01.04   Performing Arts:
          Music**
01.04-01 Instructing and
          Directing
01.04-02 Composing and
          Arranging
01.04-03 Vocal Performing
01.04-04 Instrumental
          Performing

**01.05   Performing Arts:
          Dance**
01.05-01 Instructing and
          Choreography
01.05-02 Performing

01.06   Craft Arts
01.06-01 Graphic Arts and
          Related Crafts
01.06-02 Arts and Crafts
01.06-03 Hand Lettering,
          Painting, and
          Decorating

01.07   Elemental Arts
01.07-01 Psychic Science
01.07-02 Announcing
01.07-03 Entertaining

01.08   Modeling
01.08-01 Personal Appearance

| 02 | SCIENTIFIC/
ANALYTIC |
|---|---|

02.01   Physical Sciences
02.01-01 Theoretical Research
02.01-02 Technology

02.02   Life Sciences
02.02-01 Animal Specialization
02.02-02 Plant Specialization
02.02-03 Plant and Animal
          Specialization
02.02-04 Food Research

02.03   Medical Sciences
02.03-01 Medicine and Surgery
02.03-02 Dentistry
02.03-03 Veterinary Medicine
02.03-04 Health Specialties

**02.04   Laboratory
          Technology**
02.04-01 Physical Sciences
02.04-02 Life Sciences

| 03 | NATURE (PLANTS,
ANIMALS) |
|---|---|

**03.01   Managerial Work:
          Plants and Animals**
03.01-01 Farming
03.01-02 Specialty Breeding
03.01-03 Specialty Cropping
03.01-04 Forestry and Logging

03.02 **General Supervision: Plants and Animals**
03.02-01 Farming
03.02-02 Forestry and Logging
03.02-03 Nursery and Groundskeeping
03.02-04 Services

03.03 **Animal Training and Service**
03.03-01 Animal Training
03.03-02 Animal Service

03.04 **Elemental Work: Plants and Animals**
03.04-01 Farming
03.04-02 Forestry and Logging
03.04-03 Hunting and Fishing
03.04-04 Nursery and Groundskeeping
03.04-05 Services

04 **PROTECTIVE**

04.01 **Safety and Law Enforcement**
04.01-01 Managing
04.01-02 Investigating

04.02 **Security Services**
04.02-01 Detention
04.02-02 Property and People
04.02-03 Law and Order
04.02-04 Emergency Responding

05 **MECHANICAL**

05.01 **Engineering**
05.01-01 Research
05.01-02 Environmental Protection
05.01-03 Systems Design
05.01-04 Testing and Quality Control
05.01-05 Sales Engineering
05.01-06 Work Planning and Utilization
05.01-07 Design
05.01-08 General Engineering

05.02 **Managerial Work: Mechanical**
05.02-01 Systems
05.02-02 Maintenance and Construction
05.02-03 Processing and Manufacturing
05.02-04 Communications

05.02-05 Mining, Logging, and Petroleum Production
05.02-06 Services
05.02-07 Materials Handling

05.03 **Engineering Technology**
05.03-01 Surveying
05.03-02 Drafting
05.03-03 Expediting and Coordinating
05.03-04 Petroleum
05.03-05 Electrical/Electronic
05.03-06 Industrial and Safety
05.03-07 Mechanical
05.03-08 Environmental Control
05.03-09 Packaging and Storing

05.04 **Air and Water Vehicle Operation**
05.04-01 Air
05.04-02 Water

05.05 **Craft Technology**
05.05-01 Masonry, Stone, and Brick Work
05.05-02 Construction and Maintenance
05.05-03 Plumbing and Pipefitting
05.05-04 Painting, Plastering, and Paperhanging
05.05-05 Electrical/Electronic Systems Installation and Repair
05.05-06 Metal Fabrication and Repair
05.05-07 Machining
05.05-08 Woodworking
05.05-09 Mechanical Work
05.05-10 Electrical/Electronic Equipment Repair
05.05-11 Scientific, Medical, and Technical Equipment Fabrication and Repair
05.05-12 Musical Instrument Fabrication and Repair
05.05-13 Printing
05.05-14 Gem Cutting and Finishing
05.05-15 Custom Sewing; Tailoring, and Upholstering
05.05-16 Dyeing
05.05-17 Food Preparation

05.06 **Systems Operation**
05.06-01 Electricity Generation and Transmission
05.06-02 Stationary Engineering

05.06-03 Oil, Gas, and Water Distribution
05.06-04 Processing

05.07 **Quality Control**
05.07-01 Structural
05.07-02 Mechanical
05.07-03 Electrical
05.07-04 Environmental
05.07-05 Petroleum
05.07-06 Logging and Lumber

05.08 **Land and Water Vehicle Operation**
05.08-01 Truck Driving
05.08-02 Rail Vehicle Operation
05.08-03 Services Requiring Driving
05.08-04 Boat Operation

05.09 **Materials Control**
05.09-01 Shipping, Receiving, and Stock Checking
05.09-02 Estimating, Scheduling, and Record Keeping
05.09-03 Verifying, Recording, and Marking

05.10 **Crafts**
05.10-01 Structural
05.10-02 Mechanical
05.10-03 Electrical/Electronic
05.10-04 Structural/Mechanical/ Electrical/Electronic
05.10-05 Reproduction
05.10-06 Blasting
05.10-07 Painting, Dyeing, and Coating
05.10-08 Food Preparation
05.10-09 Environmental

05.11 **Equipment Operation**
05.11-01 Construction
05.11-02 Mining and Quarrying
05.11-03 Drilling and Oil Exploration
05.11-04 Materials Handling

05.12 **Elemental Work: Mechanical**
05.12-01 Supervision
05.12-02 Mining, Quarrying, Drilling
05.12-03 Loading, Moving
05.12-04 Hoisting, Conveying
05.12-05 Braking, Switching, and Coupling
05.12-06 Pumping
05.12-07 Crushing, Mixing, Separating, and Chipping
05.12-08 Lubricating
05.12-09 Masonry

Continued

05   MECHANICAL/
(continued)
05.12-10 Heating and Melting
05.12-11 Welding
05.12-12 Structural Work
05.12-13 Cutting and Finishing
05.12-14 Painting, Caulking, and Coating
05.12-15 Mechanical Work
05.12-16 Electrical Work
05.12-17 Food Preparation
05.12-18 Cleaning and Maintenance
05.12-19 Reproduction Services
05.12-20 Signaling

06   INDUSTRIAL

06.01   Production Technology
06.01-01 Supervision and Instruction
06.01-02 Machine Set-Up
06.01-03 Machine Set-Up and Operation
06.01-04 Precision Hand Work
06.01-05 Inspection

06.02   Production Work
06.02-01 Supervision
06.02-02 Machine Work, Metal and Plastics
06.02-03 Machine Work, Wood
06.02-04 Machine Work, Paper
06.02-05 Machine Work, Leather and Fabrics
06.02-06 Machine Work, Textiles
06.02-07 Machine Work, Rubber
06.02-08 Machine Work, Stone, Clay, and Glass
06.02-09 Machine Work, Assorted Materials
06.02-10 Equipment Operation, Metal Processing
06.02-11 Equipment Operation, Chemical Processing
06.02-12 Equipment Operation, Petroleum Processing
06.02-13 Equipment Operation, Rubber, Plastics, and Glass Processing
06.02-14 Equipment Operation, Paper and Paper Products Processing
06.02-15 Equipment Operation, Food Processing
06.02-16 Equipment Operation, Textile, Fabric, and Leather Processing

06.02-17 Equipment Operation, Clay and Coke Processing
06.02-18 Equipment Operation, Assorted Materials Processing
06.02-19 Equipment Operation, Welding, Brazing, and Soldering
06.02-20 Machine Assembling
06.02-21 Coating and Plating
06.02-22 Manual Work, Assembly Large Parts
06.02-23 Manual Work, Assembly Small Parts
06.02-24 Manual Work, Metal and Plastics
06.02-25 Manual Work, Wood
06.02-26 Manual Work, Paper
06.02-27 Manual Work, Textile, Fabric, and Leather
06.02-28 Manual Work, Food Processing
06.02-29 Manual Work, Rubber
06.02-30 Manual Work, Stone, Glass, and Clay
06.02-31 Manual Work, Laying Out and Marking
06.02-32 Manual Work, Assorted Materials

06.03   Quality Control
06.03-01 Inspecting, Testing, and Repairing
06.03-02 Inspecting, Grading, Sorting, Weighing, and Recording

06.04   Elemental Work: Industrial
06.04-01 Supervision
06.04-02 Machine Work, Metal and Plastics
06.04-03 Machine Work, Wood
06.04-04 Machine Work, Paper
06.04-05 Machine Work, Fabric and Leather
06.04-06 Machine Work, Textiles
06.04-07 Machine Work, Rubber
06.04-08 Machine Work, Stone, Glass, and Clay
06.04-09 Machine Work, Assorted Materials
06.04-10 Equipment Operation, Metal Processing
06.04-11 Equipment Operation, Chemical Processing
06.04-12 Equipment Operation, Petroleum, Gas, and Coal Processing
06.04-13 Equipment Operation, Rubber, Plastics, and Glass Processing

06.04-14 Equipment Operation, Paper Making
06.04-15 Equipment Operation, Food Processing
06.04-16 Equipment Operation, Textile, Fabric, and Leather Processing
06.04-17 Equipment Operation, Clay Processing
06.04-18 Equipment Operation, Wood Processing
06.04-19 Equipment Operation, Assorted Materials Processing
06.04-20 Machine Assembling
06.04-21 Machine Work, Brushing, Spraying, and Coating
06.04-22 Manual Work, Assembly Large Parts
06.04-23 Manual Work, Assembly Small Parts
06.04-24 Manual Work, Metal and Plastics
06.04-25 Manual Work, Wood
06.04-26 Manual Work, Paper
06.04-27 Manual Work, Textile, Fabric, and Leather
06.04-28 Manual Work, Food Processing
06.04-29 Manual Work, Rubber
06.04-30 Manual Work, Stone, Glass, and Clay
06.04-31 Manual Work, Welding and Flame Cutting
06.04-32 Manual Work, Casting and Molding
06.04-33 Manual Work, Brushing, Spraying, and Coating
06.04-34 Manual Work, Assorted Materials
06.04-35 Laundering, Dry Cleaning
06.04-36 Filling
06.04-37 Manual Work, Stamping, Marking, Labeling, and Ticketing
06.04-38 Wrapping and Packing
06.04-39 Cleaning
06.04-40 Loading, Moving, Hoisting, and Conveying

07   BUSINESS DETAIL

07.01   Administrative Detail
07.01-01 Interviewing
07.01-02 Administration
07.01-03 Secretarial Work
07.01-04 Financial Work
07.01-05 Certifying

07.01-06 Investigating
07.01-07 Test Administration

07.02   Mathematical Detail
07.02-01 Bookkeeping and
              Auditing
07.02-02 Accounting
07.02-03 Statistical Reporting and
              Analysis
07.02-04 Billing and Rate
              Computation
07.02-05 Payroll and
              Timekeeping

07.03   Financial Detail
07.03-01 Paying and Receiving

07.04   Oral Communications
07.04-01 Interviewing
07.04-02 Order, Complaint, and
              Claims Handling
07.04-03 Registration
07.04-04 Reception and
              Information Giving
07.04-05 Information
              Transmitting and
              Receiving
07.04-06 Switchboard Services

07.05   Records Processing
07.05-01 Coordinating and
              Scheduling
07.05-02 Record Verification and
              Proofing
07.05-03 Record Preparation and
              Maintenance
07.05-04 Routing and
              Distribution

**07.06   Clerical Machine
              Operation**
07.06 01 Computer Operation
07.06-02 Keyboard Machine
              Operation

07.07   Clerical Handling
07.07-01 Filling
07.07-02 Sorting and Distribution
07.07-03 General Clerical Work

**08   PERSUADING/
              SELLING**

08.01   Sales Technology
08.01-01 Technical Sales
08.01-02 Intangible Sales
08.01-03 General Clerical Work

08.02   General Sales
08.02-01 Wholesale
08.02-02 Retail
08.02-03 Wholesale and Retail
08.02-04 Real Estate

08.02-05 Demonstration and
              Sales
08.02-06 Services
08.02-07 Driving/Selling
08.02-08 Soliciting/Selling

08.03   Vending
08.03-01 Peddling and Hawking
08.03-02 Promoting

09   ACCOMMODATING

09.01   Hospitality Services
09.01-01 Social and Recreational
              Activities
09.01-02 Guide Services
09.01-03 Food Services
09.01-04 Safety and Comfort
              Services

**09.02   Barber and Beauty
              Services**
09.02-01 Cosmetology
09.02-02 Barbering

09.03   Passenger Services
09.03-01 Group Transportation
09.03-02 Individual
              Transportation
09.03-03 Instruction and
              Supervision

09.04   Customer Services
09.04-01 Food Services
09.04-02 Sales Services

09.05   Attendant Services
09.05-01 Physical Conditioning
09.05-02 Food Services
09.05-03 Portering and Baggage
              Services
09.05-04 Doorkeeping Services
09.05-05 Card and Game Room
              Services
09.05-06 Individualized Services
09.05-07 General Wardrobe
              Services
09.05-08 Ticket Taking, Ushering

10   HUMAN SERVICES

10.01   Social Services
10.01-01 Religious
10.01-02 Counseling and Social
              Work

**10.02   Nursing, Therapy and
              Specialized
              Teaching Services**
10.02-01 Nursing

10.02-02 Therapy and
              Rehabilitation
10.02-03 Specialized Teaching

10.03   Child and Adult Care
10.03-01 Data Collection
10.03-02 Patient Care
10.03-03 Care of Others

**11   LEADING/
              INFLUENCING**

**11.01   Mathematics and
              Statistics**
11.01-01 Data Processing Design
11.01-02 Data Analysis

**11.02   Educational and
              Library Services**
11.02-01 Teaching and
              Instructing, General
11.02-02 Vocational and
              Industrial Teaching
11.02-03 Teaching, Home
              Economics,
              Agriculture, and
              Related
11.02-04 Library Services

11.03   Social Research
11.03-01 Psychological
11.03-02 Sociological
11.03-03 Historical
11.03-04 Occupational
11.03-05 Economic

11.04   Law
11.04-01 Justice Administration
11.04-02 Legal Practice
11.04-03 Abstracting, Document
              Preparation

**11.05   Business
              Administration**
11.05-01 Management Services:
              Nongovernment
11.05-02 Administrative
              Specialization
11.05-03 Management Services:
              Government
11.05-04 Sales and Purchasing
              Management

11.06   Finance
11.06-01 Accounting and
              Auditing
11.06-02 Records Systems
              Analysis
11.06-03 Risk and Profit Analysis
11.06-04 Brokering
11.06-05 Budget and Financial
              Control

Continued

11	LEADING/ INFLUENCING (continued)	11.09	Promotion

11 **LEADING/ INFLUENCING** *(continued)*

11.07 **Services Administration**
11.07-01 Social Services
11.07-02 Health and Safety Services
11.07-03 Educational Services
11.07-04 Recreational Services

11.08 **Communications**
11.08-01 Editing
11.08-02 Writing
11.08-03 Writing and Broadcasting
11.08-04 Translating and Interpreting

11.09 **Promotion**
11.09-01 Sales
11.09-02 Funds and Membership Solicitation
11.09-03 Public Relations

11.10 **Regulations Enforcement**
11.10-01 Finance
11.10-02 Individual Rights
11.10-03 Health and Safety
11.10-04 Immigration and Customs
11.10-05 Company Policy

11.11 **Business Management**
11.11-01 Lodging
11.11-02 Recreation and Amusement
11.11-03 Transportation

11.11-04 Services
11.11-05 Wholesale/Retail

11.12 **Contracts and Claims**
11.12-01 Claims Settlement
11.12-02 Rental and Leasing
11.12-03 Booking
11.12-04 Procurement Negotiations

12 **PHYSICAL PERFORMING**

12.01 **Sports**
12.01-01 Coaching and Instructing
12.01-02 Officiating
12.01-03 Performing

12.02 **Physical Feats**
12.02-01 Performing

2. Ranking Interest Areas

Rank the twelve interest areas from the Job Group Chart in order of importance to you:

_____ Mechanical   _____ Protective   _____ Artistic/ Creative   _____ Leading/ Influencing

_____ Industrial   _____ Physical Performing   _____ Human Services   _____ Persuading/ Selling

_____ Nature   _____ Scientific/ Analytic   _____ Accommo- dating   _____ Business Detail

List your top three:

1. _____   2. _____   3. _____

3. Top Job Group Choices

List three or more job groups from the Job Group Chart that you would like to explore further:

Number	Decimal Code	Title
_____	_____	_____
_____	_____	_____
_____	_____	_____

4. The Match Analyzer

a. Check all of the qualities required for your top job group from Exercise 3 as they appear on the Job Group Chart. Then, using your colored pencil, circle those qualities you circled in the Key Qualities Indicator.

Top Job Group Number_____ Decimal Code_____ Title_____

____M ____H 1. Logical Intelligence   ____M ____H   8. Influencing People

____M ____H 2. Intuitive Intelligence   ____M ____H   9. Finger/Hand Agility

____M ____H 3. Verbal Ability   ____M ____H 10. Whole Body Agility

____M ____H 4. Numerical Ability   ____   11. Repetition

____M ____H 5. Precise Detail   ____   12. Variety

____M ____H 6. Multidimensional Awareness   ____   13. Physical Risk

    ____   14. Status

____M ____H 7. Businesslike Contact with People

b. Is there a perfect match between qualities the job group requires and those you would like to use on the job? ____Yes ____No

c. Explain how you could overcome each quality that does not match.

_____

_____

_____

5. Researching a Job Group

Look up your top job group in the *Guide for Occupational Exploration.* Find the answers to the following questions.

a. Summarize the kind of work that you would do.

_____

_____

_____

b. Summarize the skills and abilities needed for this kind of work.

_____

_____

_____

© 1981 by United Feature Syndicate, Inc.

c. Summarize clues that tell whether you would like or could learn this work.

_____

_____

_____

d. Summarize the training needed and methods of entry into this field.

_____

_____

_____

e. List job titles you'd like to explore further.

_____

_____

_____

6. Researching Job Titles

Look up one job title in the *Dictionary of Occupational Titles,* using the nine-digit number. Summarize what you find there.

Job Title:_____ Nine-Digit Code:_____

_____

_____

_____

7. Your Expectations

Now that you've researched the job market, answer this important question: Do you want a career or "just a job"? Explain your answer.

_____

_____

_____

8. Blocks and Barriers

At this point, what could be holding you back from completing the process?

_____ In too much of a hurry to explore

_____ Have done some exercises (or pieces of the puzzle) but left others out

_____ Experiencing personal/painful traumas

_____ Afraid to look at myself; low/no self-confidence

_____ Afraid to make a commitment

_____ What else?_____

9. Portrait II: Filling in the Lines

Expand on the following and write a paragraph.
Because I am . . . [these personality types], I have . . . [these characteristics], which involve activities like . . . using . . . [the key qualities].

## CHAPTER 5

THE JOB MARKET: FACTS, TRENDS, AND PREDICTIONS

FOCUS

Explore trends in society for jobs of the future.

Relate personality types to the job market.

Consider alternative careers.

Many people are so overjoyed after they have picked a job title or two that they can hardly wait to start job hunting. But sophisticated career searchers will first investigate the job trends in their chosen field to see where they're heading. Second, they will research a variety of workplaces to find some that are right for them. Third, they will talk to people who are currently working in these fields and visit their workplaces. Then they will make a careful career decision and begin the job hunt. In this chapter you will look at job trends and predictions along with some guidelines for uncovering alternatives. In the next chapter you will learn how to examine the subtleties of the workplace.

CHARTING THE FUTURE

Job seekers are sometimes advised to "find a need and fill it." During your career search you may often find yourself wondering, "Who needs me out there?" The truth is, there is no really accurate way to predict the future needs of the job market.

Statisticians and futurists collect facts about past events to discover present trends. Understanding these trends enables them to make predictions (which are only educated guesstimates) about the future—including *your* job future. But although the trends affect your future, you will also affect the trends. If you are in tune with yourself and your deepest values, you will make wise choices and connect with others like yourself who share your aspirations. They are likely to hire you, or do business with you, or start a business with you. You may even start your own trend.

Five global explosions are affecting the job market of the 1980s and beyond—explosions in population, science, technology, information, and global consciousness.

Population: The number of people on earth has been increasing so fast that the time required for population to double has dropped from 1 billion years to 1,000 to 200 to 80 to 35 years. The world population is expected to reach 6 billion by the year 2000. (It reached 5 billion in 1986.[1]) Six billion people will impose heavy demands upon the earth's natural resources. There have never before been so many people. Supplies of resources and energy seem stretched to the breaking point. Already 25 percent of the present population do not have housing and at least 10 percent do not have enough food.[2] How will all these individuals survive, much less find enrichment?

Science: About 90 percent of all scientists who ever lived are alive today. They have split the atom and pursued its parts into quarks and even smaller elements. They have unleashed forces unimaginable a century ago—the power to redesign the human race and its companion creatures, even to redesign the structure of matter itself and then, with the touch of a button, to destroy it all. Misunderstanding such power gives birth to fear. Understanding it gives birth to even greater fear.

Technology: In a relatively few short years, modern technology has reached almost every corner of civilized life. Until the nineteenth century, human means of transportation never exceeded 20 miles per hour. Now, the speed record for a jet-powered automobile exceeds 730 miles per hour, and spaceships travel at more than 149,125 miles per hour.[3] A hypersonic aircraft now on the drawing boards will make the trip from Los Angeles to Washington, D.C. in 33 minutes at five times the speed of sound.[4] But such advances also generate formidable problems. More than half of the energy consumed over the last 2,000 years has been consumed in the last 100 years. The time it takes for technology to apply scientific discoveries to the real world has shortened from centuries to a few years and, in some cases, months. Chemical pollution of the planet increases fear pollution in the minds of earthlings as we strive to understand what technology has wrought.

Information: The average adult is bombarded by enough words and ideas every day to cause sensory overload. In 450 years, the publication of new books has increased from 1,000 a year to more than 1,000 a day.[5] In ancient times, it took years for ideas and information (data) to travel from place to place. Two California Indian tribes living in villages ten miles apart spoke completely different languages! Today we can process and transmit vast amounts of information in the twinkling of an eye. But despite the quantity of information instantly available to us, discovering facts is as hard as it ever was. Truth and accuracy are not necessarily conveyed in direct proportion to the speed of transmission.

Global Consciousness: The explosions of population, science, technology, and information—all interrelated, all the result of great social change, all creating vast challenges—are giving rise to a fifth explosion: our awareness of ourselves as inhabitants of a "global village," all breathing the same air, drinking the same water, drawing sustenance from the same earth. Astronaut Russell Schweickart described our tiny planet as seen from outer space.

> It is so small and so fragile, such a precious little spot in the universe . . . you realize that everything that means anything to you—all of history and art and death and birth and love, tears and joys, all of it—is on that little blue and white spot out there which you can cover with your thumb.[6]

Although these explosions bring exciting changes, trends in population, science, technology, and information are rapidly creating problems. Willis Harmon, senior economist and futurist at SRI International, says that global consciousness is the trend that will provide solutions.

All these trends will affect your work life. Alvin Toffler coined the term *future shock* to describe the effects of increasingly rapid change on our slow-to-catch-up psyches. If you understand the trends, you won't find yourself a victim of future shock. You'll be a shock absorber instead. You won't find your-self out on a limb clinging to an obsolete view of the world or an obsolete job. You'll develop the skills necessary for living in a fast-paced world: flexibility, the ability to learn, and the ability to use information wisely. You'll understand the need for a set of enduring values, which will enable you to maintain a broad sense of direction without being swept away by either trends or fads. And most important, you'll build a flexible, satisfying career with opportunities for growth.

TRENDS AND THE JOB MARKET

Population: What do trends have to do with you? Population studies can tell us not only how many people will be trying to enter and move over or up in the job market at any one time, but also the characteristics and probable needs of the general population that create the jobs to begin with. Consider the fifteen-year "baby boom." Between 1946 and 1961, 60 million people were added to the U.S. population, compared to 40 million born in the previous fifteen years. This group, born into unprecedented affluence, has affected such diverse areas of life as education, the crime rate, and entertainment, and its impact will continue to be strong.

Terry Kirkpatrick of the Associated Press says of the baby boomers, "They will be remembered as the generation that stood in line." Now in their late twenties, thirties and early forties, they are competing for everything—loans, housing, education, jobs, raises, promotions into mid-management. Less affluent than their parents, baby boomers are finding the American Dream of home own-ership and the other trappings of the 7 percent stereotype far more difficult to attain. And although many are having smaller families, their sheer numbers are creating a modest need for teachers, child-care workers, and all the goods and services that children require (all potential job areas). Many more are staying single, creating a market for goods that appeal to that lifestyle.

Such facts and trends can also help us predict the future. There are now over 100 million Americans in the work force. From 1980 data supplied by the U.S. Bureau of the Census, we can predict that the U.S. labor force will grow by 25 million, or about 1.6 million per year, between 1980 and 1995. Women, minorities, immigrants, and older workers who decide to work past age sixty-five are among those adding to the labor pool. Immigration for example, brings people of varied cultures together with opportunities to share their heritage, as witness the boom in ethnic restaurants.

All potential new employees through the year 2000 have already been born! Right now the people who were born the same year you were (your *cohort*), and those close to you in age, are moving along in their careers and lives in paths similar to yours. That means many of them are seeking the same sort of jobs and promotions, among other life components, as you are. But John

Naisbett reminds us that in 1992, 40 percent fewer people will turn eighteen than in 1979 and thus fewer new recruits will be job hunting.[7]

Whereas in 1950 one person in twelve was over sixty-five,[8] by the year 2000 the ratio will be one in seven of the U.S. population over sixty-five as this generation ages.[9] The number of older people will increase only slightly until the year 2000, and then it will increase by 40 percent worldwide. More elderly people will need medical and support services, adult education, travel arrangements, and all the other goods and services appropriate to older, affluent, and active people.

As more people enter the job market and the pace of life increases, the flexibility needed to change goals will become ever more important. The rate of population growth, however, is slowing down, which will result in a need for older workers to stay in the work force.

Science and Technology: Population has increased largely because of scientific discoveries and their applications through technology. In this century, the United States has been in the forefront, developing scientific and technological breakthroughs that have transformed the face of the earth. We have overpowered nature in unprecedented ways, using and often abusing its resources, all in the name of "progress." As America became the world leader in manufacturing, poets immortalized the power of its flaming steel mills, its thundering railroads, and its amber waves of grain. The American automobile, mass produced by union labor on an assembly line, symbolized a dream of universal affluence, a happy marriage of science and technology. Then the 1980s found Germany, Japan, and other nations competing in steel and auto making, American railroads in disarray, U.S. farmlands eroding (and closing out) at a rapid rate, and labor unions losing their power.

Against this background a quiet but new and powerful revolution is spreading throughout the world. It seems that the silicon chip is king, computers reign, and robots rule. Growing out of a period of tremendous scientific achievement, electronic technology—the wave of the future that touches us all—is here to stay. Smart machines are changing not only the face of the workplace but its body and soul as well. We have only seen a glimmer of the changes in work and society that are likely to take place because of the microchip. Developed in the United States, it has spawned a new age.

Information: The electronic revolution has given birth to an era of computer information systems. Formerly makers of things, we are becoming a nation of data processors—we create data, collect it, evaluate it, manipulate it, control it, and pass it on.

Every job requires data of some kind. But with each passing year, more workers are processing data and fewer are manufacturing material goods. The 1980 census shows only 19 percent of the U.S. population making such items as furniture/clothing, electrical/electronic equipment, machines/tools, chemicals such as rubber/plastics, or working in mining, construction, agriculture, and forestry. This figure is expected to drop below 10 percent by the mid-1990s.

Over 75 percent of the U.S. population, in contrast, now works in the service sector, which continues to grow rapidly. The service sector contains jobs in which people "wait on" or serve other people and things in areas ranging from nursing the sick to repairing robots, from feeding the poor to feeding data into computers. This sector includes government, education, medicine, law, entertainment and the arts, and all facets of business such as finance/banking, management, and marketing, along with repair services. The information industry provides service jobs for word processors, computer operators, programmers, systems analysts, software producers—all involved with science and technology.

Changes in the structure and content of work are creating new industries that require new kinds of skills. How will great numbers of workers retrain? Which "old" industries will be revitalized? Which should we let go?

John Peers, inventor of the talking computer concept and director of the Robotics Institute, predicts that manufacturing will return—automated, efficient, and profitable—by the end of the century.[10] Computer-controlled robots are already on-line in a growing number of factories. In short, we are experiencing the birth of a new social phenomenon—an information society in which data seems to surpass things and sometimes even people in importance.

Information is like a child's riddle: it's not only renewable but expandable; it's never scarce, doesn't wear out, uses few resources and little energy to produce, can be kept while being given away. Its utilization requires new concepts of work; its applications to every phase of life are just beginning to be appreciated.

What has happened to the people component of the data-people-things trio in this information age? Some are running mightily to stay in place; some are falling by the wayside in future shock; and some are taking night courses in computer systems. The need for skilled labor in an information society is tremendous. Ironically, after a period of high unemployment, we will have 1.5 million fewer sixteen to twenty-four year olds in 1990 than in 1980 and severe shortages of people with technical skills. Service workers also will be in demand in the next decade.

Overall, projections show an economy using smart machines and thus fewer *resources,* an economy in which two-paycheck couples will have more savings but fewer children, and thus an economy with more *capital* to build businesses, but an increasing shortage of *skilled labor,* the third essential component in employment. This adds up to a good outlook for specially skilled job seekers.[11] In the long run, then, automation should create more jobs but of a different sort. Thus population, science, technology, and information will strongly influence jobs of the twenty-first century.

With computers extending the capacity of our brains and robots giving us brawn, the work of the future should be ideal: boring and repetitious tasks, dangerous and dirty tasks can be taken over by smart machines, and "steel-collar" workers can be monitored by "gray collar" workers. New age secretaries

THE FAR SIDE / Gary Larson
Reprinted by permission of Chronicle Features, San Francisco

will manage and process data in electronic offices, a feature already present in many companies. More people will be wearing white collars and using creativity in their jobs. The reality, however, may be less than ideal if we apply the old concepts of mass production to the new technology. We can't be certain where the vast transition to technology will take us nor what it will look like when we get there. It will take time to shake out, but one thing *is* certain: workers will have to ask for what is best for them. Rapid changes in technology do not mean that human attitudes will change at the same rate and the worker risks being lost in the rush to the service/information society.

What place will education have in this scientific, high-tech information society? College degrees have been declining in value lately because increased numbers of people are obtaining them. But a degree will still have greater earning power than a high school diploma. And a high school graduate will have job opportunities that a dropout will not have.[12] By 1990, 75 percent of new jobs will require more than high school training. Jobs formerly done by illiterates can now be done by machines.[13] One study, for example, has shown skilled workers earning one and a half as much as those working in jobs that require little reading ability.[14] Degrees will still make employment, upgrading, promotions, and raises more attainable. But many degree holders will be "underemployed," that is, working in jobs that require less than their education, at least through the 1980s. Without knowledge and training, survival in the 1990s will be more difficult.

UNEMPLOYMENT: OPTIONS AND STRATEGIES

As a result of population increases, scientific and technological developments, and the emergence of the information society, full employment in the old sense (the 40-hour week/fifty-week year) may never be seen again. At some time in 1981, one out of five Americans was unemployed. The demise of many old industries and the growth of many new ones is causing a worker dislocation of enormous magnitude. Patricia Westfull, writing for the *Insider,* says that it is theoretically possible that all the goods and services the world needs could be produced by only 2 percent of the population. Robots and computers are moving into place—*our* place.

New job skills are needed to fit in with the new technology. There are many proposed solutions: slow down the change; increase the availability of part-time work for those who want it; retrain people as automation takes over; lower the hours in the work week to 30 or 35 and increase vacations to four or even six weeks. We clearly aren't ready to implement any such large-scale changes. But the resulting unemployment is frightening to many who have no alternate plans. Plant closings and permanent layoffs put 12 million people out of work between 1980 and 1984. Half of them were idle for at least six months. Of those who found another job, many were in service work, which pays about 11 percent less than manufacturing.[15] Some people predict a shortage of workers and many new jobs opening up. Others predict vast worldwide unemployment.[16]

Facts and a sense of history are of little comfort if you are presently unemployed or see a possible layoff in the immediate future. Job hunting in a tight job market with your benefits running out, the mortgage payments due, and applications that generate only rejections can undermine the strongest ego. If you are unemployed and haven't had a chance to prepare for it, now is the time to work out a plan of action to avoid sitting at home reading the want ads and feeling terrible. First, review both the you-data collected in this book and the

If I have to keep going to school, all the best jobs are going to be snapped up.

● ●

HERMAN / by Unger
Copyright 1977
Universal Press Syndicate

job market information in the Job Group Chart and related resources. Second, follow the job-hunting techniques described in the next two chapters: update your résumé, renew your contacts, and collect letters of recommendation. Third, join or start a support group. Fourth, work out a daily schedule of things to do that include not only these tasks but other important "business of living" activities like exercising and visiting friends. In the meantime, consider temporary work, part-time work, "just any job," and negotiating to share a job.

As stressful as unemployment is, if you can avoid panic and keep a level eye out for opportunities, you may find them in unlikely places. Take the steps you can take comfortably. It helps to be moneywise and have a plan for lean times. But if you don't, consider what you really *need* to survive and look for sources to fund your needs. Have a garage sale and get rid of excess baggage. Plant a garden of basics to save on food bills. Join or start a small co-op to buy food wholesale. There are many people who could share resources with you. Look at your expanded activity lists from Chapters 1 and 3 and check off things you can do now to earn needed cash.

Bartering creatively can bring astonishing results. One artist bartered stained-glass windows for expensive dental work. One young man with no money or place to stay bartered lawn care at a veterinary clinic to get shots for his much-loved dog, while a neighborhood soup kitchen and some friends saw him through some rough times. Connie Stapleton of Middletown, Maryland, asked a service station manager if he had any work she could do in exchange for repairs on her car. When that brought a negative response, she asked what he liked least about his job. He said, "Collecting bills!" She now makes collections in exchange for free car care.*

Twenty-five percent of all unemployed people lose their jobs through plant closings, by one Department of Labor estimate. One in four never returns to work, according to Dr. Lou Ferman, director of the Institute of Labor and Industrial Relations at the University of Michigan. Some workers are buying out their companies. Some are proposing the manufacture of alternative products.

As an alternative to closings and spiraling military stockpiles, unions are looking at encouraging workers to propose new products and systems. They would use the same skilled labor and machinery. In England, workers at Lucas Aerospace designed over 250 marketable and socially useful products ranging from a kidney machine to a road-rail vehicle for use in Third World countries. The company resoundingly rejected the plan and chose to close the plant. However, the programs there and elsewhere are being studied by U.S. union leaders[17] and are being implemented on a small scale.

In employee-owned companies, productivity increases along with product reliability. More and more companies now have stock option plans for employees. Even if such large-scale, risky ventures aren't for you, get together with others to share such resources as physical necessities, ideas, job leads, and support. Call your local school career center for ideas. If you are unemployed, keep busy with courage.

Unemployment "Benefits": Seeking Alternatives

A layoff can be a liberating experience—if you don't get too hungry—and a good time to reevaluate a career and make changes. Unemployed people have started businesses, often on a shoestring, found rewarding partnerships, created satisfying new careers. Many people have moved from the corporate complex to small-business ownership. From designing gas guzzlers to designing sandwiches in their own delis, from making hardware to making beds in their guest cottages by the sea, many laid-off persons are "so glad they made the change" as a result of unemployment.

People have created "new ways to work," such as job sharing, alternating male/female roles in child and house care, and "flextime." When people cut

---

*If you are interested in bartering, you can read Stapleton's book, coauthored with a Washington Post columnist, Phyllis C. Richman, *Barter: How to Get Almost Anything Without Money* (New York: Scribner's, 1982).

down their work involvement, they free up jobs for others. In California, an organization called New Ways to Work, while exploring work issues and providing resources, is helping people present themselves to employers in unique ways. The sponsors feel that "there are just not enough jobs to go around unless the work is shared." Job sharing is a good way for two people to find part-time employment, especially when child care or other commitments preclude full-time work. Not all employers are convinced of the worth of these ideas, however, so their impact on employment statistics is very small. But creative solutions are still needed to the worldwide problem of unemployment. In France, a Minister of Leisure Time has been appointed to deal with the underlying causes and problems of unemployment in a technological age.[18]

GLOBAL CONSCIOUSNESS: CATCHING THE THIRD WAVE

Global consciousness has been suggested as a solution to the problems posed by the rapid changes in society. We seem to be coming into an era in which old solutions to old problems no longer work well for us. Population increases, scientific and technological breakthroughs happening at breakneck speed, and a new age of information are creating great challenges for the twenty-first century.

A consideration of facts can help us to see trends and predict some outcomes. But just as we begin to understand the implications of a single trend, sometimes we notice a minitrend or a countertrend emerging. The population pendulum swings from baby boom to zero population growth and then back to mini-baby boom. We plan for the huge but long for the small. We've seen the sexual revolution, the women's movement, radical changes in lifestyles, increasing rates of divorce, religious movements both away from established religion and toward older and even more established religion. Each of these trends challenges our deepest values and make us feel like strangers in a strange land.

We live in a "new world" that seems to get "newer" every day. We are all people in transition. The speed of change is captured by John Peers, who has said, "We live three days a day compared to the 1950s. We do in one day what couldn't be done in a week in 1900, in a lifetime in the 1600s."[19]

In *The Third Wave*, Alvin Toffler helps us to view the current accelerated rate of change from a broad, historical perspective. He speaks of three giant waves. The first, slow and long lasting, brought about the change from a food-gathering, nomadic life to a food-raising, agrarian lifestyle. Some peoples are still making that transition. The second, faster and of far shorter duration (about the last three hundred years), has seen farm life yielding to industrial, urban life. Before much of the world was able to industrialize, the third wave began rushing in, bringing with it the information society.[20] Albert Einstein reminds us that

Courtesy of Mal Hancock

in this era everything has changed except our way of thinking and even this must change if we are to survive.

In our affluent, consumer-oriented society, success has tended to mean a job rewarding enough to support a comfortable suburban lifestyle. But there are alternative ways of defining success. Some people, for example, measure success in terms of their ability to simplify their lives. Some may try to return to nature and reject much of what technology has to offer. Others, more moderate, are like the Amish, who choose to live a nineteenth-century lifestyle, and Thomas W. Foster, writing in the *Futurist*, has said that "Amish society, a relic of the past, could become a model for the future."[21] Many groups are trying to foster the use of appropriate technology that they believe could lead to a better life.

But the power of the new is very alluring. Some societies that have used certain appropriate and valuable technologies for centuries now find a need to look "progressive." For example, in Asian societies bamboo has been well used in construction. But steel and glass are replacing this natural substance, at great cost both economically and culturally.

The following are some elements of an ideal lifestyle and sustainable society based on conservation and the wise use of technology from the perspective of global consciousness. Most products would be recycled. Factories would run on renewable, nonpolluting energy sources as far as possible and far more efficient nonrenewable energy. The raw materials and by-products of manufacturing would not damage the environment. Machinery and products would be more durable, simpler, easier to repair, and less expensive to replace. More products would be produced near consumers, saving fuel and decreasing the cost of transportation.

Things are manufactured for one of two reasons: either because we really need and want them, or because the manufacturer hopes to create a demand for them and make a profit. With our undiscriminating support, some businesses are growing bigger, but not always better. Agribusiness and nonfood conglomerates have been buying up farmland and establishing a worldwide food network that eliminates the small farmer and many of the rural poor, who flock to the cities to find work but often find grinding poverty instead.[22]

But at the supermarket checkout counter we get to "vote" on each product and the way it was made, packaged, and distributed. When we buy the product, we vote in favor of each company involved in its production. We endorse the company's ethics and approve its advertising. As we consumers become more conscious of our market voting power, we will choose products that are caring of the planet.

Small Is Beautiful. The number of Americans living in urban areas has increased steadily throughout the last 150 years. But one trend may indicate a longing for a "Small is Beautiful" lifestyle in a healthy world: the 1980 census shows that the number of Americans living in urban areas increased only 0.1 percent in the 1970s, compared to 3.4 percent in the 1960s. More people are moving to rural areas, and fewer are leaving. The U.S. Department of Agriculture reported a 17 percent increase in the number of farms of less than 50 acres between 1978 and 1982, some carved out of larger farms by part-time farmers.[23] In 1982, to reserve land for small farmers, Nebraska passed a law restricting the sale of farmland to large corporations.

A company in San Jose, California is importing the British concept of the minicondominium. These 440-square-foot studio apartments are a departure from the American Dream of a house with a two-car garage in the suburbs. But minicondos can be a good way to get a start on home ownership. Some people enter into shared ownership and appreciate their escape from the struggle to maintain a home and yard alone.

Add minicars to minihomes, minicities, minicomputers, and minibusinesses, all for the minifamily. About 88 percent of all new jobs in America in the last five years were created by companies with twenty or fewer employees.[24] Small companies often have the added advantage of being less alienating. Minitrends may foretell the future. According to Toffler, everything will come in small, variable parts, "de-massified and diversified," instead of large homogeneous clumps.

Industrialized society required obedience to authority, repetition, and mass production. Information systems require more autonomy, responsibility, commitment, flexibility, and creativity, and in these areas the social-investigative-artistic personality types will find their niche.

As *things* become less important to those who have enough, emotional, intellectual, and altruistic wants can surface to a greater degree. There may be more *being* and less *doing,* more cooperating and less competing, more communicating and less achieving, more listening and less producing, more sharing and less grabbing. If robots and computers take some of the tedium and danger out of work, we might look forward to a more enriched life on all levels.

We need to consider new ideas often dismissed at first as unrealistic and impractical. James Benson of the Council of Economic Priorities, for example, recently estimated that in the Nassau-Suffolk area of Long Island, New York a low-cost energy package aimed at installing insulation, storm windows, and solar hot water systems could provide 270 percent more employment and 206 percent more energy over a thirty-year period than the same amount of money spent to construct and maintain nuclear power plants.[25]

If we can "telecommunicate" sometimes instead of commuting to work and school, we will use less energy in transportation and also less personal energy. Air quality would improve, land use would be less, and a variety of other costs could be reduced. Entrepreneurs could consider setting up neighborhood computer/office centers with a variety of services to offer the telecommuter. Social life, missing at home, could be supplied there!

In *The Third Wave,* Toffler notes that as second-wave institutions crash about our heads, we tend to see only decay and breakdown. "Yet social decay is the compost bed of the new civilization. In energy, technology, family structures, culture, and many other fields, we are laying into place the basic structure that will define the main features of that new civilization."[26]

Because of the trends, countertrends, and minitrends, it is important to know what *you* believe in, so that as you begin to choose your future you can put your energy to work in a job that is consistent with your values and that has a positive impact on the world. But in the meantime predicting the job market becomes increasingly difficult as these movements occur ever more rapidly. It is awesome to visit automated warehouses, power plants, and other work sites where silent computers initiate, direct, and terminate complex and heavy work, where "gray-collar" workers act as technicians and diagnosticians. But watch for the countertrend: increasing costs of automation and high unemployment are causing some employers to delay investing in this technology. Some are hiring low-cost human labor instead.

Nobody can predict the future with absolute certainty. And few people want to acknowledge trends or listen to predictions that seem totally out of harmony with their view of the world. Not many people in the 1950s and 1960s believed that we would ever have an energy shortage. In the oil-rich mid-1980s, many people still think of oil as an infinite resource. And many people still don't see the connection between pouring a harmful chemical down the drain or on the ground, and the pollution of their own water supply. But major trends have a tremendous impact on the job market and on the quality of our lifestyles.

As you consider a "thought-full" career and lifestyle decision, you can remember that trends are trends because people choose them. Your own life and work will have an effect upon the earth and its people. You will be a "future-maker."

FAST-GROWING JOBS FOR THE 1980s AND 1990s

Now that we have examined some long-term trends, you realize that job openings in manufacturing and agriculture are decreasing throughout the United States. Many fast-growing jobs can be found in the service/information industries. After studying trends in employment, the Department of Labor published lists of jobs that are expected to be among the fastest-growing occupations until 1995.[27] Labor market predictions are based on dated statistics and random samples, not on 100 percent of the population; yet they are surprisingly accurate.

"Fast growing," however, does not always mean easy to get. The availability of jobs is affected by competition, geographical limitations, educational requirements, and the state of the national economy. Jobs that have a high salary potential and few openings are in demand; competition for them may be fierce. This category includes positions in advertising, commercial art, fashion merchandising, industrial sales, personnel, and public relations. If you are interested in such work, check the number of jobs available in your area. Local trends may be more important then national trends. Talk to people and consult the state employment office to learn the dynamics of your job market. Women are moving into high-paying jobs in greater numbers. Advertising, for example, formerly a male province, now employs 53 percent women.[28]

Figure 5-1 lists fast-growing jobs related to the six personality types— realistic, investigative, artistic, social, enterprising, and conventional. Perhaps you will find an intriguing job in this list. (But remember, some of these areas are highly competitive.)

Researchers Marvin Cetron and Thomas O'Toole went out on a limb to predict the following fast-growing and (occasionally strange-sounding) new jobs for the 1990s:[29]

Bionic-electronic technician

Computer axial tomography technician

Energy technician/auditor

Genetic engineer

Hazardous waste management technician

Holographic inspection specialist

Housing rehabilitation technician

Industrial laser process technician

Industrial robot production technician

Materials utilization technician

Nuclear medicine specialist

Positron emission tomographer

• •

FIGURE 5-1 The Fastest-Growing Jobs, 1980–1995

REALISTIC

*Aircraft pilot

Automobile/motorcycle
  mechanics

Broadcast technicians

Chefs/cooks

Computer service
  technicians

Corrections officers

Diesel mechanics

Dispensing opticians

Electrical/electronic
  technicians

Engineering
  technicians

Glaziers

Guards

Office equipment
  repairers

Photographic processors

Tool programmers/
  numerical control

INVESTIGATIVE

*Architects

*Computer programmers

*Computer system analysts

*Dentists

*Engineers

  Aerospace

  Chemical

  Civil

  Electrical/electronic

  Industrial

Mechanical

Metallurgical/ceramic/
  materials

Optometrists

*Physicians

Podiatrists

Veterinarians

ARTISTIC

*Actors/actresses/directors/
  producers

Dancers/choreographers

Designers

Graphics/fine arts

Photographic/camera
  operators

*Writers/editors

SOURCE: U.S. Department of Labor, Bureau of Labor Statistics, *Occupational Outlook Quarterly,*
Spring 1986, p. 10.

An ad by Champion International Corporation[30] suggests the following even stranger future job titles:

Android physiologist

Artificial intelligence tester

Computer psychiatrist

Cyberg mechanical engineer

Deep sea mining engineer

Epizoothic therapist

Fusion engineer

Laser dentist

Microastronomer

Oceanic/space hotel manager

Planetary geologist

Quarkologist

Tectonic statistician

According to Alvin Toffler, the "big four" growth areas are electronics, space, oceans, and gene research, both application and technology. Moreover, the energy-producing industries will need more workers worldwide—mining, chemical, and petroleum engineers; metal workers; offshore rig construction workers; synthetic fuel plant construction workers, and biotechnologists. Satel-

• •

SOCIAL

Bartenders

Chiropractors

Corrections officers

Cosmetologists

Dental assistants

Dental hygienists

Dietitians/nutritionists

Electro-encephalographic
  technologists/
  technicians

Flight attendants

*Health services
  administrators

Medical assistants

Nurses' aides/orderlies

Occupational therapists

Physical therapists

Psychologists

Radiologic technologists

Recreational therapists

Recreation workers

Registered nurses

Respiratory therapists

Social workers

Teachers

  Preschool

  Elementary

Waiters/waitresses

ENTERPRISING

*Lawyers

*Public relations specialists

*Securities/financial service
  sales workers

Travel agents

Wholesale sales workers

CONVENTIONAL

*Accountants and auditors

Actuaries

*Bank officers and
  managers

Cashiers

Computer operators

*Hotel managers/assistants

Legal assistants

Medical records
  technicians

Underwriters

---

*Jobs that have a high salary potential (*Working Women,* January 1987, p. 53).

lite-based telecommunications and the construction and maintenance of earth stations will be big business. Information technology will bring financial, library, and entertainment data into every home. There will be an increase in small businesses. Money management, sales, and franchising will be important.[31] These trends should mean new jobs for men and women of each personality type.

PERSONALITY TYPES IN THE JOB MARKET

Realistic Type

Jobs for the realistic type generally involve handling things, using body skills, and dealing with whatever data is required. Examples range from various trades and crafts to professional sports. Careers in sports, of course, are extremely competitive and limited to the most talented. Since realistic personalities provide food, clothing, shelter, and transportation to all of us, such jobs are basic, necessary, and highly visible. Although automation and imports will increase in some areas, the employment outlook ranges from good to excellent for many jobs in the realistic category, especially for persons that are service oriented or do highly skilled and specialized work.

If you belong to this personality group, you might consider indoor or outdoor jobs in industry or with public utility companies. You may need special vocational training, although on-the-job training is sometimes available. In the building trades, you may be required to join a union as an apprentice. Cutbacks in government spending have limited the number of outdoor jobs available to people who like to work with nature.

Volunteering is a way to get training and work experience in some of these jobs. Sometimes realistic persons build unique and creative careers through such practical activities as cooking, tailoring, or cabinetmaking at home.

Investigative Type

Jobs for the investigative type are high-data jobs and, except for jobs in health care, have little involvement with people except as coworkers. They usually require above-average intelligence and verbal or mathematical skills. Except for some technical areas, most jobs require at least a four-year college degree. Most jobs in this area require *thinking* about things rather than handling things, but they are nevertheless thing oriented.

Many investigative jobs in the sciences are not directly "productive" because they deal with "pure research." When there are no products or direct services to be sold for profit, funding tends to be less abundant. Engineers and medical researchers are generally well paid, however, because they do research that applies directly to practical problems. Hence more jobs are available in these categories. In fact, there are good job possibilities in all investigative occupations except pure research. Investigative types who are not scientifically or technologically oriented can apply their investigative talents to other areas. Many work settings can profit from the research and analytical skills of the investigative person.

Artistic Type

Most jobs for the artistic type require special talent along with special training. They are usually high-data, high-thing jobs, with no deep involvement with people. Artistic persons enjoy creating new things but often dislike the mass producing and marketing aspects of earning a living because business pressure often militates against creativity. Many highly creative people also find it hard to work in structured settings doing work for others, such as architecture, advertising, and various other design jobs. Technical writing would fit the scientifically minded creative person and that area is growing. Because most artisitic jobs tend to be highly competitive, the artistic type should plan alternatives. New developments in electronic media will provide opportunities for some creative people.

Social Type

Social personality careers deal primarily with people. The data necessary to do the job will range from simple to complex, depending upon the degree of involvement with people. Workers should be good with people, concerned with people's problems, or at least comfortable providing services. Many people have a strong desire to do socially useful work, such as caring for children or solving problems of the disabled and the elderly.

The need is great, yet many of the jobs in the social services area are government funded and are now scarce because of tax/budget cutbacks. Some government jobs in human services defeat the purpose of helping people; workers in some settings are drained by large numbers of clients with serious and chronic problems. With little support, few resources, and yards of red tape, the worker needs strong motivation to succeed. People with good business sense and enough funding sometimes start private practices or community organizations.

Health care has been a growing field, but growth is now slowing. In many localities entrance into training programs is limited. Traditional health care also requires thing involvement and tends to be conventional. People with social concerns find that their special talents can be used in a variety of settings, however, because all employers hire people and need to solve employee and customer problems.

Enterprising Type

The enterprising type is usually a person of energy, courage, and confidence who loves the "game" of selling, persuading, risking, and motivating. Enterprising personalities, by their very natures, seem to have the inner drive to "connect" with the people and events that help them get ahead. And there is always a need to organize and sell goods and services in the world of things and data. Purely enterprising types are out there, already involved.

Generally, men have been socialized to strive for success with courage and confidence—whether they like it or not—but women have been socialized for a commitment to people instead of accomplishment. The most effective person for the enterprising jobs achieves a balance between striving to accomplish and being sensitive to people. These are all high-data jobs requiring intelligence and good verbal skills.

Conventional Types

Conventional personality careers require steadiness, orderliness, and accuracy in dealing with data. They require tolerance for paperwork and at times involve business contact with people and the use of machines. Workers who favor this orientation rarely seek promotions and additional responsibility. Experience may build their confidence and give them the courage to advance, but generally they do well in supportive roles.

Many careers demand the steadiness and order of the conventional personality. Now that we have become a nation of data keepers and processors, jobs in this area are abundant, visible, and usually easy to find and can become well paying by finding the right setting.

SIAs and Other Combinations: The Hard Cases

The realistic, conventional, and enterprising types and various combinations of these personalities have the easiest time starting careers: the realistic because their jobs are concrete and visible, the conventional because they tend to follow established patterns, and the enterprising because they are willing to take risks. Generally speaking, the SIA personalities—social, investigative, artistic, or some combination of these—have a harder time choosing and launching a career. People who work with ideas or feelings have no tangible product to show their employers.

But all SIA personalities gravitate toward work in which they can deal with people to solve problems by creating new systems. This need may arise in just about any work setting with any group or type of workers. SIA jobs call for transferable skills, such as analysis and communication. Satisfying jobs in this area are usually on a highly competitive, professional level. A college education is almost a must for the successful SIA personality. The beginner will need some supporting work-specific skills that relate to the work place. If you are applying to a computer firm, for example, know something about computers. If you plan to get a four-year liberal arts degree, take electives in such subjects as business, technology, or health. Or obtain a two-year vocational degree at a community college before transferring to a university.

The social and investigative person with conventional rather than creative characteristics enjoys working with people to solve problems by following established guidelines. Guidelines are provided in personnel and labor relations work, probation and law enforcement, health care, and sales. Travel agents and bank clerks are often required to investigate and state rules for customers.

The enterprising and social combination are people with both "drive" and "good people skills." Those who have or can develop both traits will usually be successful with people in business and public service administration. Often the SIA personality has enough enterprising skills to work happily in many of the social/enterprising areas—for example, in teaching. Teachers must be "people sensitive," but must also be able to organize and motivate people. They must be willing to be key figures in a group, as well as using their investigative and creative qualities.

Be clear on the main function that your highest personality components enable you to perform with enjoyment:

Realistic: Do the practical, physical work required

Investigative: Gather the information (research) and solve problems

Artistic: Create fine arts but also create systems in many settings

Social: Help people with problems of all sorts

Enterprising: Initiate the work/project to be done

Conventional: Follow the guidelines of others to get the work done

When you can state what it is you wish to *do,* finding it will be much easier.

Regardless of your personality type, analyzing your transferable skills in depth and zeroing in on your strengths are important steps in choosing a career. Consider various careers that utilize the same skills and offer similar satisfiers. No one can guarantee you a job after you have invested many years and dollars training for it. How much are you willing to risk? How motivated are you? Have you looked for ways to use your training in alternate choices?

If you need some help in being your own futurist, you will find that the *Occupational Outlook Handbook,* published by the U.S. Department of Labor, is one of the best beginning references to explore trends. Generally available in any library, the handbook provides a good overview of 800 of the most popular careers in the United States. It outlines the nature of the work, average earnings, training requirements, and places to write for further information, along with the projected employment outlook. But no matter what the trends, it's always wise to have some alternate choices and to keep your options open.

BRAINSTORMING ALTERNATIVES

Choosing a career is no problem, you think. You have decided on *the* career. Ever since high school when Mr. Yesteryears turned you on to the Peloponnesian Wars, you have wanted to be a history teacher just like him. You could hear your students sighing, "Wow, I never knew history could be so great!"

Slowly into your fantasy bubble seeps the news that there are hundreds of unemployed history teachers. The bubble bursts.

But wait. All is not lost. Have you considered alternatives? Think over the various elements that make up a career. For example, where in the world are you willing to go to teach history? Germany? Australia? Does Alaska need you? The Peace Corps?

List all the functions of a history teacher (or whatever career you are exploring). Then check the functions that you think you'd enjoy the most. Do you like history, or appearing before an audience, or both? What can you do with a history background besides teaching high school or college students?

Consider developing a unique lecture series on a topic of current interest—such as the architectural history of Victorian homes in Dubuque—to present to community groups. Consider tutoring, learning to be a docent, working as a tour guide, working as an historian for a state park department, getting involved in politics.

If you can get along without teaching, consider developing a tour series on tape or by map—for example, a walking tour of Atlanta—writing news articles about historical subjects such as the Indians of the Upper Michigan Peninsula, working in a library, publishing company, or bookstore and specializing in historical books "on the side," or planning historical tours.

Perhaps, after thinking it over again, you will decide that teaching is more important to you than history. Consider teaching other subjects (check school districts for local trends); volunteer in schools, recreation centers, senior citizen centers; work as a teacher aide; teach small classes at home in cooking, macramé, vegetable gardening, or house plant care; try teaching these or other subjects to community groups such as the Parent-Teacher Association or Girl/Boy Scouts.

With a little work some of those activities can be parlayed into a lucrative business, but others cannot. A job must fulfill the needs and wants of other people to such an extent that they will part with something, usually money, to fullfill them. For people who would like to teach and earn a more secure living, an often overlooked area is industry. Larger industries, especially, have training programs/orientations for new employees and in-service training for continuing employees. Someone must be "teacher" in these industrial settings.

The First Thing
to do in life is to do
with purpose
what one proposes to do.
PABLO CASALS

• • • • • • • • •

Working in marketing and sales, public relations, or personnel, including such areas as job development or affirmative action, can involve you in many situations similar to teaching: giving site tours, helping people find employment, and working with other people problems that arise. Again, know what functions you would like to perform, and many more options may be visible.

Go back to the Key Qualities Indicator and the Job Group Chart and consider the factors that are important to you. Consider related jobs again and *brainstorm, brainstorm,* with friends, relatives, neighbors, acquaintances, strangers, anyone who will give you five minutes of their time and a dip into their experience pool. For just about any career you choose there are alternative jobs that can offer you most of what you would enjoy.

If you still want more then anything to be a history teacher, or some other career that is highly competitive, don't be afraid to face that competition. Develop some unique skills by getting involved in some of the above alternatives, but keep to your chosen goals.

Here are some other ideas to give you a start in your career:

- Volunteer experience can be extremely valuable in skill development. It wouldn't do to stay in the back room and lick stamps, however, unless learning to lick stamps is your goal. Pinpoint the skills you would like to develop. When you volunteer, ask for experience doing these things; for example, public relations, fund raising, supervising people, organizing materials or activities, and such. Be specific. Be aware, however, that volunteer organizations usually are just as accountable for time and money as any business and cannot always accommodate your needs.

- Be sure to review your volunteer experience for skills you've already developed: writing good letters, directing membership drives, and so on. Be very specific about your accomplishments.

- Don't overlook entry-level or support-service job skills, such as typing and cashiering, to gain access to businesses of interest to you. Often you can then work into jobs closer to your interest field in places from art galleries to auto shops by beginning "at the bottom."

- Take skill courses that can help you gain access to jobs. For example, most banks train tellers on the job but might prefer to hire someone with training in accounting or computers.

- Use your main career interest as a hobby while you work at something else to support yourself. Who knows where it will lead? Walter Chandoha pursued a business degree while maintaining an interest in photographing cats. He has been a professional animal photographer for fifteen or more years now and is doing better than he ever dreamed.[32] Maybe his business background has been a help! He also writes occasional articles published in organic gardening magazines, another use of his creative talent.

- Investigate training programs in various industries and government agencies.
- Consider earning extra money, perhaps at home, through cooking, hobbies, and crafts—or by teaching them. For example, think about:

Catering, special food services	Embroidering clothing
Cake decorating	Sewing alterations
Picture framing	Knitting
Dried flower arrangements	Crocheting
Sculpture	Painting
Auto repair	Furniture refinishing
Weaving	Stained glass
Hand puppets and dolls	Decoupage
Doll clothes and jewelry	Pet care

- Consider teaching recreation skills:

Dancing	Skiing	Bridge
Yoga	Massage	Tennis
Music	Riding	Golf
Exercise	Swimming	

Advertise your skills and classes through friends, supermarket bulletin boards, local community groups. Donate samples and demonstrations.

Here are some careers to do at home:

Typing/word processing, perhaps in a medical, technical, scientific, or legal specialty

Bookkeeping

Computer programming

Translating

Telephone wake-up service

Singing messages

Designing stationery, business cards, party favors, what else?

Recycling clothes, furniture, household appliances

Income tax service

Tool/gadget repair and maintenance

Consider direct selling for companies such as Avon, Tupperware, Shaklee, Cutco, and others of good reputation, where you can virtually be your own boss. Write for member list and information by enclosing a long, stamped, self-addressed envelope to: Direct Selling Association, Suite 610, 1730 M St. NW, Washington, D.C. 20046. Write for free *Tips on Work at Home Schemes* and

Tips on Mail Order Profit Mirages from the Council of Better Business Bureaus, Inc., 1150 17th St. NW, Washington, D.C. 20036. Request *Small Business Bibliography No. 3,* "Selling by Mail Order," and *Free Management Assistance Publications* from the U.S. Small Business Administration, P.O. Box 15434, Fort Worth, TX 76119, or pick up copies at any local field office. Ask advice from friends who have sold such items as cosmetics or cleaning products. Consider franchises. They exist in a wide variety of fields from construction to specialty foods.

Consider temporary employment, a growing area that provides flexible time, a sense of independence, and in some cases many employee benefits. One of your local agencies can provide a way to survey businesses, make contacts, and make money on your own schedule in a wide array of jobs.

Keep your options open. The wider your "satisfaction band," the more likely you are to achieve satisfaction. When you have done everything you can but end up with a job you don't care for, you still have some choices.

• Watch for opportunities within the business you are in.

• Retrain at night or get further training on the job.

• Create your own career within a career—some people have found exciting things to do in apparently the dullest and most stifling of situations.

Some people create so much joy within themselves—despite facts, trends, and predictions—that they are happy anywhere. Perhaps that joy, after all, is the key to success.

Self-Assessment Exercises

Predicting Your Future

1. Define future shock. Tell how it affects you.

_____

_____

_____

2. Circle your three highest personality types: realistic, investigative, artistic, social, enterprising, conventional. According to this chapter, what are some job possibilities for your personality types?

_____

_____

_____

3. List your first tentative job choice and several alternatives.

_____

_____

4. Is your first job choice in manufacturing or service/information? _____

5. Look up your first job choice in the *Occupational Outlook Handbook* and summarize what it says about the possibility of future job openings under "Job Outlook."

_____

_____

_____

6. If few job openings are predicted for your career area, what will you decide to do?

_____

_____

7. What effect would a college degree have on your job prospects? On salary? On job satisfaction?

_____

_____

8. Describe how your lifestyle will affect trends in society. _____

_____

_____

9. What positive contribution will your career make to society?

_____

_____

10. Define "global consciousness" in your own words.

_____

_____

_____

_____

Group Discussion Questions

1. Name ten specific changes happening around you as a result of the five major trends. How have these trends affected the world during your lifetime?

2. Which problems resulting from these trends concern you the most?

3. How can your career contribute to the solution for these problems?

4. How might your job be affected if 40 percent fewer recruits enter the work force in 1992?

5. What does John Peers mean when he says, "We live three days in one compared to the 1950s. We do in one day what couldn't be done in a week in 1900, in a lifetime in the 1600s"? Give examples.

6. Give present-day examples of first-, second-, and third-wave jobs.

7. Can we afford to let all our manufacturing go overseas? To become totally an information and service society? Could our data processing go "offshore" also?

8. Is training everyone for the high-tech/information society desirable in the long run? If not, what are the alternatives?

9. If you could repair or build things by directing distant robots from your living room, what kinds of goods or services would you like to provide?

10. In what ways do technology and modern life conflict with biology?

11. If we could provide goods and services through automated electronic systems, might cities and their business activities become obsolete? Describe how work communities might be organized.

12. How would you cope with a reduced work week and a slightly diminished paycheck?

13. What contribution does each personality type make in the job market?

14. Fantasize a third-wave world in 2025 in which all robot-made products are durable and beautiful. People purchase only goods and services that enrich their lives. Many people provide some basic needs for themselves. Many work at home via microchip devices. How would the world be different? Would there be more unemployment or could everyone find work? What kind of work? How could people use their leisure time? What resources would be conserved? How would you feel about that world?

15. Can you choose your future? How? Can you describe it?

WORKPLACES AND WORK STYLES: SCANNING THE SUBTLETIES

F O C U S

Connect personality types with the seven categories of workplaces.

Look at the rewards of work offered in various settings.

Explore and evaluate workplaces and work styles.

..... Deciding on a career is a big step. But even with a job title in mind, you still need to decide on, first, the type of workplace where you can do what you enjoy, and second, the work style that will suit you best. You may be surprised to learn that there are only seven categories of workplaces: business, industry, education, communication/entertainment, health, government, and military. Each of these categories has hundreds and some have even thousands of jobs, many of which have similar characteristics. If you're still unable to choose a job title, just being able to pick one of these seven is a huge step in narrowing down your choices. Let's look at each of these broad categories.

SEVEN CATEGORIES OF WORKPLACES

Business includes every desk from an executive suite to a tiny space in the back of an auto repair shop. Business is not limited to desks in office buildings. It occurs wherever two or more people get together to trade goods and services. Its workers range from the retail clerks in your neighborhood record shop to the shipping tycoon who has offices around the world; from one person word processing at home to a complex international organization. Labor relations, personnel, contract negotiations, consulting, accounting, marketing, and hundreds of other functions make up the work of the business world and its many support systems.

The enterprising and conventional types are most at home in business, but all types can find expression there: the social person in dealing with people and their problems, the artistic person in advertising or creating new designs, the realistic person in managing products and production, and the investigative person in research and problem solving. Choosing business, then, will narrow down your choices yet leave the door open to a variety of careers.

To facilitate the flow of goods and services in business involves both paper data and mind data. *Paper data* includes writing it, reading it, typing it, data/word processing it, filing it, along with *mind data*—researching, analyzing, and teaching it. General clerical skills will enable you to enter the field of business in positions such as filing or shipping clerk. When you feel the need for more training, you can attend workshops and seminars or take college courses at the AA or BA level. Or you might go directly to college to earn a BA in business, in a field such as accounting or marketing. Even with a BA or an MBA degree, however, most people must start near the bottom of the ladder and work up—unless a serious shortage of personnel exists or you have special expertise or experience.

Industry can be defined loosely as a concern with products, not with people or paper (if you exclude the "business end" of industry). Repairing cars, flying planes, pouring concrete, and raising wheat are industries in this sense, along with testing and quality control and quality assurance of products. Even the artist making clay pots at home is involved in industry. Working with machines and tools and tangible materials attracts the realistic person to industries of all kinds. Those realistic persons with an investigative bent will enjoy scientific research directed toward "practical" problems and engineering.

To enter jobs in this area, take related high school and community college or adult education courses or programs. And look into on-the-job training (OJT) in industry or apprenticeship programs through trades such as those in construction.

Education offers many careers besides teaching in schools and colleges. Computer companies hire specialists to develop learning programs, and business and industry carry on employee training programs of all sorts. People who teach various skills or crafts at home or at community centers also participate in the field of education.

The enterprising and social personalities enjoy the task-oriented interactions of teaching, leading, and motivating others. Those with a realistic bent enjoy teaching such subjects as physical education, military arts, and shop, whereas artistic types drift toward humanities and fine arts, crafts, and design classes. Investigative interests are needed for scholarship and research along with teaching the liberal arts and sciences, whereas conventional personalities do well in teaching "the basics." In fact, all personality types can be found in education—it helps to be a "jack of all trades" when you are teaching.

The *communication/entertainment* workplace ranges from circus tents to TV studios, but opportunities tend to be more limited than those in any other area because generally these fields are highly competitive. In order to succeed here, you need exceptional ability, great quantities of luck, and lots of courage. Artistic personalities are naturally attracted to communication and entertainment but may be unsuccessful unless they possess some of the qualities of the enterprising type (or possibly a good agent). Such areas as the electronic media with their business administration, clerical, engineering, and research functions are growing along with the creative positions. But because they usually like to work alone or in unique places, creative people may find it difficult to work in a very structured setting doing routine work even though it may be a creative workplace.

Realistic types may enjoy careers such as industrial design, whereas conventional types may do well in such areas as computer-assisted drafting. Enterprising artistic people may open their own galleries or become book publicists. But with the incredible rise of the information society, opportunities will open up for the creative person who is technically talented, wordwise, and/or number-nimble.

Health suggests a hospital or doctor's office, but in fact health care workers also find employment in business, industry, education, and military settings. The health profession has expanded rapidly as specialization trends and technological advances have increased. But it slows when recession and unemployment pinch health care budgets. The investigative person with a good social orientation will enjoy the challenge of helping people solve their health care problems, whereas conventional/social persons will like the routine systems found in some health care facilities. There may be a great deal of physical work, which may be attractive to the realistic person who likes to work with people. Several hundred job titles are associated with health care delivery.

Government employs people of all types in every setting from agricultural stations to hospitals, from prisons to the great outdoors. You must usually pass a "test" to become employed at the federal level (and often at state and county levels, too). The test may combine an oral interview and a written examination with points added for years of education, military service, and past work experience. Any type of personality can find satisfiers in one of the great variety of government jobs that include narcotics agent and food program specialists, museum curators, and public health specialists. Your state and other employment offices have information about these civil service jobs.

Traditionally, a government job has implied security but low pay. In past years the pay increased along with the number of jobs. But now the taxpayers' mood prevails, and low pay and insecurity have entered the picture for many employees of the government. It takes persistence to obtain these jobs, but some are still there for the person who has patience to try for them.

Military operations and procedures appeal most readily to realistic and conventional personalities, but here again people of all types can find opportunities of many varieties, from cooking to hospital laboratory work to sophisticated industrial research and design. For those so inclined, the military provides a good living with training in a variety of skills.

As you review these categories, begin visualizing the size of workplace you might enjoy. This will also tend to focus your choice even more. Is a multinational corporation for you, or a tiny business at home? Gather job titles that would work in these places.

Then, before you cast off some job titles, be sure you aren't stereotyping them in a way that distorts the possibilities. Food services might seem to mean frying hamburgers, but if you stop there you miss management at local, regional and corporate levels, finance, accounting, marketing and planning, and all the functions of any corporation. And the possible work settings include industry, schools, hospitals, airlines, and even executive dining rooms where highly professional food services personnel work a five-day week entertaining upper management and their guests.[1]

Of approximately 102 million workers, about one-fourth work in goods-producing jobs, including about 6 percent in mining and construction and about 19 percent in manufacturing of durable and nondurable goods; services-producing jobs account for about three-fourths of workers and include approximately 24 percent in wholesale/retail trade, 6.5 percent in finance, insurance, and real estate, 5 percent in business services, 6 percent in health services, and 16 percent in federal/state/local government; about 8 percent are self-employed; about 2 to 3 percent are agricultural workers.[2]

Choosing a type and size of workplace focuses your career exploration and can even get you started on a basic college curriculum or training program. Keep in mind the main functions your personality combination enjoys:

R: working with things	S: helping people
I: solving problems	E: initiating projects
A: creating new systems	C: following guidelines

WANTED: REWARD ON ALL LEVELS

As we watch the frantic activity in the work world we've created, a disturbing question arises: What is happening to the individual in the workplace? Many work situations prove far from ideal on the personal level.

First, subtle changes have placed barriers between us and natural things. We drive and park along heavily concreted wastelands. Many people work in buildings without windows, far from sunlight and breezes. They have little say about what happens to their souls and bodies during the workday and on what schedule. What are some of the rewards to look for?

Workplaces provide pay and benefits, which supply basic needs and some of the wants on your agenda. But work also brings intangible rewards on many levels. Self-esteem, prestige, caring relationships, and opportunities to actualize your unique potential are powerful motivators that draw people into the work world. Many people find pleasure in working and would continue some kind of work involvement even if they were wealthy.

You will find that workplaces have personalities just as people do. Some are austere, rigid, demanding; others are lavish, casual, easygoing. They reflect various combinations of the six personality types and tend to attract people who enjoy being together. Before you choose a workplace that matches your unique need/want/value/personality combination, consider these areas of reward: opportunities for climbing the career ladder, fringe benefits, and some emotionally subtle satisfiers, including a supportive atmosphere, autonomy, and compatible values.

• •
FIGURE 6-1 The Career Ladder

Position	Responsibility	Education	Support Staff
Top level			
Top management and professionals, such as Presidents Board members Doctors Lawyers	The decision makers, who are responsible for nearly everything. There is more independence at this level.	Ph.D, DD, MD, MBA, etc. Technical and professional expertise	Operates at all levels to provide auxiliary services such as Personnel Finance Communications/Graphics Legal Counsel Research Purchasing Marketing Data Processing Secretarial/Clerical Maintenance
Middle level			
Middle management and professionals, such as Department heads Engineers Nurses Teachers Product managers	Shares responsibility with the top level and enjoys some independence.	MA, MBA, MS, BS, BA, etc. Middle-level expertise	
Lower level			
Lower management and technicians, such as Supervisors Lead persons Legal assistants LVNs	Responsible for a small part of decision making. May supervise others.	AA, AS, vocational, or on-the-job training	
The workers			
Basic production and service work, such as Trades, crafts Assemblers Machinists Waiters/waitresses	Responsible for a particular function. Entry level jobs, often repetitive work.	High school, apprenticeship. Usually *some* training or experience is needed.	

The Career Ladder

You may find it rewarding to match your satisfiers with one of the levels in the career ladder in Figure 6-1. The chart identifies four levels that can be found in many work settings. In some settings, such as the military, the structure is rigid. In others, the levels are less formal and less evident.

All workplaces, no matter what size—a lawyer's office, a large catering service, a hospital, or an international manufacturing corporation—have similar structures, sometimes repeated over and over in various divisions. A small staff might consist of the boss, who has many management functions and one assistant who does the rest. Some places "contract out" certain jobs like data processing, accounting, income tax, and maintenance service. Some firms are turning such areas as personnel services and personnel over to a company who then "leases back" the employees.

Julie Pitts has been a medical assistant in a doctor's office and her job has included billing, typing, personnel, a little family counseling, public relations, tax work, research, and even interior decorating. Still, many days brought surprises to her work: the latest, consulting for a doctor who wanted a more efficient management system for her office. In a larger workplace, entry-level workers can expect to do a more limiting and specialized job, whether it is putting lettuce leaves on a thousand sandwiches, soldering a link in a thousand electronic circuits, or word processing a thousand letters.

So size and complexity of the workplace can be a very important factor in your job choice. In a larger workplace a specific position may be subject to more limitations; possibilities for change, however, including moving both over and up, are greater. Research shows that mid-size companies often outperform huge corporations, create many more jobs, and are usually more flexible and innovative. In a smaller workplace tasks may be more varied and responsibility greater, but options are narrowed. Small businesses employing fewer than twenty people make up 89 percent of U.S. firms.[3]

Generally, the higher you climb on the career ladder, the higher your salary, but education/training/experience factors are also higher. Where do you wish to fit in this scheme of things? How far up the ladder do you want to be? (It may be lonely at the top, but it's also exciting and challenging—and not everyone can get there. It's more comfortable at the bottom but often not so rich or so interesting!) If you know where you want to be a few years from now, you will not limit yourself by neglecting present opportunities or choosing dead-end jobs.

Don't Overlook Benefits

Generally, salary is the prime benefit most people look for. But fringe benefits are not just a minor attraction. They represent a considerable, if hidden, part of your pay. Health care, for example, can include dental and vision care in addition to hospital care. Paid holidays and several weeks vacation with pay, use of a company car, expense accounts, child care subsidies, education subsidies, and even use of vacation resorts are just a few of the benefits offered by some companies. Some offer benefits "cafeteria style" and allow employees to choose whichever combination suits them. Also consider a company's record in career "pathing" or developing and the quality of their training programs.

Although retirement can seem a century away to the beginning worker, it's never too early to look at various options and plan accordingly. There have been many changes, some of them related to reduced or deferred income taxes like Individual Retirement Accounts, or IRAs. Some pension plans, especially for nonworking spouses, have been highly discriminatory of women. Reforms are moving slowly in this area.

If a company is very sensitive to personal needs, its managers may include fringe benefits that help with the ever more complex "business of living," a term that refers to the endless but absolutely necessary tasks each person must perform in regard to: (1) financial matters such as banking, taxes, insurance, real estate, and other investments; (2) medical/dental care; (3) personal care, including food, clothing, and shelter; (4) child care in all of these categories; and (5) education—"keeping up with your field." Concern about such problems drains energy, awareness, and creativity.

Some large corporations have begun to hire people to assist workers with these areas. For instance, some places have doctors or nurses for short-term consultation, financial services such as credit unions, courses for work improvement, recreational activities and even dry cleaning pick-up and delivery.

Staff Support: The Emotional Contract

Most workers want to feel they are valued not only for the work they do, but also for themselves as persons. When you are hired in a workplace, you agree to an unspoken, unwritten "emotional contract" that can seem almost as real as a legal document. This contract pertains to the way you will be cared about and respected, how personally supportive the atmosphere is, how fairly you will be treated. It's the kind of thing you pick up intuitively from people who work there, from the environment, suggesting that emotional rewards will be forthcoming. You are tapping into the corporate culture or climate. *Corporate culture* can be defined as a common and shared set of beliefs that create and shape attitudes and behaviors and make for reduced conflict and greater efficiency. This state of affairs could also create stagnation if everyone were quite content with the status quo. Your work life will be more satisfying if you choose an environment with just enough support for you. On the other hand, some people have exaggerated expectations about the role the workplace and their coworkers should play in their emotional lives.

Sometimes the interpersonal characteristics of a job can change. One newly divorced mother enjoyed working in a small savings and loan office. An older woman gave her much understanding; the boss was great, and the younger workers were a delight. But the boss, who had decided to work harder at "moving up," began to be more restrictive, even to the point of pressuring workers

"This is not the kind of perk I had in mind."

to stay overtime without pay. The older woman was "phased out" when the company decided to hire a "security guard/teller." The work atmosphere of the job changed from fun to funk—but later it went back to fun when the now-experienced working mother became the manager. In general, over the long term a workplace will probably not supply a good part of a person's emotional needs.

No matter how carefully you plan your career, at some time you are likely to have a job that does not supply all your needs and wants. Cultivating a reasonable amount of independence and a moderately strong skin can protect you against the ups and downs of the work world. At the same time, be aware of your particular needs and aim for a match.

Autonomy Dimensions: Who's Boss?

Old industrial-style management techniques gave bosses complete authority over employees. In the information age many workers are taking on responsibility for their own decisions. More of this sort of autonomy is predicted into the twenty-first century.

An attitude of responsibility and trust between employer and employee generally increases autonomy and decreases alienation. Some autonomy can do a lot to ease systems pained at all levels, global to personal. Employees can make the really *"major"* decisions, such as who will go to lunch when, who can have the most computer time, and how many times a day you can use the copier. These are the decisions that affect personnel personally where it hurts—in the every day.

The *"minor"* decisions include whether to expand company operations in Pakistan, invest a million in a new widget/gidget, or buy a shipping line. The majority of workers will be touched by these types of decision only in that less sensitive spot called the "long run," which is not today. What directly affects *me, now,* has highest priority in the mind of the individual worker.

Erving Goffman wrote in *Asylums* that simply by reason of sheer numbers institutions tend to become dehumanizing.[4] But large size doesn't always mean depersonalization. Within many a large organization we can discover small, cohesive, caring groups of people looking out for each other's interests. This kind of support would not be found even in a small business if it is run by a tyrannical leader.

Barbara Garson studied three workplaces in New York. She reported that two well-known companies showed extremely restrictive policies for workers: no talking to other employees during work time, no personal phone calls about family emergencies, and other rigid rules. In contrast, the report described the accounting office of a community college where five older women worked very hard, often staying late to complete their tasks. They managed to fit in noon parties, trips to the hospital to visit sick family members, and other personal ventures.[5] No want ad or job description will ever deal with this kind of "fringe benefit" or "perks."

Robert Schrank, a Ford Foundation work specialist, believes that attempts to relieve worker boredom by letting them have a say in diversifying tasks have limited value when the tasks themselves remain repetitive and dull. He worked on an assembly line himself and points out that every detail is predetermined in a modern production line. The workers cannot introduce variations. Schrank suggests that workers, especially blue-collar people, be allowed time to socialize

"INSPECTORS, ROBINSON, DO NOT
EXPRESS OPINIONS."

on the job to relieve boredom, if they can still complete their work on time. He uses the word *schmooze* to describe the amenities that professional and white-collar workers enjoy: time to make a phone call, talk wih coworkers, take some extra time off at lunch. Schrank believes these minor privileges would be more rewarding to the worker than diversified tasks or other current attempts at motivation.[6]

But some companies continue trying to make the workplace a more autonomous place. At United Motor Company in Fremont, California workers carry briefcases instead of lunch boxes. They are part of decision-making teams. Access to data, formerly the property of mid-management, gives the workers more autonomy. Some people feel that having access to computers and thus to all levels of personnel in a company may further blur the lines on the career ladder.

Much management training today concerns just such creation and use of decision-making teams. More worker involvement increases productivity, especially when supported by profit and benefit sharing. Communications skills are the key to effectiveness in today's management. The openness necessary to encourage trust requires constant cultivation and much sensitivity to human needs.

Because the number of workers with college degrees is increasing, and because these workers are often underemployed, they are likely to challenge old-style management techniques. When their survival needs are fulfilled, they focus on emotional needs for self-esteem, prestige, and recognition, as well as the intellectual need to use their minds creatively. And often they become altruistically more aware of the needs of people and planet. Increasing autonomy involves risk, but the majority of people (even small children) act responsibly when given a chance. The momentum lies in this direction, and only a prolonged economic depression or other disaster will stop it from happening.

The alternative, an arbitrary use of power, can stifle growth and initiative and defeat the ultimate goals of the workplace. But workplaces tend to be conservative. "Work is hard work," a serious enterprise mainly geared to profit and/ or public service. Shared decision making means we have to *think, adapt, relate, create,* which takes *time,* and *time* is *money.* What's more, some workers themselves would prefer to keep the status quo and not get too involved. When Joe Rodriguez, a ten-year Ford employee, took part in an experiment at Saab Engine Plant in Sweden designed to maximize worker involvement in decision making, he said, "If I've got to bust my ass to be meaningful, forget it. I'd rather be monotonous."[7] Thus tension arises between employers' needs to get on with it and their dependence on worker goodwill to get the job done. Such tension is not likely to disappear. There is need for the right balance between autonomy and supervision.

Corporations that use people and resources wisely perform better. For example, are secretaries considered part of the team, encouraged to think, be responsible, move up? Are young people given a foot in the door with entry-level jobs, summer job training? Are resources used to better the community? Denying support and advancement to its own workers, as well as ignoring its larger impact on the community, sabotages a company's overall effectiveness in the long run.

The human potential is out there, just waiting to be tapped by creative, positive leadership in cooperation with workers. It's a lofty goal, but worth aiming for.

Workplace Values

You will invest time and energy getting yourself set up in just the right job. But what would you do if you found your employer involved in some illegal, unethical, or immoral actions that clash head-on with your value system? And suppose you further found that you were expected to participate either actively or by keeping quiet?

Such dilemmas can usually be avoided by doing a little research ahead of time. Some investors are pulling their money out of companies that make faulty products, pollute, treat employees poorly, or practice fraud. A "social screen" has been developed by the U.S. Trust Company of Boston for use in advising concerned investors. They gather information from a number of sources: annual company reports, Securities and Exchange Commission reports, findings of the Investor Responsibility Research Center, the National Labor Relations Board, the Council on Economic Priorities, Inform, and the Interfaith Center on Corporate Responsibility, among others. They use the following questions to test and grade the social performance of corporations or other issuers of securities. You can use this social screen to tune you into a given firm's corporate culture:

- Do they produce and market safe, pure, quality products?
- Do they produce in ways that respect and preserve the natural environment?
- Do they provide a safe, healthy work environment?
- Do they provide equal employment opportunities for women and minorities?
- Do they have fair labor practices and allow the participation of workers in management, encouraging cooperation instead of confrontation?
- Do they operate nuclear power plants or provide products for those plants?
- Do they operate under and depend upon a repressive government—in particular, South Africa?
- Do they depend upon military weapons contracts?
- Are they willing to disclose information that gives us answers to all these questions?

For example, the South Shore Bank in Chicago has been noted as a socially responsible bank working for the good of the community. *Working Mother* magazine puts it in the top thirty companies, with thirteen of twenty-four management positions going to women.[8] The South Shore Bank is further using its resources to build housing and businesses in a ghetto area.

······ **WORKPLACE TAKE-CHARGE GROUPS**

These groups are working to influence and change workplaces. Write for information if you are interested.

Association for Workplace Democracy
1747 Connecticut Avenue N.W.
Washington, D.C. 20009

Center for Community Self-Help
P.O. Box 3259 413 E. Chapel Hill Street
Durham, NC 27705

COOP America
2100 M Street N.W. Suite 310
Washington, D.C. 20063

Good Money: Newsletter for Socially Concerned Investors
Also: *Netback and Catalyst*
Box 363
Worcester, VT 05682

Industrial Cooperative Association
58 Day Street, Suite 200
Sommerville, MA 02144

National Center for Employee Ownership
426 17th Street, Suite 650
Oakland, CA 94612

9 to 5, The National Association of Working Women
1224 Huron Road
Cleveland, OH 44115
(216) 566–9308

9 to 5, The Working Woman's Guide to Office Survival, by Ellen Cassedy
New York: Penguin Books, 1983

Philadelphia Arm for Cooperative Enterprise
2100 Chestnut Street
Philadelphia, PA 19103

Twin Streams Educational Center, Inc.
243 Flemington Street
Chapel Hill, NC 27514

As a concerned potential employee, ask around about the integrity of a company. It can be amazing how much employees know about the ethics of their own company. And if you have reason to suspect a company of unethical practices, library research, including a review of the business section of newspapers and magazines, can turn up a great deal of information. The question, "Can a company do well when doing good?" (that is, be both ethical *and* profitable) has been answered with a resounding "Yes!" It's important to find a company whose values match yours.[9]

Company Buy-Outs

One way to ensure that a company's value system matches yours is to buy it out! In the event of plant closings, workers are beginning to consider this option and in some cases are making it work for them. In addition, a "Fed Co-op" plan has been revived to allow federal workers to bid on contracts if they feel they can reduce costs. The rule, Circular A-76, affects about 600,000 employees who do everything from automatic data processing to running a cafeteria. Such "privatization" would save the government a great deal of money.[10]

ALTERNATIVES TO NINE-TO-FIVE

We work on schedules that don't match our natural rhythms. We are continually caught in a time bind in an increasingly complex world of ever longer commutes, more complicated personal business transactions, more involved maintenance of homes and gadgets. Most people work on a rigid schedule with little leeway for personal needs.

Some people are convinced that such stress even causes death. In the book *Type A Behavior and Your Heart,* Meyer Friedman and Ray H. Rosenman deal with behavior characteristics of the individual who is prone to heart attacks. We see a profile of the striving American doing six things at once and all the while fearing failure.[11] Our biology tries to catch up with our technology. We have much evolving to do to learn to blend with technology without losing our identities or our health. Yet it would hardly be feasible to give it all up. We need technology. How about "biorhythmic technology," moderated and more humane?

Work takes time. It can occupy a large part of a day, a week, a year, a lifetime. For many people the 40-hour week and the fifty-week year are the center of life. Flexibility for many is nonexistent and leisure hard won. But John Kenneth Galbraith says, "Only if an individual has a choice as to the length of

"Night work! You mean when it's dark?"

• •

HERMAN / by Unger
Copyright, 1977, Universal Press Syndicate. Reprinted by permission.

his working week or year, along with the option of taking unpaid leave for longer periods, does he or she have an effective choice between income and leisure."[12]

Many people feel that work uses too much of their prime time. Work plus family demands and the "business of living" leave them with little time for other enriched choices. Studs Terkel quotes a steelworker who says, "If I had a 20-hour work week, I'd get to know my kids better, my wife better. Some kid invited me to go on a college campus. On a Saturday. It was summertime. Hell, if I have a choice of taking my wife and kids to a picnic or going to a college campus, it's gonna be the picnic. But if I worked a 20-hour week, I could do both. Don't you think with that extra 20 hours people could really expand?"[13] Perhaps in the future we will see that such expansion could not only enrich many individuals but the planet as well, as people use time to explore and solve current issues.

Many workplaces creak with rigidity. For example, most employers are fearful of letting people leave work early when they are caught up. To avoid such struggles, the 40-hour week has become sacrosanct and is further regulated by professional and union rules about who does what when. Thus it is

Listen, if you want to eat in the office, BRING SANDWICHES!

HERMAN / by Unger
Copyright, 1977, Universal Press Syndicate. Reprinted by permission.

reported that the workers in a little state office in one small Midwestern town, when they occasionally finish all assigned work at 4 or 4:30, don hats and coats and sit in their darkened office until 5 o'clock. Probably they use the time to worry about children at home alone and what to have for supper.

A secretary at one of the world's largest corporations sits at her desk at 11:30 a.m. facing a day with little or no work because of a slowdown. Her boss had previously told a visitor that business was booming. Asked if she is permitted to go home early in such a case, she is horrified. "Never, in a company like this!" With a spectacular view of San Francisco, its bay, ocean, and bridges all around, she sits surrounded by little portable walls, seeing nothing, doing nothing. To knit or read a good book—even a book on how to be a better secretary—would violate a taboo. What a strain to fear being seen without work lest one's job disappear!

The late Hal Boyle of Associated Press estimated that most people who spend 8 hours in their offices could get their required work done in 2 hours.[14]

Self-Employment

Many people dream of becoming their own bosses, creating their own work environment by starting their own business either at home or outside. What services does your locale need that you might provide? A unique system to determine new business opportunities has been designed by the Council for Northeast Economic Action in conjunction with the First National Bank of Boston. Dr. Judy Appelt, a geographer with the project, can tell if a certain type of business will succeed. We have had few such ways of making good predictions for the beginning entrepreneur.

The person with a product or service to offer and the energy to "do it all" can find great satisfaction in being an entrepreneur. Molly Bauer, who began Communi-Speak, a firm that teaches people to speak more effectively, attributes a large measure of her success to having a good business advisor. Jessica McClintock, designer/owner of Gunne Saxe Fashions, cautions, "Hire a helper only when you're ready to drop." There is no question that beginning a business may be hazardous to your health on many levels. But from the farmer in a communist country marketing vegetables on the side to the weekend do-it-yourselfer remodeling the American kitchen, self-interest is a powerful motivator for getting work done.

The Gallup Organization found that 58 percent of business owners are "very happy" with their work; only 35 percent of employees feel the same way. During the last serious recession in 1980–1982, small businesses actually created 5.8 million new jobs while big businesses lost jobs.[18] Ten percent of Americans work for themselves. In 1980 women owned 22 percent of all sole proprietorships with $6.2 billion in net income, and those numbers are increasing.[19] Between 1975 and 1985, the number of self-employed women increased three times faster than the number of self-employed men. The most successful earn as much or more than their salaried counterparts.[20] Though women own 25 percent of

And Tony Shively (pen name, Thorne Lee), writer and philospher, says, "The average person is only capable of 4 productive hours of work a day. The rest is spent filling time. Society often demands more of a man's nature than it can give." In a walk through many workplaces, one can observe people finished with their four essential hours. In *The Fires of Spring,* one of James Michener's characters advises a young man, "A lot of nonsense is spoken about work. Some of the finest men I've known were the laziest. Never work because it's expected of you. Find out how much work you must do to live and be happy. Don't do any more."[15]

small businesses, they generate only about 10 percent of total business receipts,[21] but we can expect that number to increase as women learn the "knowhow" of business.

You will hear a great deal of advice about starting a small business. Some advisors encourage the budding entrepreneur to start with a flourish; others counsel going slowly and in small steps. Each case is unique, but the facts show that many small businesses fail in their first year through lack of planning and experimenting as well as lack of capital.

You can avoid investing a small fortune; you can start small by investing in a simple business card at $3/hundred.*

Then begin handing them out to friends and relatives, charging little or nothing for your services. Despite all our media efforts, the best advertisement is word of mouth by satisfied customers. Use evenings and weekends to test the waters while keeping your paying job as a backup. Richard Patocchi advises the beginner to rent office space part time and fill up that segment with clients; only then should you expand into more time per week. Be sure to check local zoning, traffic, and licensing laws before business starts booming or if you intend to use dangerous materials. Many local colleges and adult education centers provide workshops and counseling for the prospective entrepreneur.

Buying or leasing a franchise can provide a person with a business but also with a great deal of support and training. Franchising sales have increased 72 percent since 1980. These businesses have moved far beyond the fast food arena into such growing areas as fast-cut beauty salons, copy shops, and computer stores.[22] Many people find that getting a few years of work experience and contacts behind them is a good way to start their own businesses. And they find their qualifications develop and grow as they do. Learn about business before starting a business! Here is an overview of the process. Use what applies to your own situation.

*A catalog is available from Walter Drake and Sons, Inc., 94 Drake Bldg., Colorado Springs, Co. 80901.

Most of us need *some* structure in our lives, even though we might like to think of ourselves as free spirits. Work is the basic organizing principle for most people. But for the past fifty years, the nine-to-five 40-hour work week has been virtually set in solid concrete. Now that tradition is slowly changing.

And when we look at basic needs and wants and compare them with the work that is being done, we might be tempted to say that *much of the work that we do is not the work that needs to be done.* Aware people are evaluating their own work to see if it not only meets their own needs, wants, and values but is socially responsible as well. After a certain point, they may wonder if the

······

TIPS ON STARTING YOUR OWN BUSINESS

Is Small Business for You? Your Qualifications Summary:

- Are you fairly enterprising: confident, enthusiastic, optimistic, persistent, good with people?
- Are you trustworthy, energetic, hard working, flexible, independent, balanced, organized?
- Are you a responsible leader, good decision maker, self-starter?
- Are you willing to learn, take advice, observe and study other options?
- Can you develop a good support network: family, friends, associates?
- Do you get an idea and get it "off the ground"?
- Do you know when to move on, not stay in one place forever?

Information Gathering:

- List ideas that you might turn into a business.
- Describe each one in a paragraph.
- Put each one through the decision-making process described in Chapter 8.
- Rank them in order of total desirability and likelihood.
- Evaluate each product or service: is it innovative, of good quality, desirable?
- Contact people listed in the telephone directory yellow pages and newspaper financial pages who run similar or related businesses or franchises. Use the information interviewing techniques discussed later in this chapter.

money is worth the *time*. They begin to explore alternatives to the nine-to-five schedule and end up creating a variety of new work styles: full-time and part-time entrepreneurs, intrapreneurs, worksteaders, and prosumers involved in creative careers (all to be dealt with later in this chapter).

Some experimentation with new work schedules is taking place. *Flextime,* for example, allows workers to work for any 8 hours between specified times, such as 7 a.m. to 6 p.m. People can take care of the "business of living" in their off-hours when others are still at work to serve them. Those whose biorhythms make them either early or late risers are accommodated. Compressed work schedules such as four 10-hour days per week is a variation on flextime that has yielded similar good results. Some companies are even experimenting with three 12-hour shifts, enabling college students to work three weekend nights and still attend classes or working parents to share child care.

- Attend workshops for small businesses at local colleges, the Small Business Association, or other centers. Go to meetings of business people in your areas of interest. Read related books.
- Do market research; sometimes just asking around can give you an idea of the market before hiring someone to do it professionally.
- Explore locations/types of spaces available.

Financial/Legal Planning:

- Begin with clear statement of purpose.
- Develop a sample product or prototype.
- Cost out possible expenditures: goods/services/equipment/real estate; keep good accounts.
- Work out a financial plan as carefully as a résumé or term paper: complete description of the business, estimate of cash flow, one- and five-year projections, your own financial assets/liabilities.
- Talk to a knowledgeable financial planner about various funding options.
- Get to know your banker; getting credit is one of the largest hurdles, especially for women!
- Develop a credit rating by paying a small personal loan back promptly.
- Look into: loans from banks/private foundation; taxes, partnerships, stocks, qualifications of staff needed.
- Negotiate the terms of loans and other contracts and expenses; don't just accept the first suggestion.
- See a lawyer about various legal aspects of the business.

Job sharing, another option, enables people to choose shorter work hours while getting the job done with a partner. Some companies allow people to work at home on their own time. Though such flexibility may add to the work and cost of management, research shows that absenteeism drops and productivity rises in these situations.

Many more people could be employed if some people worked fewer than 40 hours per week, fifty weeks per year. The loss of income might be offset in many ways (even financially): saving energy and resources, enjoying a more enriched life, having more time for the business of living.

Today one out of six Americans works part time regularly and by choice. Over 2 million part-timers are professionals, managers, and administrators.[16] In 1981 a Louis Harris survey of American families found 28 percent of all working men and 41 percent of all working women preferring part-time work over full-

······ **SMALL BUSINESS RESOURCES**

American Women's Economic Development Corporation The Lincoln Building, 60 East 42nd Street New York, NY 10165 (212) 692–9100

Be Your Own Boss: The Complete Indispensable Hands-on Guide to Starting and Running Your Own Business, Dana Schilling (New York: Penguin Books, 1984)

Big Profits from Small Companies, Steven Popell (Lomas Publishing Co., Mountain View, CA 94043, 1985)

Consumer Information Catalog, U.S. General Services Administration, Consumer Information Center–Z, P.O. Box 100, Pueblo, CO 81002

Entrepreneurial Mothers, Phyllis Gillis (New York: Rawson Assoc., 1984)

The Entrepreneurial Workbook, Charlotte Taylor (New York: New American Library, 1983)

The Entrepreneur and Small Business Problem Solver: A Reference and Guide, William A. Cohen (New York: John Wiley & Sons, Inc.: 1983)

In Business–for the Independent, Innovative Individual and *Sideline Business: Your Monthly Guide to Moonlighting Success* Box 323, 18 S. Seventh Street, Emmaus, PA 18049

Invest in Yourself: A Woman's Guide to Starting Her Own Business, Peg Moran (New York: Doubleday, 1986)

time or volunteer work or work at home. Percentages were highest in the over-fifty-five age group.[17] Such an arrangement keeps the permanent core of full-time workers more stable. Disadvantages to the part-timer are the lack of benefits and pension rights.

Temporary work is a growing alternative. Some people find that working full time at intervals is quite to their liking. Some temporary agencies even provide a variety of benefits.

How important is schedule for you? Single parents, especially, carry burdens that demand attention not always amenable to a nine-to-five schedule. One woman engineer noticed several male colleagues consulting on what she assumed was their project. On closer inspection, she found these newly divorced males discussing the merits of the microwave for the working parent!

Journal of Small Business Management, International Council for Small Business, P.O. Box 6025, West Virginia University, Morgantown, WV 26506

Kessler Letter, $5/yr. 6 issues, P.O. Box 67A47, Los Angeles, CA 90067

National Association of Women Business Owners (NAWBO), 500 N. Michigan Avenue, Chicago, IL 60611

Real Money from Home, Valerie Bohigan (New York: New American Library, 1985)

Small Time Operator: How to Start Your Own Small Business, Keep Your Books, Pay Your Taxes, and Stay Out of Trouble, Bernard Kamoroff, CPA (Bell Springs Publ. P.O. Box 640, Laytonville, CA 95454, April 1985)

Starting and Managing a Small Business of Your Own, Wendall O. Metcalf (Washington, D.C.: U.S. Small Business Admin., 1982)

Successful Small Business Management, David Siegel and Harold Goldman (Fairchild Publ., 7 E. 12th St., New York, NY 10003, 1982)

Starting on a Shoestring: Building a Business without a Bankroll, Arnold S. Goldstein (New York: John Wiley & Sons, 1984)

1987 U.S. Industrial Outlook, U.S. Dept. of Commerce, International Trade Administration, Washington, D.C. 20230

U.S. Small Business Administration, P.O. Box 15434, Fort Worth, TX 76119

A key need for many people is time. Yet not everyone could slow down and enjoy leisure even if more were available. For some, work is life. Instead of getting in touch with other facets of their personalities, the total technologist eschews social gatherings; the confirmed clerk avoids art. In the extreme, a highly successful person could be leading a life impoverished on many levels.

Worksteads

People who do work at home—typing, translating, editing, and now data entry—are *worksteaders.* Either working for a company or on your own, it is now possible to do much of that work at home by computer. Telecommunications can bring people within sight and sound of each other even though they are hundreds of miles apart. One production plant was kept running all weekend even though the human in charge was ten miles away. Equipment thousands of miles in outer space can be operated and repaired from the earth by remote control. The Japanese have an experimental farm run by computerized robots. Who knows what goods and services will be produced from the "electronic cottage" of the future? Here's what some worksteaders say:[23]

> There are a whole bunch of soft industries that are information oriented or technologies that have no pollution whatsoever. . . . These kinds of industries could be right in our neighborhoods. . . . I've always lived where I work.
>
> —Peter Ziegler, Earth Lab Institute

> If a person is going to leave a job to work at home, he needs a very clear attitude about how he is going to live. I set up a rather modest goal of the kind of security I wanted to have before I left the law firm. I don't buy expensive clothes, for instance. I enjoy cooking so I don't go to restaurants much. If you have a place to live, where you can also work, you can get along on very little. The rest of life doesn't really take too much money if you have a place to be.
>
> —George Hellyer, Attorney

Productivity increases for those who work at home. Single parents, the elderly and disabled can possibly find new opportunities "worksteading"! Lack of safety guides, however, and possible exploitation by an employing firm— meaning low wages, no vacations or benefits, and long hours—are cause for some concern. Isolation is another issue to consider. And unless you are running a creative business or have a good job, your career is not likely to develop at home. Combining child raising with work at home can also prove a stressful alternative for some people. In some cases workers may become responsible for equipment lease or purchase along with office furniture. They may find their utility bills (e.g., telephone linkup) and energy costs rising. Some companies, finding long distance work so attractive, have moved their data processing work "offshore" to Third World countries where worker wages as well as worker protection are minimal, thus subtracting from the available pool of jobs in the United States.[24]

Third Wave Prosumers

When a truck driver with a college degree was asked what he intended to do with his education, he replied, "I will practice living, I will develop my intellect, which may incidentally contribute to the elevation of the esthetic and cultural levels of society. I will try to develop the noble and creative elements within me. I will contribute very little to the *grossness* of the national product."[25]

Some prefer not to contribute to an economy they feel encourages mindless consumption of goods, wastes energy and resources, and contributes to a poor quality of life. These nonconformists, called *prosumers* by Alvin Toffler, are riding in on the Third Wave. Do-it-yourself and self-help tasks, bartering, and sharing are all parts of their diversified lifestyle.[26] The psychologist who helps people grow at the office may come home to a small farm and grow vegetables for self and sale. A veterinarian's varied schedule includes part-time spaying of dogs and cats at an animal shelter along with research, writing, and private consulting. He and his artist wife grow many of their own vegetables and repair their own car. Richard and Susan Pitcairn are thus third wave prosumers. Their book *Natural Health for Dogs and Cats* reflects their caring lifestyle.[27]

Prosumers Pat and Bill Cane live a largely self-sufficient lifestyle raising chickens, bees, and raspberries, making jam and honey. Their bountiful garden provides food for table and barter. A monthly nine-course gourmet meal for a group of friends provides their basic expenses. While Pat barters beautiful stained glass for a variety of goods and services, Bill writes. In *Through Crisis to Freedom,* a book about life transitions, he says, "In crisis, you are somehow enabled to get in touch with sources of life deep inside yourself—sources you never knew were there. And then mysteriously, like the blades of grass, you begin to know how to grow."[28] These new "old" lifestyles aren't for everyone but are options in a nine-to-five world for those willing to take the risk. Many people lived this way years ago. In the technological future, we may be able to do less work and enjoy more of life's good things.

Other Work Alternatives

Most people, especially males, begin work after graduating from high school or college and keep at it until age sixty-five. But even the most exciting of career fields can pall after many years. Steps must often be taken to keep up motivation: going back to school, seeking promotions, changing positions or companies, looking for a unique approach to your job, finding enriching hobbies, fostering personal growth on all levels all help to keep up your work energy. Some industries have experimented with leaves of absence for social action projects and part-time or full-time educational leaves, either paid or unpaid.

For some people the opportunity to work after age sixty-five is most welcome. To others retirement (as early as possible) means liberation to do other things. We are just barely beginning to consider the possibility of integrating work and leisure. Some husbands are taking time off while their wives work; some people are "easing into retirement" with reduced schedules. Total involvement in work, then, may not be essential in an affluent information society.

Most workers have experienced the two extremes—either total work or no work—rather than a balance of the two. But in 1969 we passed the era of full employment based on a 40-hour week. Now we need creative schemes that will allow education, business, industry, and government to train more workers for fewer hours of work per week. The cost will be great, but the benefits may be even greater. In a work-oriented society, where the unemployed feel inadequate, crime and mental illness increase when the unemployment rate is high. The quality of life is diminished. Taxes must be increased to pay for welfare and related problems, including law enforcement and health care. With productivity sagging nationally and unemployment plaguing us, creative lifestyle and work style options are fast becoming a necessity.

Cooperatives

Cooperatives and *collectives,* group-owned and democratically run enterprises, are a rich and growing option for people to improve their work environments. These joint undertakings often result in increased motivation, sense of control, and greater productivity. Some companies, while maintaining control, do share power and profits by means of employee stock option plans or ESOPS, which remain in effect until an employee leaves. And some employees have bought out their companies successfully in cases of plant closings.

THE INTRAPRENEUR

An intermediate position between the cold, cruel corporation and the cold, cruel world on one's own is filled by the *intrapreneur,* a term coined by Gifford Pinchot III, a consultant to such companies as Exxon, to describe the "*intracorporate entrepreneur.*" Intrapreneurs remain company employees while contracting their services to their employer. Using company resources and support, they act as self-employed persons often developing services or products that the company is unwilling to commit to with large-scale expenditures. Intrapreneurship may take some capital but involves less risk than entrepreneurship. Even a small work section within a company could perform this role: a typing pool could set up its own system in return for a lump sum payment; an engineer could gather a team to do creative research. A company benefits since it does not lose a valued employee who might otherwise move to a competitor, taking the idea along.[29] Flexibility and more independence from the company can also result when employees are "leased" back to their companies by an agency that has taken over all hiring of permanent employees. Look around your workplace for a possible intrapreneurial opportunity.

Creative Careers

As you interview people and observe them on their jobs, look for those who have taken an ordinary job and brought it to life in a creative way, sometimes within a very structured bureaucracy. The position "store manager" with its attendant duties may sound formidable or dull. But Monique Benoit of San Francisco gave it new life. Well known for her community involvement, she loved to shop in expensive antique shops and boutiques. She also cherished her independence and loved to travel. Monique managed to satisfy a number of these divergent likes by creating her own job: she carefully composed a letter and sent it to managers of her favorite stores, offering to "shop sit" if they had to be away from the store for business or personal reasons. She received a good response and subsequent offers of part-time employment.

"Susie Skates" indulges in her favorite sport while delivering messages. "Flying Fur" delivers pampered pets around the country, while "Sherlock Bones" searches for missing pets. From Rent-a-Yenta, Clutter Cutter, and Rent-a-Goat, to Mama's Llamas, Rent-a-Thief, Choco-Logo, Nanny Pop-Ins, and Sweet Revenge, people create careers with imagination instead of capital. Some groups like Nanny Pop-Ins Trade Association provide services for its members or clients: consulting, insurance coverage, accounting, discount purchasing and warehouse storage are some of these services.

Here are a few other creative, though not always lucrative, careers: house-sitting, pet sitting, providing travel/transportation companions, creative child care that includes instruction in a craft or hobby, shopping and transportation for the elderly and disabled, photography at special events, house calls on sick plants, giant cookies, tasty diet candy, exercise groups for the elderly, masquerading servants at parties, teaching do-it-yourself auto repair. Add producing and marketing very special gourmet homegrown/homemade food and herbs, and the possibilities are endless. The mark of a fulfilling job is the invigorating and energy-giving feelings it provides.

THE INS AND OUTS
OF WORKPLACES

Begin *now* to collect information about workplaces. Become career aware! First, get a view from the outside by reading about workplaces and eliminating those that don't match your needs and wants. The next step is the information interview: getting the inside story about careers and companies by talking to people "on site."

Information about companies is available from many sources. Most libraries have a business reference section, and most local librarians love to help people and take pride in knowing where to find data. Texts like *Standard and Poor's* or *Thomas Register* may be helpful but more technical than you need or want. Look for books like *Everybody's Business: An Almanac,* the irreverent guide to corporate America by Milton Moskowitz, Michael Katz, and Robert Levering, *Rating America's Corporate Conscience,* by Steven D. Lydenberg, Alice Tepper Marlin, and Sean Strub with the Council on Economic Priorities, Reading, MA, Addison Wesley Publishing Co., Inc.: 1987. *Who's Who in Commerce and Industry* will give you key names. Business and professional journals in your field provide a wealth of information. An *Encyclopedia of Associations* lists groups promoting their own wares and even a *Directory of Conventions* is available.

Publications like *Community Jobs,* a newsletter of want ads (1520 Sixteenth St. NW, Washington, D.C. 20036) can give you an idea of what is out there when you are beginning the search. Professional organizations themselves hire personnel, for example, in public relations and finance. Look at chambers of commerce, Better Business Bureaus, real estate boards, and trade associations at the national, state, and local levels not only for information but for possible jobs.[30]

The U.S. Bureau of Industrial Economics has information on trends in various fields available from the Industry Publications Division, Trade Development, Room 4424, Herbert C. Hoover Building, Washington, D.C. 20230. Your local chamber of commerce has information about all the businesses in your town. College career center libraries, placement offices, and state employment offices are often stocked with material about companies. Some companies have public relations departments that send information if you write or call.

The yellow pages of your phone book are a gold mine of ideas because just about every business in your area is listed there according to what it does. If you read the business section of your local newspaper regularly, you will know who is doing what and where in the work world in your area. Don't be afraid to call or write to people who sound interesting. Ask them to tell you more about what they do or congratulate them on some accomplishment or promotion. People appreciate positive feedback. Let them know if you are sincerely interested in some aspect of the company. The applicants best prepared for a job interview are those who not only know the company they want to work for but also have a broad knowledge of the work world. Knowing some of the basics about a company, an industry, and its competition gives you confidence during the job hunt.

Information Interviewing

After doing library research, many people still feel some pieces are missing from the puzzle. Some are disappointed because many jobs described in occupational guides sound dull. But those descriptions are the bare bones of the job. You can put flesh and blood on those skeletons by visiting workplaces and interviewing people about what they do. So from here on in it's important to be *out*—out talking to everyone about their jobs, out observing work environments.

How often have working friends given you a blow-by-blow description of life at Picky Products, Inc.? If *you've* worked for a company, you have information about it that's not easily available to an outsider. You know the people who are likely to help beginners; you know how tough or easy the supervisors are, how interesting or boring the work is—what it's *really* like!

A key part of the career search process is interviewing people about their jobs and observing them in their workplaces to get that inside information. You want to answer two questions: One, is this a job you would really like? Two, is this a place you would really like to work? Unless you are an experienced and sophisticated jobseeker with a broad knowledge of jobs, it is important to gather as much firsthand information as you can before you choose a career and per- haps plan courses and get a degree. The job may require education or special training. Why not find out all you can before spending time, energy, and money on training for a job you may not like? You can also eliminate misconceptions about the preparation you need in order to be hired.

If you feel timid about approaching a stranger, practice by interviewing people in your family, then a friend or neighbor about his or her job. Talk to everyone you meet about what they do and who they can introduce you to in your career field. Ask people you know for names of willing interviewees. It's amazing how you can usually find someone who knows someone who knows someone. . . . Your college alumni office is often in touch with graduates in different fields. An instructor in a field of interest may know someone "out there" who will talk to you. Seek someone close to the level at which you are applying. Don't ask to see the president of a company if you are searching out information about safety engineering. Rather, find a person who is a safety en- gineer or industrial technologist or technical supervisor. It's much better to make an appointment ahead of time at that person's convenience. If you want the interview to go smoothly, do not drop in unexpectedly on a busy person.

If you feel uncertain about going to an interview alone, ask a friend to introduce you, or ask someone with a mutual interest to go along. If it seems appropriate, invite the person you will interview out for coffee or lunch after you visit their workplace.

•••••••   ## What to Look for in a Growth Company

- Sales growing at 30 percent a year
- No acquisitions of other companies
- Little or no debt
- Positive cash flow
- Five consecutive years' higher earnings
- One-of-a-kind product or service
- Special niche without competition
- Lowest cost producer*

And although some companies are not publicly owned and may resist sharing information about how profitably they are doing, you still need to persist and get some idea of how they are doing financially.

*Mark O'Brien, "How to Pick a Growth Company," *Business Week's Guide to Careers,* October 1984, p. 75.

Use the information interview sparingly, not casually. Wait until you have done all your homework carefully and have some idea of your direction. Most people are sincerely interested in helping information seekers but sometimes they cannot spare the time. Don't feel discouraged if you are refused an interview.

Following your skills and interests may lead you into work environments ranging from serene to frenetic. As a writer, for example, you might find yourself either researching in a library or risking your life as a war correspondent. There are many things you thoroughly enjoy but might hate if you had to do them under pressure—a thousand times a day—in a hot, crowded, noisy, and otherwise unpleasant place—for an irritable boss with ulcers! You may enjoy cooking but be fairly certain you would not enjoy serving some of a billion hamburgers every day. You might not like cooking regularly for any large group, even in the most elegant setting. You can find out by visiting various kitchens, talking to the cooks, and observing what they do. Barbara Rosenbloom and Victoria Krayer, owners of a charcuterie in Berkeley, California showed one visitor the huge pots of heavy paté that had to be mixed, emptied, and cleaned. The visitor learned that cooking is sometimes physically demanding.

Find out whether the company you are interested in (or one like it) gives tours. In some cases you can spend a whole day observing someone doing a job you might like. Remember, when you talk with people in your career field of interest, you are gathering all their biases. Each person likes and dislikes certain things about the job. Each one will give you a different view. Keep your antennae out to receive the emotional content of their messages. Then weigh all these messages against your good feelings and reasoned judgment.

There are other ways to meet people in your field of interest. Many professional groups welcome students at their meetings and have special rates for student/lay participation; the Society of Women Engineers is one of these. (The *Occupational Outlook Handbook* lists names and addresses of such organizations.) Throughout the United States, the American Society for Training and Development has chapters that hold monthly meetings and annual conventions. At such meetings you can meet people who have access to local business information and contacts. Chambers of commerce and other community organizations hold regular luncheons with speakers. In social settings like these, it's possible to make contacts easily and explore possibilities for on-site visits. At workshops or classes in your career area of interest, speakers and participants can share information with you both formally and informally.

Much of your success will come from keeping your eyes and ears open. Begin to wonder what just about everyone you meet is doing. Almost every media news item is about people's doings. Which activities attract you? How can you learn more about these activites? Keep on looking, listening, asking questions—it's your best source of information. Eventually you will be talking to people who are doing work you would like to do. Something will click as you begin to share experiences and enthusiasms. You will make a network of friends who may later wish to hire you.

One caution. Most people are happy to answer most questions about their jobs until you come to salary. A direct question about a person's earnings would rarely be appreciated. But there are ways to get an idea of what you might expect. Some possible approaches: "What is the approximate salary *range* for a position like yours?" How much might an entry-level person expect to earn in this position?" A call to a local/state employment office can also provide approximate salary levels.

At first many people hesitate to call a stranger in a large company—or even an acquaintance in a small one. One student, whose talents were apparent to everyone but herself, was terrified at the prospect. She grimly made the first phone call. To her amazement, the interview was delightful—that is, until she was advised to explore a graduate program at a nearby university. She forced herself to see the department head that same day. Another warm reception! Elated, she rushed out to call her career counselor from the nearest phone booth. She was chuckling, "Here I am thirty-five years old and as excited as any kid over talking to two human beings!"

Another student given the same class assignment simply didn't do it. She had been a psychology major with a love for art, but changed to business which seemed more "practical" although it didn't seem to fit her creative "people" needs. Then she discovered organizational development and told someone about it—who knew a management consultant who used graphic arts in his work. Her reluctance to interview vanished as possibilities began to open up.

Perhaps not everyone you meet will be helpful. You may meet a "Queen Bee" or a "King Pin"—someone who has made it and is unwilling to help others. Sometimes people are just having a bad day, are truly too busy, or have yet to learn what all self-actualizing people know: "The more you help others, the more successful you'll be." But if you don't give up, you will find warmhearted people who understand your needs, your confusion and YOU! Keep on searching for those who are sensitive to YOU.

When people have spent time with you, follow up with thank-you notes. This courtesy will be appreciated and help employers to remember you when you begin the job hunt. The information interview process puts you in the hiring network. It can be an adventure—and it can be very profitable.

Work Experience

Probably the best way to get the inside story is to get a little firsthand experience in the work environment—even if you have to volunteer. Try your school or state employment placement office for positions at different workplaces. Or sign up at a temporary employment agency with a good reputation to survey businesses, make contacts, and make money on your own schedule. Once inside, you can get acquainted with people in the cafeteria, for example, and watch the bulletin boards for job announcements.

Internships are sometimes available for students to do course research and cooperative work experience, sometimes with pay. They can be just a day or two or a whole semester or even yearlong. While these sorts of activities give you a chance to survey companies, they also give employers a chance to get to know you. Such contacts may be valuable resources for you in the future.

With some actual work experience, a young person who "loves animals" may find working at the local vet's office either exciting or, with sick animals and worried owners, traumatic. On the other hand, every job will gradually (or quickly) demonstrate some unpleasant aspects. Basically, work is often hard work. You must function within the economic and time parameters of an organization or, if self-employed, meet client and societal demands. When both time and money are in short supply, deadlines and shortages create pressure.

As you become familiar with the workplace, your confidence will grow. By the time you are ready for an interview, you will understand the job and its problems. You will know the latest techniques in your trade or profession. You will know people in the field who may recommend or even hire you. Remember: The Department of Labor has estimated that 70 to 80 percent of all jobs are acquired by word of mouth. And with your newfound self-confidence, that first job interview will be duck soup—not sitting duck!

• • • • • • • • • • • • • **Self-Assessment Exercises**

The following exercises will help you decide what kind of workplaces and work styles you prefer and then locate those that match these preferences.

1. Where Do You Fit In?

a. Number the categories of workplace in order of importance to you:

_____ Business   _____ Health

_____ Industry   _____ Government

_____ Education   _____ Military

_____ Entertainment/Communication

b. Check the workplace size that most appeals to you:

_____ Very small   _____ Moderate   _____ Very large

_____ Multinational

c. Check which you prefer:

_____ Indoor work   _____ Outdoor work

_____ A combination

d. How far up the ladder do you think you want to go? Explain.

_____

e. Check your work style preference(s):

_____ Career creator   _____ Third wave prosumer

_____ Entrepreneur   _____ Traditional nine-to-fiver

_____ Intrapreneur   _____ Worksteader

f. Describe an alternative to the nine-to-five work style that interests you.

_____

_____

g. List three businesses in your field of interest from the phone book yellow pages:

_____

_____

_____

2. Researching Workplaces

Using library resources, research one workplace in your career area.

Name of workplace:_____ Phone Number:_____

Address:_____ City/State/Zip:_____

Organization:

Divisions and locations:_____

_____

Products/services:_____

Number of employees:_____ Job titles of interest to you:_____

_____

Performance

Past and present market:_____

_____

Company earnings as of past year:_____

Future projections for growth and profit:_____

Stability:_____

Competitors:_____

Other Factors

Reputation/integrity:_____

Environmental record:_____

Social concern:_____

3. Workplace Checklist

Rate one workplace of interest to you on the following checklist. Put a (+) in front of the ten qualities that are of most interest to you.

Company name:_____ Phone number:_____

Address:_____ City/State/Zip:_____

Management characteristics: Good   Fair   Poor

_____ Honesty   ____   ____   ____

	Good	Fair	Poor
_____ Respect	____	____	____
_____ Objectivity	____	____	____
_____ Openness	____	____	____
_____ Cooperation	____	____	____
_____ Goal orientation	____	____	____
_____ Flexibility	____	____	____
_____ Scheduling	____	____	____

Use of skills/interests

	Good	Fair	Poor
_____ Encourages growth/autonomy	____	____	____
_____ Provides varied experience	____	____	____
_____ Supports efforts	____	____	____
_____ Acknowledges achievements	____	____	____
_____ Open to transfers/promotions	____	____	____
_____ Offers educational opportunities	____	____	____
_____ Provides training/development	____	____	____

Environment

	Good	Fair	Poor
_____ Location/setting	____	____	____
_____ Appearance of buildings	____	____	____
_____ Work stations	____	____	____
_____ Cafeteria	____	____	____
_____ Restrooms	____	____	____
_____ Colors	____	____	____
_____ Light	____	____	____
_____ Furnishings/equipment	____	____	____
_____ Safety	____	____	____
_____ Compatible coworkers	____	____	____
_____ Friendliness	____	____	____
_____ Orderliness	____	____	____

Salary/benefits	Good	Fair	Poor
_____ Salary	___	___	___
_____ Medical/dental	___	___	___
_____ Fitness facilities	___	___	___
_____ Life/disability insurance	___	___	___
_____ Vacations/holidays	___	___	___
_____ "Business of living" time	___	___	___
_____ Maternity/paternity leaves	___	___	___
_____ Child care	___	___	___
_____ Profit sharing	___	___	___
_____ Moving/travel expenses	___	___	___
_____ Flextime	___	___	___
_____ Retirement benefits	___	___	___
_____ Traval benefits	___	___	___

The community

	Good	Fair	Poor
_____ Recreational/cultural facilities	___	___	___
_____ Medical/dental facilities	___	___	___
_____ Acceptable schools	___	___	___
_____ Transportation	___	___	___
_____ Cost of living	___	___	___
_____ Other amenities	___	___	___

   a. Complete this statement: I would (or would not) like to work there
      because:

   _____

   _____

4. Workplace Values

   a. Rate these corporate values H, M, or L meaning High, Medium, or Low in
      importance to you as a potential employee.

      _____ Produce and market safe, useful, pure products

_____ Use production methods that respect/preserve the environment

_____ Provide a safe, healthy work environment

_____ Make equal opportunities available for women and minorities

_____ Maintain fair labor practices

_____ Allow workers to participate in management

b. Would you turn down a job because of violations of any of these issues?

Yes_____ No_____ Check which ones.

Information Interview

Interview in a career field that interests you. Write the results of one such interview either here or on a separate sheet of paper.

_____

Name of Person   Company Name

_____

Job Title   Address

_____

Phone Number   City/State/Zip

Here are some questions you might ask:

a. Why did you choose this field?

_____

_____

b. How did you get your job?

_____

_____

c. What do you really do all day?

_____

_____

d. If you could redesign your job, which parts would you keep? Which would you get rid of?

_____

_____

e. If you had it to do all over again, what would you do differently in your career? What decisions do you regret?

_____

_____

f. What were your most positive career decisions?

_____

_____

g. What are the major issues in your career field? The important books, journals, organizations?

_____

_____

h. What is the entry level job title and its salary range?

_____

_____

i. What is the outlook for this field in job growth?_____

j. What are the requirements for the job: training, certificates, licenses, degrees, tools, union membership?

_____

k. Will your company have openings in this field soon? _____Yes _____No

l. Could you recommend someone else I might interview?

_____

Name of Person   Company Name

_____

Job Title   Address

_____

Phone Number   Cite/State/Zip

Group Discussion Questions

1. What have you learned about various workplaces?
2. What insights did you gain from the information interviewing process?
3. What factors prevent workplace environments from improving?

4. In what ways is your household a workplace? Consider goods and services, management, finances, maintenance, communications, personnel, labor negotiations, your degree of commitment, emotional climate, skills you use, and functions you perform. Does your household respect the rights of its members and care for the natural environment?

5. Ask for career information from members of your study group. Trade resources.

6. What changes in the workplace (e.g., in schedules) could help solve the unemployment problem?

7. What changes in society could help solve the unemployment problem?

8. Will there always be unemployed people who would like to work?

9. How can they be taken care of? Should they?

10. Explain: "Much of the work we do is not the work that needs to be done."

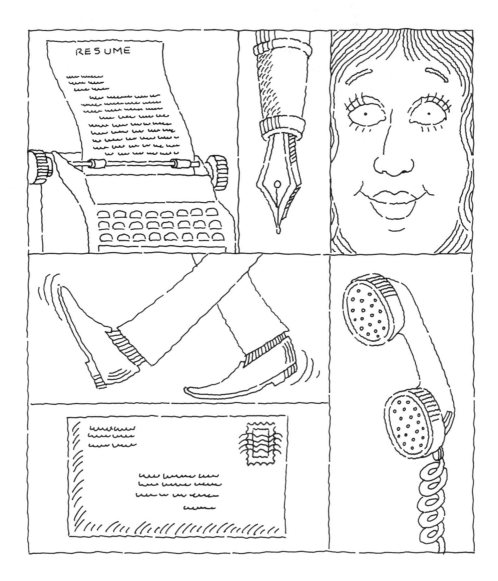

THE JOB HUNT: TOOLS FOR BREAKING AND ENTERING

. . . . .

F O C U S

Learn about creative job hunting including networking.

Gather information about yourself into a good résumé.

Prepare for an effective interview.

•••••

Y ou have thoroughly assessed your needs, wants, shoulds, values, and interests. You have envisioned your ideal lifestyle. You have researched your skills so thoroughly that you now have a marvelous list of your own accomplishments. You have begun to collect words to describe yourself. You have looked over the whole job market and found many jobs that would suit you well. You have interviewed people, researched companies, explored workplaces. You have considered the "job versus career" issue, the career ladder, possibilities for future goals, creative careers, and owning your own business. You have zeroed in on a job title or two and some companies where you have contacts. In short, you are ready, at last, for the job hunt!

Job hunting is often a full-time job. And like work, it is often hard work. Networking, résumés, letters, applications, phone calls, and interviews can make your head swim. The challenge and excitement of a career search may wear thin as you travel this long and sometimes weary road. Keeping your wits about you and keeping up your courage are two essential skills.

Some people find it helpful to join a support group or start one at this time. Friends can be a source of ideas and emotional support if and when the going gets tough. Ask for help and understanding. It also helps to keep several options open—developing possibilities on your present job, taking a course or two, inching toward starting your own business—while you interview in several different areas.

There is no one way to job hunt. Many employers use want ads and employment agencies, and many people walk through these doors to find jobs. Use all the help you can get. But be aware that private employment agencies are like used car dealers: some are reliable, and some are only there to put bodies behind the wheel and collect a fee. Some are less than honest. They may put false ads in the newspaper to attract clients and use excessive flattery to get your signature on a contract. They may be able to collect their fee even if you find a job on your own without their help. Check with people who have used the services. Read the fine print before you sign over a big chunk of next year's paycheck for a job that may not be right for you.

If you have followed all the steps in the career search process, you should be able to do your own job hunting. Perhaps someone you've contacted in your information interviewing is just waiting for your résumé and application to hire you. Sending out dozens of résumés to personnel departments is the least effective strategy, especially if you are looking for a job in a competitive field. You may get a nibble or two but not too many people are hired this way. Here is where your information interviewing will pay off to get you into the hiring network.

NETWORKING

Networking is a new "old" word. Whatever it's called—the buddy system, the old boys' network, or the new girls' network—the fact is that employers have always passed jobs along to people whom they know. It has even been estimated that 80 percent of all jobs are obtained by word of mouth and often not advertised. People are networking when they shake hands and exchange business cards—something that many men do automatically and women are learning to do. Men talk business everywhere—in the hallways, over coffee, in the men's room. These casual conversations may sound trivial, but they strengthen the links in the old boys' network.

Where do you stand in the networking game? If you are new at creative job hunting, the inner circle may look like a closed circuit that doesn't include you! But think again—how often have you or people you know heard about a job opening from a friend? And bring it close to home. Suppose you want to hire someone to do work of great importance: take care of a child or ailing parent, fix your much needed car, clean the house that contains everything you own. No doubt you feel safer when you ask around and get a referral from a friend. Employers feel better, too, when they hire someone they know or someone recommended by a trusted friend or colleague. If you have already done information interviewing, you have a good start on networking. Use the same process and the same contacts to find out about job openings and how to approach a given workplace. These insiders can offer you the inside story as well as moral support. Also consider contacting school friends, social contacts, anyone who knows you.

Even if you haven't developed a network of personal contacts, call on as many companies (or clients) as you can and apply for possible openings. Make contacts instead of staying at home alone reading the want ads all day. Now is the time to keep your energy up. Plan a schedule: exercise, eat well, get plenty of rest, and talk to as many positive people as you can. In a tight job market it's important to keep up your courage. Remember that rejections are part of the game and they do not mean you are unacceptable. Chances are you are just one of many good candidates. Later the company you are interested in may offer you a different job than the one you had in mind. If the company is a good one, it may even be worth taking a different job just to get inside where changes in position are more easily arranged.

You can use networking to find out about openings. It can assist you in obtaining information that can help you be more successful in getting hired. But be aware that employers are required to follow affirmative action guidelines. They must advertise widely and screen an adequate number of applicants to

• • • • • •   **RÉSUMÉ FORMATS**

1. Name, address, home phone, business (or message) phone.

List this information prominently at the top of the page. Be sure to give useful phone numbers; a prospective employer should know where to reach you, day or evening. If you do not wish your present employer to know you are job hunting, ask someone to take messages for you when you are at work.

2. Position objectives, as specific and brief as possible.
3. Qualifications in brief: highlights of your education, experience, skills.
4. Experience summary.

The type of presentation may be chronological, functional, or a combination of the two.

Chronological:

Begin with your most recent job and work backward.

March, 1986–Present: COMPANY, City, State, Job Title. Add a brief, concise description of what you did.

In this type of résumé, you may wish to include a section on community service, military service, or whatever applies (see Figure 7-4 and the Appendix).

Functional:

The information is arranged by areas of competence, expertise, or effectiveness, such as public relations, management, organization, program development, sales.

(continued)

give as many people as possible a fair chance at the job. Networking is not meant to give less qualified people an unfair advantage over others, though it sometimes does. Asking for help is legitimate. But employers are not allowed to discriminate against another well-qualified applicant. They will try to ensure that the help they give is available to all prospective employees. (Some employers will simply be equally "unavailable" to all!)

No one ever said the job hunt would be easy! Work on your résumé, schedule your time, set goals, and keep moving.

The Résumé

A résumé is a summary of personal information relevant to the job you seek. A good résumé marks you as a serious job seeker. Much has been written about the résumé. Some regard it as a sacred cow, *the* most important item to use in

List functions that are related to your position objective.

Follow each category with the businesslike action words you've collected, such as "planned" and "classified"; then give a summary of the type of things you accomplished. You may either list employers and dates at the end or note them on the company's application form (see Figure 7-2).

Combination of chronological and functional:

If this format suits your experience, be sure that special skills relevant to your position objective are highlighted (see Figure 7-3).

5. Educational background (this could go before work experience if it is more job-related.)

The purpose of listing educational background is to indicate general and specific training for a job. A person who has little or no educational training would omit this item.

COLLEGE NAME, City, State, Degrees, majors, dates. If you received no degree or you are presently attending college, give the number of units completed (or say, "degree candidate"), major, date, place.

High school: List if you have not attended college. Add dates, and areas of speciality.

Also include: Relevant workshops, adult education, vocational training, either in summary form or in chronological order.

6. Personal paragraph

You may wish to include a statement describing personal attitudes toward work that make you a valuable and unique employee (see Figures 7-3 and 7-4).

---

presenting yourself; others believe preparing a résumé is a worthless exercise. Still, many employers require them, so job hunters, an obliging lot, will continue to oblige.

Writing a résumé can be a very rewarding experience even if you never use it. It forces you to state clearly how your education and experience relate directly to the job you are seeking.

There are two kinds of basic résumés: chronological and functional. If your work experience was fairly continuous and in related areas, use a *chronological* résumé, which lists your work experience in reverse order. A *functional* résumé, developed on the basis of three or four skill areas, can be used if you were in and out of the job market at various times or your work experience does not appear directly related to the job for which you are applying. Writing both kinds of résumés may benefit you because this exercise gives you two different perspectives on yourself. Samples are shown in Figures 7-1 through 7-4 and in the Appendix.

• •
FIGURE 7-1 Chronological Résumé of a College Student

KEVIN DONOVAN
643 Eagle Drive
Dubuque, Iowa 52001
(319) 555-6789

JOB OBJECTIVE: Customer Service Management Trainee

QUALIFICATIONS IN BRIEF:

Learn job routine quickly. Possess ability to deal effectively with the public and flexible
enought to work alone or in a team effort. Good driving record. Not afraid of hard routine
work. Primarily interested in a swing shift to allow time to further my educational goals.

WORK EXPERIENCE:

K-MART, Dubuque IA   1987 to present
Customer Service/Bagger

Help customers with merchandise, stock shelves in warehouse, maintain appearance of
the store, bring carts from parking lot into building, and bag merchandise from
checkstands.

DUBUQUE GYMNASTIC ASSOCIATION, Dubuque, IA   1986
Gym Instructor

Sold memberships and equipment, outlined programs for participants, gave tours of the
facilities to potential customers and guests, balanced monies and accounts daily,
answered phones, and took responsibility for maintaining a smooth operation of the gym
facilities, adding a professional tone.

S & S WELDING, East Dubuque, IL   1985
VAN'S FURNITURE AND MATTRESS CO., Dubuque, IA   1984
Warehouse Worker

Moved furniture, paint, and equipment; helped with inventory control; assisted customers
in making proper selections.

EDUCATION:

LORAS COLLEGE, Dubuque, IA
                                                                        1986 to present
Major: Business/Liberal Arts

DUBUQUE HIGH SCHOOL, Dubuque, IA
                                                                        1982-1986
College Preparatory

REFERENCES: Provided upon request.

• •
FIGURE 7-2 Functional Résumé of a Teacher in Transition to Industry

BETTY A. BUG
5403 W. Monroe Street
Chicago, Illinois 60644
(312) 555-9829

POSITION OBJECTIVE: Industrial Employee Trainer

QUALIFICATIONS IN BRIEF:

BA in English, Mundelein College, Chicago, 1980; eight years elementary teaching; fluent in Spanish; demonstrated skills in instruction, supervision, communications, human relations.

EXPERIENCE SUMMARY:

INSTRUCTION: Planned, organized, presented language and mathematics instruction material to elementary students; developed instructional modules to solve specific learning problems; developed computer programs for instruction, and instructional audio-visual material, used equipment such as Apple IIe and Macintosh Computers, overhead and movie projectors, audio and video cassettes; did extensive research in various curricula; member of curriculum development committee; introduced new motivational techniques for students. Conducted staff inservice workshops, including installation of a downlink for a teleconference.

SUPERVISION: Supervised student groups, teacher interns, and a classroom aide; evaluated students, peers, and programs; moderated student activities. Interviewed, trained, and evaluated support personnel, volunteers, and teacher interns.

HUMAN RELATIONS: Did effective problem solving/conflict resolution between individual students and between student groups; initiated program of student self-governance; acted as a liaison between families of diverse cultural, ethnic, and economic backgounds and school personnel/services; conducted individual and group conferences to establish rapport with parents and to discuss student progress. Represented school to the community.

COMMUNICATIONS: Presented new curriculum plans to parent groups; sent periodic progress reports to parents; developed class newsletter.

CURRENTLY EMPLOYED: Austin Elementary School, Chicago, Illinois

REFERENCES: Provided upon request.

. . . .

FIGURE 7-3 Functional/Chronological Résumé with Personal Paragraph of a Senior Citizen/ Housewife Returning to the Job Market

---

HELEN B. BELL
432 Spruce Street
Junction City, Kanas 66441
(913) 555-7035

POSITION OBJECTIVE: Office Manager with Accounting Responsibilities

EXPERIENCE:

Successful Accounting Work: Managed payroll, payroll taxes, accounts receivable, accounts payable, bank reconcilation, and executive credit card expense account; handled data entry. Acted as full-charge bookkeeper through monthly and annual profit and loss statements.

Supervision and Management: Directed office functions such as secretarial, accounting, customer relations, sales, employee performance, and schedules.

EMPLOYERS:

KINDERGARTEN SUPPLIER, USA, INC., Wichita, KS Accountant	2 years
ELECTRA CORPORATION, Wichita, KS Receptionist	1 year
RIDEGWAY COMPANY, Topeka, KS Accountant/Secretary	1 year
ROD'S VAN AND STORAGE COMPANY, Topeka, KS Accountant/Secretary	2 years
HUMPHREY MOTOR COMPANY, Junction City KS Accountant/Secretary	9 years
SCOTT STORES, Junction City, KS Bookkeeper	1 year

PERSONAL PARAGRAPH:

The accounting field with its attendant and complex problems is fascinating and thoroughly involving for me. I am interested in ensuring smooth flow, efficiency, and accuracy of accounts in a moderately sized, growing company.

REFERENCES: Provided upon request.

• •

FIGURE 7-4 Résumé of a Technical Person, Including Personal Paragraph

---

ANTOINETTE GAYLE SALAS
295 Alviso Avenue
Santa Clara, California 9505l
(408) 555-l2l2

JOB OBJECTIVE: Graphic Arts Computer Specialist

EDUCATION: MISSION COLLEGE, Santa Clara, CA.: AA Candidate, Graphic Arts with CAD/CAM
EVERGREEN COLLEGE, San Jose, California

WORK EXPERIENCE:

AMERICAN MICROCONDUCTOR, Sunnyvale, CA.   6/80 to present
Components Scheduler for Central Material Control

Organize and improve reporting procedures for CMC planners. Track and expedite
material movement, generate computer input sheets, and interface with various product
groups. Handle key operator responsibilities, office supplies, and answer phones.

Product Verification Specialist/Discrete Operations   6/78-6/80

Verified and dispositioned CMR paperwork and material using the Lorlin tester and
correlating bench testers. Provided feedback to correct the actual cause of the returns.

Transistor & FET Buildsheet, Document QA/Transistors   10/76-6/78

Organized a system to simplify the buildsheet outlines of department's dice and
packages. Documented control books and tab reports. Handled key operator/clerical
duties.

Wafer Fab (diffusion/masking) Specialist/LST Division   5/76-10/76

Specialized in all diffusion and masking operations, utilized CV Plotters, Elipsometer,
Terminal, and ET Machines.

Encoder and File Clerk/LMSC Data Bank   10/69-5/76

Audited, edited, and posted data. Received, interpreted, and encoded miscellaneous
Polaris data for the computer system.

COMMUNITY EXPERIENCE: Boy Scouts of America: Hostess, committee chair, den leader.

PERSONAL PARAGRAPH: I enjoy solving problems by organizing and simplifying any
challenging task. I like to work with my hands, using creative abilities. Effective interfacing with
people is one of my strong skills.

REFERENCES: Available upon request.

There is no single prescribed way to write a résumé, but some good basic guidelines to follow are: (1) be brief, (2) be clear, (3) be neat, (4) be honest. The best résumé describes your qualifications on only one page. A reasonable résumé, which should rarely require two pages, states succinctly, the education and work experience that specifically relate to the job for which you are applying. It is easiest to read in outline form with plenty of "white space," good spelling, punctuation, and grammar, well printed and reproduced. Although it is important that you be truthful, a résumé isn't the place for true confessions. Emphasize your good points! Ask experienced friends to read and criticize your rough draft, but have confidence in your own judgment about what is right for you.

If you have access to a computer, use it to do your résumé or have it done. The advantages are many: you can tailor-make each version to a particular job and/or company, corrections and up-dating are a breeze, and you can use some subtle touches like **bold print** or *italics* that will add to its sharp look if not overdone. If you must type your résumé, you can erase, use correction fluid, and even cut and paste sections in with tape; a copy shop can still produce a copy that will look perfect. Use a good off-white, gray, or beige-tinted paper. If you plan to mail it, prepare a carefully typed, matching envelope addressed to the correct person. For a final touch, add a handsome commemorative stamp. You want your résumé to get a second look rather than the usual 30-second glance.

Some people send a résumé with an individual letter addressed to a specific person in a company. Sometimes the résumé is attached to an application, or requested after an application has been received. The general idea is to give the employer a preview of you before an interview takes place. Always have your résumé handy and bring a copy to the interview.

You may spend from 12 to 15 hours writing a good résumé. Because there are an almost infinite number of ways to describe yourself, doing a résumé means picking a winning combination that exactly fits the job you are seeking. Yes, it's true! You *do* need a separate résumé for each job title and sometimes even for each company!

If you have been developing a list of file cards for each job, a résumé will be not only easier to do but easier to adapt. Start with lists you made of all your favorite activities and skills in Chapters 1 and 3. The ten basic skills empower you to perform many different tasks in many different settings with data, people, and things because the skills are transferable. The key question to answer when you go job hunting is, "What can you *do*?" The most important words to use on your résumé, then, are action verbs that tell what you've done, what you've accomplished, and therefore what you *can* do. Action verbs have an impact when they are relevant to the job you want. Collect businesslike nouns, adjectives, and adverbs to use with the action verbs. A woman who worked for a sanitation district said she "gave messages to the guys in their trucks." On her résumé this phrase was translated to "communicated by radio with personnel in the field."

Many-faceted skills such as management can be divided into a variety of functions and subfunctions, which in turn relate back to the ten basic skills. Management involves only three of the basic skills: medium to high intelligence, verbal ability, and sometimes (but not always) medium to high numerical ability. Yet many action verbs would apply: advise, arrange, budget, communicate, control . . .

As you polish your résumé, try to make each statement very specific. Here are four different versions of the same sentence, which becomes more effective with each revision:

1. Designed a program . . .
2. Designed a marketing program . . .
3. Designed an effective marketing program . . .
4. Designed an effective marketing program that resulted in a 60 percent sales increase.

COVER LETTERS

Some say that a well-written cover letter (see Figure 7-5 and the Appendix) is an excellent door opener for an interview. The letter that accompanies your résumé should be brief, clear, neat, and honest. It should be addressed to a specific person, and it may amplify an important aspect of the résumé. Use your cover letter to form a chain linking you to the employer:

- *Connecting:* State your reason for writing and your employment objective. Mention the person who referred you to this employer or the source of the reference, such as a classified ad.

- *Add more links:* Describe your experience in brief.

- *Solder the links:* State what you can do for the company and tell how you will help this employer solve his or her problem.

- *Hold onto the chain:* Prepare the way for the next step by requesting an interview and indicating when you will call to set it up. Sometimes you will get a negative response when calling for an interview. Rather than answering with a stunned silence, be ready with a positive answer to reinforce your possible contribution to the company. For example, to "We don't hire people without experience, your reply might be, "I do learn very quickly," or, "I have had a great deal of experience as a student doing such similar tasks as . . . "

After the interview, write a letter to thank the interviewer, encourage a reply, request more information, accept or decline an offer.

• • • • • • • • • •

I AM RATHER

like a mosquito in a nudist
camp; I know what
I ought to do, but I don't
know where to begin.
STEPHEN BAYNE

• • • • • • • • • •

LETTERS OF REFERENCE

Be prepared to supply the names of people who have written or will write letters of reference for you or who will answer questions by phone. Do not name someone as a reference unless that person has agreed to be contacted. The people you ask should be professional people, former employers—individuals who are acquainted with your work skills. Some college placement offices keep letters of reference, a current résumé, and transcripts on file for their graduates and send them out to prospective employers for a nominal fee.

When you apply for a job, the usual procedure with references is to provide names if they are requested or to bring copies of letters along to the interview. If letters are on file at a college placement office, have them sent to the prospective employer either right before or soon after your interview. But if the competition is fierce and you are almost certain this is a job you want, it may be appropriate to ask a couple of key people to write letters or even make phone calls to the person who may hire you. Ask a teacher or counselor who knows your skills, an acquaintance in the company to which you are applying, or some other professional acquaintance known to the interviewer or to the person you will be working for to speak on your behalf. But understand that this is not the usual procedure and should be used with discrimination.

THE APPLICATION FORM

The application form provided by the company may determine the employer's first impression of you. It must look sharp. Carelessness or sloppiness may cause you to be eliminated. Be sure to fill out an application as clearly, completely, and neatly as possible. Try to obtain two copies ahead of time. (Sometimes

companies will mail them to you by phone request.) Use one copy for practice and keep it for your file.

Applications vary from one company to another, but each form requires an accurate record of past work experience and education. Prepare a minifile containing all relevant information. Check it carefully for accuracy. You will need names, addresses, and dates for both education and work experience. Obtain this information now if you do not have it. Employers often verify these facts, and they should check out. The more careful you are, the better you look. Be clear if you are asked what you did. Know exact job titles, the types of machines you've used and the salary range you are interested in. Here are some helpful hints to remember.

- Read the *whole* application form before beginning to fill it in. Follow all directions, and note the fine print.
- Print with a pen or, better still, type answers, carefully, completely but succinctly.
- Fill in all blanks. Write in N/A (not applicable) if a question does not apply to you.
- You need to obtain a Social Security number if you do not have one. Have it available. Some companies ask for a driver's license as identification. (Revocation or denial of a driver's license can be a clue to some physical or mental problem.)
- Your reason for interest in the position should state an advantage to the employer. Research the company and know what you can do for it.
- An arrest is not a conviction. Arrests need not be mentioned.
- Provide accurate names and addresses of those who have given you permission to use their names as references. Have original reference letters available, plus copies to leave if requested.
- Reread the application carefully.
- Sign the application.

THE INTERVIEW

Although it has been denounced by some as a barbaric custom and by others as "proven ineffectual," the interview is likely to remain an employer ritual for some time to come. Usually an employer interviews persons whose applications, letters, or résumés have proven interesting and those who have made a personal contact or have been referred.

An interview is a "structured conversation" between an employer or delegated interviewer and a prospective employee. Its purpose is to exchange information. The interviewer needs to find out if the interviewee has the qualifications necessary to do the job. The applicant needs to make sure that he or she understands the job, the company, and what is expected. Here we will cover the key points in the interview and review a set of practice questions and answers.

The interviewer may be a department head, project director, or even a series of people familiar with various aspects of the job. A group of staff members may act together as an interviewing committee. In a small business you may be interviewed quite casually and briefly by the owner. A large corporation employs professional interviewers. Reputable companies want their interviewers to present a positive image. They want you to leave with a favorable impression of the company, to feel that you were treated well. Interviewers want to do a good job, too, by hiring the best person. Their jobs depend on it!

An interview is not a time for game playing or for one person to try to trap the other. It will be counterproductive for both parties if they deceive each other. The interviewer will end up with an employee who "doesn't fit." The worker will be dissatisfied.

Like a good English composition, the interview usually has a beginning, a middle, and an ending. Introductions and casual conversation begin the interview and are designed to help you feel at ease.

After a few minutes, most interviewers will guide you to the purpose of the meeting and will then begin inquiries about your qualifications. A good interviewer will also give you information along the way to help you make your decision. The interviewer may discuss: job duties, hours/overtime, salary/benefits, vacation/sick leave, opportunities for advancement, company policies and procedures.

Some interviewers also will give you a tour of the workplace. Depending on the level for which you are being considered, an interview might be over in fifteen minutes or last several hours. Most information can be exchanged in 30 or 45 minutes. Interviewers bring these meetings to an end and usually give information about when you will be notified. They are generally seeing other people, sometimes many others.

A successful interview might be one in which you *don't* get the job. In some cases, the interview turns up the information that hiring you would not be good for either you or the company, which only means that the interview has accomplished its purpose. In any event, you will want to appear at your best.

Getting Prepared

When you are meeting someone you wish to impress, common sense and courtesy are your most reliable guides. Lean slightly toward the conservative in dress and manner if you have any doubts along this line. Prepare what you will wear ahead of time. Be sure that your outfit is clean, pressed, polished, and *comfortable*. When purchasing your "dress for success" suit, try sitting in it, moving in it. Then, wear it a time or two, perhaps to an information interview.

A word to the wise includes the research done by Seattle University Professor of Business William L. Weiss, who says, "In a race for a job between two equally qualified people, a nonsmoker will win 94 percent of the time.[1]

The very best preparation for an interview is practice. Practice talking to people about their jobs; practice calling for appointments to see people in order to ask for career information. If you have done information interviewing and networking, you will be used to sharing enthusiasm about the career of your choice, and this enthusiasm will come naturally at the interview. Go to interviews even if you think you might not get a job, and then honestly assess your performance.

More immediately, do homework on the company you are approaching. Many have brochures; many are listed in standard library references. A call to the public relations department can sometimes result in a wealth of material. Talk to people who may know the company. Ask questions. Try to see how you best fit in. Know the important facts about the job, including the salary range. Prepare to bring relevant examples of your work, such as sketches, designs, writings.

In some career areas, salaries are nonnegotiable and not an issue—teaching and union jobs are examples. In others, they are negotiable. In such cases, the interviewer may ask what salary you expect. If you have no idea of the range and were not able to find out ahead of time, ask. Unless you are a superstar, don't ask for the top of the range, but don't undervalue yourself, either. Know the minimum you'll accept—and know your worth. Place yourself somewhere in the middle and leave it open to negotiation. Also, you might ask for a salary review in six months or so.

Don't be afraid to ask about salary and benefits such as medical, dental, and disability coverage as well as life insurance, vacations, and retirement if these are vitally important. A better way is to check out all this information before the interview. Ask the personnel office for brochures on company benefit plans.

Interview Behavior

As a job seeker, you should approach each interview by being yourself, being true to yourself, and trusting your own judgment about the style that suits you best. You can build self-confidence by practicing ways of talking and listening effectively and by learning to answer an interviewer's questions. Here are some key points to practice.

- *Good eye contact:* Don't avoid this form of personal contact. If you like your interviewers, your eyes will communicate warmth and interest.
- *Appropriate body language:* Be relaxed and open, interested and attentive. Notice how bodies speak! Become aware of ways in which your body sends messages of boredom, fear, enthusiasm, cockiness, nervousness, confidence.
- *Appropriate voice melody:* Try to come across with vitality, enthusiasm, and confidence. Remember that low tones convey confidence and competence; high tones convey insecurity.

INTERVIEW OVERVIEW

Get Ready

Check: The company (from reference section of library, public relations department of firm, contacts, friends)

- Location
- Products/services
- Potential market
- Earnings/benefits
- Policies

Check: Important items you wish to cover:

- How you fit in
- Your strengths
- Your experiences
- Your interests

Get Set

Check: Items for your application:

- Social security number
- References (personal and professional)
- Name of person to notify in case of accident
- Details of past experience:
  - Name of company
  - Full address and phone number of company
  - Dates worked
  - Salary
  - Job titles
  - Supervisors
  - Duties, projects, skills
  - Education (dates, majors, degrees)
  - Military experience (if any)
- Copies of résumé and, if relevant, examples of work

Check: Exact time, date, location (building and room) availability of parking

- Name of interviewer (and its pronunciation)
- Go alone

Go

Check: Your appearance:

- Neat, clean, conservative outfit
- No gum, no smoking, no fidgeting
- Sit comfortably straight, at ease
- Your attitude: a serious job seeker
- Definite goals
- Willing to work and work up
- Reasonable approach to salary, hours, benefits, or other aspects of the job
- Uncritical of past employers, teachers, coworkers
- Evidence of good human relations
- Sense of humor
- High personal values
- Wide interests, openness, flexibility

Your manner:

- Confident, not overbearing
- Enthusiastic but not desperate or gushy
- Courteous, attentive
- Good voice, expression
- On-target answering questions
- Shake hands firmly
- Leave promptly after the interview

• •

FIGURE 7-5 Résumé with Cover Letter

5401 Monroe Street
Mobile, Alabama 36608
April 11, 1989

Ms. Jill Jones
Director of Marketing
PTT Corporation
Dogwood, AL 36309

Dear Ms. Jones:

As a word processor at Datatime Company last summer, I had occasion to meet with people from PTT. It was your sales representative, Joan Carl, who referred me to you. I was impressed with both your product and your personnel. This June I will receive my bachelor's degree in marketing and sales from Peachtree University. I would like to be considered for a training position in marketing with eventual sales responsibility at PTT.

I am an energetic, enthusiastic person with a commitment to whatever I take on. My involvement in student affairs led me to plan and execute a successful campaign for student body vice-president. In this capacity I met and negotiated with faculty representatives and board of trustee members and hosted visiting guests of the college. My senior project in marketing won departmental recognition while my 3.2 GPA put me on the dean's honor list.

With these qualifications I feel that I can make a positive contribution to PTT. I look forward to meeting your campus recruiter, A. J. Lupin, next month to explore a marketing trainee position.

Sincerely yours,

Chris Cross

Chris Cross

• •

FIGURE 7-5 (continued)

CHRIS CROSS
5401 Monroe Street
Mobile, Alabama 36608
(205) 555-1212

<u>POSITION OBJECTIVE</u>: Marketing Trainee with Eventual Sales Responsibility

<u>QUALIFICATIONS IN BRIEF</u>:

B.A. in Marketing and Sales. Won departmental honors in Marketing. Word processor for three summers on PTT Systems. Good human relations, energetic, goal oriented.

<u>EXPERIENCE SUMMARY</u>:

DATATIME COMPANY, Mobile, Alabama   Summers: 1987-89
<u>Word Processor</u>

Did data entry for marketing and sales department; logged product sales, sales personnel progress, and regional growth; interacted with service representatives.

McDOUGAL'S HAMBURGER SHOP, Mobile, Alabama   October 1983-May 1985
<u>Part-time Waitress</u>

Waited on customers, handled cash, oriented new employees. Suggested successful coupon marketing strategy that raised long-term sales by five percent. Occassionally acted as hostess, manager.

<u>COMMUNITY EXPERIENCE</u>:

PEACHTREE UNIVERSITY STUDENT BODY, Peachtree, Georgia   1988-89
<u>Vice-President</u>

Planned and executed campaign, worked extensively with faculty, administration, and board of trustees; hosted visiting college guests; spearheaded senior projects like: Homecoming Dance and Career Day. Participated in student activities all four years.

BLOSSOM HIGH SCHOOL, Mobile, Alabama
<u>Senior Class Secretary</u>   1984-85
<u>Junior Vice-President</u>   1983-84

Participated throughout high school in student body activities, science club, and intramural basketball and soccer.

GIRL SCOUTS, Mobile, Alabama   1973-81
<u>Member</u>

Mapped out a winning sales strategy for Girl Scout Cookies for three years. Won a variety of merit badges; taught crafts and counseled younger members at camp.

<u>EDUCATION</u>:

PEACHTREE UNIVERSITY, Peachtree, Georgia   June 1989
B.A.: Marketing and Sales; GPA: 3.2

<u>REFERENCES</u>: Provided upon request.

- *Active listening:* Indicate that you have heard and understood what the interviewer has said. For example, if the interviewer mentions tardiness as a problem, say, "It must be difficult to have employees who are late all the time. I can assure you I'll make every effort to be on time."
- *Good choice of words:* If you do your interview homework and practice, the right words should come easily. Much of what you "say" will of course be conveyed by your manner, not your words.[2]

Practice Questions

You will be asked questions about your previous work experience and education, your values, and your goals. You may possibly be asked questions about your family life and leisure activities, but very personal questions are not appropriate in an interview.

Questions dealing with factual information should not be a problem if you have done your homework. Have on hand your own card file of all education, previous jobs, and other experience, with correct dates, place names and addresses, job titles and duties, names of supervisors, and other relevant information in case these might slip your mind. Usually this information is on the application. The interview centers on clarification of points on the application and résumé.

If you have been working regularly and successfully in your field for a period of years, the interview will be mainly a chance for you to tell what you have done. If you are a young graduate, the discussion may focus on your education, interests, and casual jobs.

If you have been in and out of the job market or have had problems in the past, the interviewer will want to explore the reasons. Be relaxed and not defensive. Look upon the interview as a chance to make a fresh start. Assure the interviewer that you will not be a problem but a solution. All the questions in the interview are different ways of asking, "Can you do the job?" It's not fair to expect to be hired if you can't do the job well. If you keep that clearly in mind, you will be able to support your answer, "Yes, I can do the job," with all sorts of relevant data.

Practice answering interview questions until you feel comfortable. Prepare concise answers so you won't ramble. Omit inappropriate personal information and especially any negative information about your past job and employers. Some people get carried away and start talking about their childhood, personal problems, and all sorts of irrelevant data that wear interviewers out and hardly charm them. Before the interview, tape your answers and replay them or at least practice them out loud, either alone or with someone who will give you honest feedback.

Here are some typical, commonly asked questions, along with answers for you to consider.

Tell me something about yourself: This request, one of the most frequently asked by interviewers, could be followed by a dismayed silence as you race your mental motor trying to find something to talk about. If you are prepared, you will hop in happily with the reasons you feel your skills, background, and personal attitudes are good for the job and how you see your future with the company. You will seldom have a better opportunity than this to talk about yourself.

Why are you leaving your present job? (Or: *Why did you leave your last job?*) If the circumstances of your leaving were unpleasant or your present conditions are unbearable, these personal problems will be the first answers to pop into your mind—but they should be the last answers you give. Everyone leaves a job for more than one reason, and negative reasons can be made positive. If your boss was oppressive, coworkers disagreeable, or the job was too difficult, a move can provide opportunity for growth in a variety of ways. It's difficult for anyone to improve on a job when feelings are all negative. Some possible replies:

- "I seemed to have reached a point where there was little potential for growth."
- "I have learned my job well and would like to try new dimensions of it in a growing [or larger, or innovative] company."
- "I decided to change careers, and I just got my degree."
- "I left to raise a family, and now I am ready to return to work permanently."
- "I moved [the company reorganized or merged or cut back or slowed down]."

Your application indicated that you have been in and out of the work force quite often (or haven't worked in some years). What were you involved with in those periods of unemployment? Here the interviewer has several concerns. One is that you might be likely to leave after being trained for this job. Another is that your skills might be rusty. Be prepared to give assurance that you plan to stay with this job and that your qualifications are such that you can handle it. Knowing your abilities and what the job demands can clarify this subject for you.

What are your weaknesses and what are your strengths? Smile when they ask this one. Have a list you have memorized about what you do best, such as, "I work well with other people on a team basis." If the job you are applying for matches your personality type, your weaknesses will be in areas not important for the job. On a conventional job (C), for example, artistic strengths (A) would

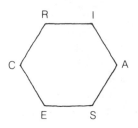

get in the way. So you might say, "I'm not very creative. I prefer to follow a set routine." Or if the job calls for machine work (R), you might say your communication skills (S) aren't the best. Whatever personality type the job calls for, weaknesses of the opposite type on the hexagon can be turned into plusses!

Do you have any physical limitations that may interfere with your performance? If you do not, there is no problem. If you do have a physical limitation or a past history of serious illness, be prepared to show that it will not interfere with your work. A doctor's statement might be helpful here.

Made-up situations that test a person's knowledge of the job may begin with questions like, "What would you do if . . . ?" The quality of your solution is not nearly as important as your attitude. A calm approach is a best bet. It's better to cushion your statements with answers like, "One of the things I might consider would be . . ." If you commit yourself to a process of what you *would* do, and it isn't one *they* would like or consider, you are in an awkward position. Give your answer a cushion of several possible choices, and indicate that you would carefully assess the situation.

How did you get along with . . . ? This question can be asked about supervisors, coworkers or subordinates, even teachers. If you generally get along with people, say so. If you had a problem with someone, there is usually no need to tell the whole tale here. Simply say that occasionally you've had to work out difficulties with people. Be positive, not blaming or complaining.

Would you accept part-time or temporary work? Employers are more inclined to hire for full-time work from a part-time or temporary employment pool than to take a person from the outside. If you plan to stay with the company, ask if a temporary or part-time job may result in a permanent hire before you say yes. If you want a temporary job and are offered a permanent position, however, consider their cost of training you, only to have you leave. It takes most employees at least several months to begin to earn their pay. "No" is a better answer if you really want temporary or part-time work when you are offered a permanent, full-time position.

Why do you want to work for our company? Most people looking for a job are more interested in getting a good job than in being particular about where they work, and it does come across that they don't care about the company. One of the most important things you should do before you go to an interview—or ask for one—is find out all you can about the company. Identify some positive aspects of policies, procedures, or products you can discuss with interest. Do your homework—so that you will have work to come home from.

How long do you expect to work for us? The truth is that a company will not keep employees past their ability to use their skills. And you are not going to work for a company past the time that it is good for you. The best answer might be, "As long as it is good for both of us."

Do you have any questions about the company or the job? An interview doesn't have to be one-sided. Be ready for this question by preparing some questions of your own ahead of time to show your interest. Employers, down at the bottom of their company hearts, believe the myth that good people are hard to find. If they are asked to define a good person, that person is always someone who is really interested in the company and in the job he or she does. So this is an ideal time to relate your interest, enthusiasm, and commitment to the company and the job.[3]

Questions to resolve honestly ahead of time:

- Are you willing to/can you move or travel, work overtime, take a temporary or part-time job?
- Do you have plans for your next job, your next few years, starting your own business, changing fields, going back to school? In every case the real question is, *Can you do the job?*

Sometimes you may be asked questions that startle you. If you feel unprepared, it's wise to say, "I need a few moments to think about that." Then take a few deep breaths, relax, and begin confidently. If it should happen that you still draw a blank, be prepared to deal with the situation. Possibilities: "Maybe we could come back to that later," or "I really should be prepared to answer that but I'm not." It's a learning experience and you learn that you can keep cool.

Be prepared for some difficult ("Whew!") questions if you have ever been convicted of a crime or fired for serious problems, or if you have a poor work record. Take a deep breath, relax a minute, look at the interviewer, and say in your own words something like this: "Yes, I made a mistake [or have done poorly in the past] but I learned my lesson, and I'm determined that it won't happen again." Then stop. Do not keep on explaining. If you sound confident and not defensive, the interviewer will be more likely to accept your answer.

Perhaps you can include some recent experience as evidence that you've made some changes in your life. Again, you need to reassure the interviewer that you are capable of doing the job.

You might be startled by inappropriate questions that appear to have nothing to do with job qualifications or even illegal questions that indicate discrimination. The interviewer should not ask questions about age, race, religion, nationality, or disabilities unless the answers are job related. Also inappropriate are questions that discriminate between males and females, for example, questions about family planning, child care, or pregnancy. Even questions about education may be discriminatory if not related to job performance.

Decide in advance how you will answer such questions if they are asked. If the issue is not really important, you might prefer to answer the question rather than risk alienating the interviewer with a refusal. If you'd prefer not to answer, you might say, "I wasn't aware this was a requirement for the job," or "Can you explain how this question relates to the job?" You can appeal to the law in obvious cases of prejudice; in less serious instances, a good sense of humor and respect for others can be enormously helpful. Don't win the battle and lose the war!

Nelva Shore, a California employment specialist, says, "It really doesn't matter what questions are asked as long as you can talk!" Be ready to talk positively about yourself, your goals, and your reason for applying. Practice talking. There is no other way. One woman who stood out in an interview later told about how she had practiced sitting down in front of a mirror; she practiced talking out loud, answering questions, eye contact, voice melody, every phase of the interview until she felt totally at ease. Her enthusiasm came through unspoiled by anxiety. You can learn these skills, too.

At the end of the interview feel free to ask when you will hear the results if you aren't told. Follow up the interview with a thank-you letter that encourages a reply, perhaps asks for more information, or accepts or declines an offer (see Figure 7-6). Then call after a week or so if you haven't heard unless you have been given a different time line.

Sometimes there is a delay in hiring someone after an interview. Several months may go by because of changes inside the company. A key employee may decide to quit or retire, for example; or an employer may decide to fill another position first; or a complex reorganization may take more time than planned. Tactfully keep in touch with your contact in the company or with the personnel department until you are certain there is no opening for you or you are hired.

After you are hired, you may be asked to supply such items as a birth certificate, proof of citizenship, a photograph, and proof of age. Have these items ready if you feel they might be required.

JOB OFFERS: TOO MANY OR TOO FEW?

You probably will not get a job offer during your first interview. But suppose you do get a job offer—or two or three—in this early phase of your career search. Maybe you had planned to do personnel work, but the welding shop

• •

FIGURE 7-6 Thank-You Letter Following an Interview

411 Park Drive
Rutland, VT 05701
November 20, 1988

_____

Ms. Margaret T. Caitan
Title Insurance and Trust
4l0 Coates Drive
Winooshi, VT. 05404

Dear Ms. Caitan:

It was a pleasure meeting with you on Friday. Thank you for the opportunity to interview for a sales position.

I was pleased with what I learned about Title Insurance and Trust and your approach to sales. Your attitude toward professionalism in sales reflects my view completely.

I am excited about the possibility of working with you and hope to be considered for one of the positions available.

Sincerely yours

Marie Mello

Marie Mello

Here's one! Sophisticated, attractive, well-groomed, typing experience—
too bad we can't type.

● ●

BOBBY SOX / by Marty Links
Copyright Marty Links

would welcome you! Beware of such decisions. You can easily get carried away with excitement and leap into the first job that comes along.

Some jobs sound rewarding in terms of personal growth opportunities, but the salary is so low you could not live on it without making sacrifices. Another job pays very well, but the work sounds dull and disagreeable. You might even be offered a temporary job; it would fulfill your immediate needs, but you'd be back on the job market in six months or so. Should you accept one of these less desirable jobs just to get hired or to get experience?

Now is the time to review your needs, wants, and values and become very clear about what you want the job to do. Perhaps your goal is just to get into a special company that you've chosen. Taking a job you don't particularly like could give you this chance. Many companies promote from within before they open jobs to outsiders.

If you aren't hired for the job you really want right away, you may be only one of many well-qualified applicants. In a competitive field it can take six months or more of continuous job hunting to find a job. Whether you should take a less desirable job depends on how long you can afford to wait and continue the search. If you job hunt for many months without a nibble, you may need to consider alternatives: other careers, new training, other opportunities in your present position, additional paid or volunteer experience that might be useful in a different kind of job.

Choosing may be difficult because you have in mind a portrait of the perfect workplace. But when you actually go job hunting, you will find that perfection doesn't exist. You need a job because the rent is due and you have a car payment to make.

You may have to start at the bottom and work up to the job you want. Suppose you, a business major with a fresh degree from a good university, are offered a job as a mail clerk. Or you have a master's degree in computer programming, but you are offered a job as a computer operator. You may feel such offers are beneath your dignity. But before you ride away on your high horse, consider these facts: One major oil company makes a practice of hiring as mail clerks new grads who are candidates for all management and public relations jobs. Because many excellent companies promote from within, they have a chance to look you over before entrusting a more important job to you. And you have a chance to network inside and explore possibilities before getting too entrenched. Be wary of turning down a job that fails to meet your expectations. Ask some company employees what the offer means. Ask the interviewer what the growth potential of the job is and whether you might be given a performance review in three to six months for a possible promotion.

Job hunting requires that you keep involved at all times in some part of the process. The more exacting your requirements, the longer you will job hunt and the more often you will be turned down. But if you can accept some frustration as a normal part of the job-hunting process, you will not be discouraged. Keep in mind a clear picture of the place you would like to work in so that you will recognize it when you find it. Focus on the changes you can make to begin to experience more satisfaction in the workplace.

Self-Assessment Exercises

1. The Job Hunt Begins

    a. Begin your résumé. Write a rough draft of some items you will use. Then polish and type a good copy.

Name:_____

Address:_____

Home Phone:_____ Work Phone:_____

Position Objective:_____

Qualifications in Brief:_____

_____

_____

Experience Summary:_____

_____

_____

_____

_____

Education:_____

_____

_____

Personal Paragraph:_____

_____

_____

_____

Special Notes: (honors, works published, organizations, etc.):_____

_____

_____

b. Write a cover letter to accompany your résumé.

c. Fill out a sample application, such as Figure 7-7.

2. Practicing an Interview

Some interviewers use a rating scale to grade your performance on various points of importance to them. Figure 7-8 shows a scale used by recruiters who come from various workplaces to interview students on the campus. Role-play an interview. Then rate yourself or ask someone to rate you on your interview skills. Here are some what/how/why practice questions.

Work Experience: What have you done to get where you are?

What were your major responsibilities on your last job? (Or last military experience)

What did you like most about that job?

What did you like least about that job?

What problems did you face? How did you overcome these problems?

What did you learn on your last job?

How do you feel your last job used your ability?

Why did you leave your last job?

What impressions did you leave behind on your last job?

Why do you want to work for us?

What do you feel you can contribute?

Education

What were your favorite courses (workshops, seminars)?

Why did you choose your major?

How would you rate your instructors?

What activities and clubs were you in? How did you participate?

How did you finance your education?

What further education are you planning?

Skills and Values

How do you get along with people (supervisors, coworkers, instructors)?

What are your transferable skills?

What are your work-specific skills?

What are your personality-responsibility skills?

What are your strengths?

What are your weaknesses?

How important is money to you?

How well do you work on your own?

How many days did you take off last year for sickness and personal business?

How do you feel about overtime? Flexible hours? Part-time work? Temporary work?

Travel? Moving to a new location?

What do you do when a coworker is behind schedule?

What kind of decision maker are you?

Goals

What do you see yourself doing in five years?

How do you plan to get there?

What areas of growth and development do you plan to work on?

What salary would you like to earn?

Family/Leisure

What are the most important qualities in your family?

What do you do in your leisure time?

What books have you read lately?

What newspapers and magazines do you read regularly?

What kind of vacations do you enjoy?

Tell me about yourself!

3. The Application Form

Carefully fill out the application form in Figure 7-7 and sign it.

4. The Job Hunt Checklist

If you are job hunting now, establish a goal: e.g., you will contact fifty people by information interviewing, networking, applying for jobs, writing letters, making telephone calls, and sending résumés upon request. To check your progress, answer the following questions *yes* or *no*.

_____ Have you interviewed 25 people to obtain information about jobs and companies?

_____ Have you applied for work directly to 25 companies?

_____ Have you written an effective résumé for each job title?

_____ Have you contacted a network of at least 25 people who could help you?

_____ After each interview, do you critique yourself honestly?

_____ Have you written letters to thank the people who interviewed you?

● ●
FIGURE 7-7 Sample Application Form

HEWLETT **hp** PACKARD
1501 Page Mill Road, Palo Alto, California 94304

EMPLOYMENT APPLICATION

HEWLETT-PACKARD IS AN EQUAL OPPORTUNITY EMPLOYER AND ALL APPLICANTS ARE WELCOME.

PERSONAL INFORMATION

NAME: _____   Social Security No.: _____ – _____ – _____
　　　　Last　　　　　　　First　　　　　Middle

Address: _____
　　　No.　　　　Street　　　　　　　　City　　　　　　State　　　　Zip

Telephone No. _____   Message No. (If necessary): _____
　　(Area Code)　　　　　Number　　　　　　　　　　　　　(Area Code)　　　　Number

Other name(s) under which you have worked: _____

Have you ever applied for employment at HP?:　Yes ☐　No ☐　If "yes", Location: _____　Date: _____

Previously employed with HP?:　Yes ☐　No ☐　　　If "yes", Location: _____　Date: _____

Names of relatives employed here: _____　Relationship: _____　Location at HP: _____

How were you referred to HP? _____

If not a U.S. citizen, please name type of visa: _____

Have you ever been convicted of a felony?:　Yes ☐　No ☐　If "yes", give date, place, offense, and outcome: _____

Previous convictions do not exclude an applicant from consideration for employment.

Are you between the ages of 18 and 70?　Yes ☐　No ☐.　All applicants under the age of 18 must submit a work permit.

TYPE OF WORK APPLYING FOR

CHECK:　☐ Electronic Tech.　☐ Machinist　☐ Tech. Maint.　☐ Stock　☐ Custodian
　　　　☐ Shop Helper　☐ Computer Op.　☐ Assembly　☐ Office　☐ Other _____

State specific type of job in the area you checked and your qualifications: _____

Shift(s):　Day _____　Swing _____　Grave _____　Hours:　Full-time _____　Part-time _____

Do you have any physical condition which may limit your ability to perform the job(s) applied for?　☐ Yes　☐ No

OFFICE	SHOP	OTHER
Typing Speed _____ WPM	List tools and machines you feel qualified to use without further experience:	What specific skills or abilities do you have?
Shorthand Speed _____		
Office Machines _____	_____	_____
Keypunch/Data Proc.: _____	_____	_____

EDUCATION

CIRCLE LAST GRADE COMPLETED — Grade　1 2 3 4 5 6 7 8 9 10 11 12　　College　1 2 3 4

Name(s) of School(s) other than high school:	Location	Major	Dates	Degree (if any)

Is there anything else you would like us to know about you? _____

US MILITARY

BRANCH	LAST RANK	DATE OF SEPARATION

Your most important duties and training during service:　(include schools attended) _____

6-170175　(6/78)　　　　　*All Information Treated Confidentially*　　　　　(continued)

● ●

FIGURE 7-7 Sample Application Form (continued)

<table>
<tr><td rowspan="4">WORK EXPERIENCE</td><td colspan="4">LIST PREVIOUS JOBS STARTING WITH YOUR PRESENT OR MOST RECENT ONE. PLEASE DESCRIBE DUTIES AS COMPLETELY AS SPACE ALLOWS.</td></tr>
<tr><td>

Present or
Last Employer: _____

Address: _____
Number — Street

_____
City — State — Zip

Telephone No.: _____
(Area Code) — Number

Your Duties: _____
</td><td>

Reason for
Leaving: _____

_____

_____

Supervisor: _____
</td><td>

Dates
Start
/ /
Left
/ /
</td><td>

Salary
Start
$
Left
$
</td></tr>
</table>

One of HP's pre-employment steps is to contact your previous employers.
May we contact your present employer? ☐ Yes ☐ No
REFERENCES IN THE SPACE BELOW PLEASE LIST PERSONAL REFERENCES WHO CAN COMMENT ON YOUR EDUCATIONAL OR JOB RELATED EXPERIENCE: (DO NOT GIVE RELATIVES OR YOUR EMPLOYERS LISTED ABOVE)

NAME _____ PHONE NO. — 8 AM–5 PM

NAME _____ PHONE NO. — 8 AM–5 PM

NAME _____ PHONE NO. — 8 AM–5 PM

LOCATION PLEASE CHECK LOCATIONS WHERE YOU ARE WILLING TO WORK:
☐ Palo Alto ☐ Cupertino ☐ Mountain View ☐ Santa Rosa
☐ Santa Clara ☐ San Jose ☐ Sunnyvale

SIGNATURE THIS APPLICATION IS NOT COMPLETE UNTIL THE FOLLOWING STATEMENT HAS BEEN READ AND SIGNED:
I certify that all of the information furnished on this form is true, complete, and correct to the best of my knowledge. I understand that such information is subject to verification by Hewlett-Packard.

_____ SIGNATURE   _____ DATE

EMPLOYMENT OFFICE COMMENTS

_____

DISPOSITION OF APPLICATION:
Post Card _____   RLC _____
Date   Date

FIGURE 7-8 Interview Rating Scale

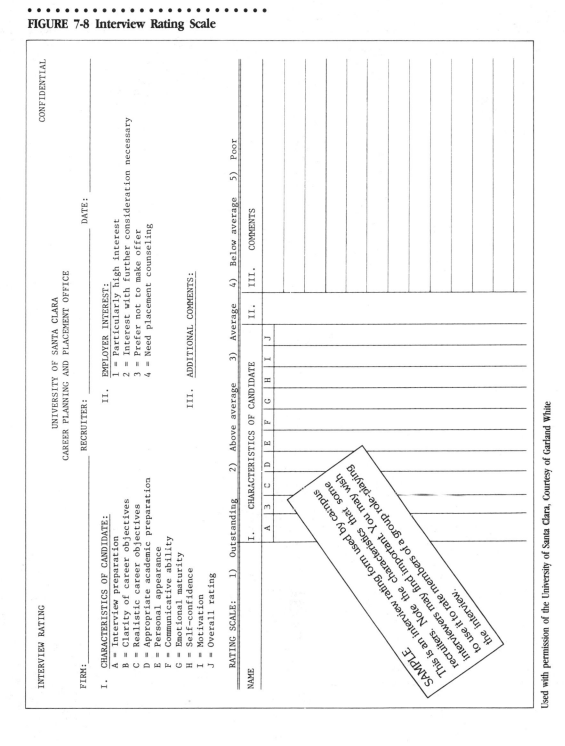

Used with permission of the University of Santa Clara, Courtesy of Garland White

DECISIONS, DECISIONS: WHAT'S YOUR NEXT MOVE?

F O C U S

Survey the options.

Weigh them in a decision-making process.

Define success.

•••••T he last step in the career search process is making a good decision. Will you go back to school, start a new job, keep the same job but with a new approach, or keep the status quo by deciding not to decide? Decision-making is easier if your values are clear. It also helps to be aware of the behavior characteristics of your own personality type when faced with a decision.

Each personality type has its own decision-making style. The social person acts out of caring for others but is not always "practical." Both the realistic and the conventional types tend to stay within societal norms. The conventional type follows the lead of others; realistic types will decide independently, often disregarding people's feelings but generally staying on the conservative side. The creative/artistic person, on the other hand, will see so many possibilities— including some that follow no known guidelines—that it's hard to choose. And whereas the enterprising person leaps first and gets the facts later, the investigative type seems to do research in the library forever.

We can fantasize a perfectly self-actualized person bringing all of these factors into balance: caring for others, with just enough "hard-headed" realism; creating new systems while following guidelines when appropriate; searching out just enough facts before risking the decision. Since most of us aren't troubled with such perfection, we often need help with decision-making. In this chapter we will consider the *decision-making dozen:* four attitudes, four options and, a four-phase decision-making process.

ATTITUDES

To deal with attitudes, the first rule is *keep calm*. If possible, make your career decision when you are not under pressure because of a crisis in your life. In times of crisis, a million fantasies may arise: quit work altogether and drop out; start your own company; join the Marines; end your marriage; run off with your secretary; sell everything, hitch up the wagon and head West! The uncertainties are as numerous as the fantasies: Am I okay? Is this all there is? Will my health hold up? Will my kids ever get settled? Will I? Will I look like a fool if I go back to school? Can I keep on succeeding? Do I even want to? Sometimes turbulent thoughts can seem like part of the decision-making process. You can practice letting them go, however, just like leaves in the wind.

Second, *take small steps with courage and persistence*. Making a life choice is a zigzag process, rarely a straight line. It can take time to sort out all the possibilities. Remember that you don't have to put a decision into action immediately and in one leap! You can set a reasonable time line and proceed by taking tiny steps. Just as you analyzed past activities, you can analyze a decision into its minicomponents. If a decision to get a four-year degree seems overwhelming, looking at college catalogs in the library may be a manageable first step.

Third, *keep perspective*. Review all the relevant facts you've been collecting and record them in the space provided at the end of this book. You can use Maslow's hierarchy from Chapter 1, for example, to identify the weak spots in your life. For example, some people feel they want material success after long periods of "doing without"! Others wish to move away from materialism so that they can develop nurturing relationships, grow intellectually, search for more meaning in their lives.

Where are you on the Career Choice Continuum?

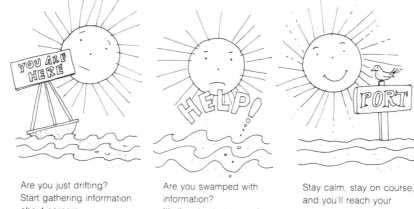

Are you just drifting? Start gathering information about careers.

Are you swamped with information? It's time to start narrowing the choices.

Stay calm, stay on course, and you'll reach your destination.

Fourth, *be confident*. Know that you can take the necessary steps to make your decision happen. If you look at your past honestly, you will see that you have made good decisions. Since you cannot know the future, every decision involves risking, and then trusting that it will work out. In order to improve your life, you change what can be changed, accept what can't be changed, and hope you have the wisdom to know the difference. You have to take the first step, however small.

Let's approach the first step by examining the options.

BACK TO SCHOOL

For the first time in the history of the United States, more than half of all U.S. workers have white-collar jobs. As the need for unskilled labor decreases, more adults choose to go back to school to upgrade their skills. In 1984, more than

73.3 percent of all Americans twenty-five years and older had graduated from high school, and 19.1 percent had completed four years or more of college.[1] The concept of lifelong learning encourages adults to change and grow on many different levels. In today's fast-moving technological world, workers need to "keep up." Learning to learn, to be a generalist, to have a broad view of the world are essential skills for the future.

You may be wondering if you should return to school. Or you may be in college and wondering what subjects to study if you continue. You could take courses to improve your basic skills, to explore various majors (areas of specialty), to prepare for possible careers, or just to foster personal enrichment and growth. Do not let your age or your previous school record discourage you. The average age of all adults returning to school is rising to the thirty-year-old level, and there's no ceiling in sight. One newspaper article described a man of ninety-two receiving an AA degree.

Twenty years after publication of Betty Friedan's classic, *The Feminine Mystique,* women who have worked little or not at all for pay outside their homes are still returning to college in record numbers. Studies show that the great majority of such women, as well as returning men, are fearful: "Am I too old to learn, too old to compete with young college students?" The surprise comes when, with few exceptions, the reentry person reports a great growth in confidence and the discovery of new-found goals. Many returning students, both men and women, have previous school records that qualify as disasters. But now, because they are mature and motivated, (though they don't always *feel* that way), they can reach their goals. So can you. One college provided an orientation for prospective students. After the series of meetings those attending were told that they had earned a half unit of college credit for the work that they did. It seemed like a modest beginning, but for one older woman that college credit was a dramatic breakthrough.

If your high school education was incomplete or deficient, consider basic skill courses in language and math at adult education centers or community colleges. The community college (junior college) is also a good place to explore and begin various majors and prepare for a career. Obtain a catalog at the college bookstore and look for introductory courses. The titles of these courses frequently include terms such as "beginning," "orientation to," "introduction to," or "principles of." The catalog will tell you the required courses and general degree requirements for each major. Usually advisors or counselors will be available to help you through the maze of choices. Search for someone who understands exactly where you are now, and how you feel about it.

If you want a college degree at the four-year level, you can go directly to a four-year institution or you can attend a community college for two years and then transfer to a four-year college or university to complete your junior and senior level courses. The four-year "package" can be outlined as follows:

First year: General education (GE), introduction to a major, and electives (free choice courses)

Second year: Major exploration, GE, and electives

Third year: Major requirements, electives, and remaining GE

Fourth year: Major requirements and electives

You will probably need more math if you are interested in science, four-year business or technical fields, architecture, or engineering. The usual sequence is as follows:

High school: Arithmetic, introductory algebra, plane geometry, intermediate algebra, trigonometry, college (pre-calculus) algebra or "senior math"

College: College algebra, analytic geometry and calculus (two to three semesters or five quarters), other advanced courses as needed and required

First, check to see how much math you need for various programs. (You may not need any at all.) Then try to start where you left off or where you feel most comfortable. Before you try to enroll in a course, however, find out whether you must complete any prerequisites. (A *prerequisite* is an elementary course that you need to take before enrolling in a more advanced course.) Experience can substitute for some prerequisites.

Adult education programs offer math courses at the high school level and sometimes beyond. Community colleges offer not only high school level courses but also most of the college courses at the freshman and sophomore level. Both offer remedial arithmetic.

You can find courses for personal growth and enrichment in colleges, adult education programs, and community centers. Many are noncredit courses, which provide an easy way to start back to school.

If returning to school seems impossible—because of distance, for example—investigate tutoring services, correspondence courses, and courses by TV. Some colleges and universities administer tests like the College Level Examination Program (CLEP), which enable you to earn credit by examination. Some give credit for work experience. You may be required to attend the school in order to complete courses, but such credits decrease the time you need to spend on campus.

If finances are a problem, apply for financial aid. Sometimes students of all ages can get grants and low-interest loans for education. Some people change their lifestyles, mortgage or sell their houses, sell their cars and ride a bike.

Remember, too, that much learning takes place off campus. You can teach yourself many things, and you can find others who will help you learn. Much depends on having a goal and working toward it—and being flexible enough to see alternatives.

· · · · · ·   **ALTERNATIVE ROUTES TO EDUCATIONAL CREDIT**

High School Credit

Adults can earn high school equivalency certificates through the General Educational Development (GED) program:

GED Testing Service
One Dupont Circle, N.W.
Suite 20
Washington, D.C. 20036-1163

College Credit

At various colleges, look for flexible alternatives such as TV courses, weekend programs, credit by examination, and credit for work experience.

Credit by Examination

You can take examinations to earn college credit. Contact the College-Level Examination Program (CLEP) for information:

CLEP
CN 6600
Princeton, NJ 08541-6600
(215) 750-8420

Or contact the Proficiency Examination Program (PEP):

ACT: PEP
P.O. Box 168
Iowa City, IA 52243

Credit for Noncollege Learning

The Center for Adult Learning and Educational Credentials at the American Council on Education evaluates courses given by private employers, community organizations, labor unions, government agencies, and military education programs. Contact:

American Council on Education
The Center for Adult Learning and Educational Credentials
One Dupont Circle N.W. Suite 1B-20
Washington, D.C. 20036-1163

(continued)

Credit for Experience

You can apply for college credit for your work experience. Contact the Council for Adult and Experiential Learning:

CAEL
Suite 203
10840 Little Patuxent Pkwy.
Columbia, MD 21044
(301) 997-3535

Educational Testing Service (ETS) publishes *How to Get Credit for What You Have Learned as a Homemaker or Volunteer*. It may be purchased for $5. Contact the Educational Testing Service:

ETS
Publication Order Services (T0-1)
CN 6736
Princeton, NJ 08541-6736

Credit for Correspondence and Independent Study

The Division of Independent Study of the National University Continuing Education Association (NUCEA) sponsors a wide variety of correspondence and independent study courses and programs, which are available through its membership institutions. The Association publishes *The Independent Study Catalog: The NUCEA Guide to Independent Study Through Correspondence Instruction, 1986-88.* ($8.95):

NUCEA
Suite 420
One Dupont Circle, N.W.
Washington, D.C. 20036-1163
(202) 659-3130

To order the publication, contact:

Peterson's Guides
Department 6217
166 Bunn Drive
P.O. Box 2123
Princeton, NJ 08543-2123

(continued)

•••••• | **ALTERNATIVE ROUTES TO EDUCATIONAL CREDIT** (continued)

Home Study Schools

A book entitled *Bear's Guide to Nontraditional College Degrees* (1987) is available for $9.95 from:

John Bear
P.O. Box 11415
Marina del Rey, CA 90295

Another relevant publication is *We Succeeded Through Home Study,* by Dr. G. Howard Poteet, available for $6 from:

National Home Study Council
1601 18th Street N.W.
Washington, D.C. 20009

For additional information on accredited home study schools, contact the following organizations:

National Home Study Council
1601 18th Street N.W.
Washington, D.C. 20009

Regents College Degrees
Cultural Education Center, 5D45
Albany, NY 12230

(continued)

Remember that most jobs require only average to somewhat above average skills. Talking to people "in the field" can help you to assess your motivation to go on, especially if it looks as though you'll need years of training. Remember, however, when you meet a competent professional who is all trained, experienced, and "way up there," that he or she didn't get there in one step. Most valuable in acquiring high-level ability is the patience to stay with it until you learn it. But hard work is fun if you are doing what you enjoy.

As you go along, new horizons will open up. You can also float to your level—that is, choose to stop at a point where you feel comfortable. Instead of going straight on to become a certified public accountant, for example, you might try work experience as an accounting clerk, which might lead you in a direction that you hadn't seen before. Or you may find along the way that you'd like to float sideways to a different area with similar satisfiers. The more homework you've done on your interests, the more quickly you'll be able to make such changes.

Thomas A. Edison College
New Jersey College for External Degrees
101 West State Street
Trenton, NJ 08625

International University Consortium
University College
University of Maryland
College Park, MD 20742

Specialized Programs

To learn about educational opportunities on small farms (apprenticeships and degree programs), write:

New Alchemy Institute
237 Hatchville Road
East Falmouth, MA 02536

For the publication *A Woman's Guide to Apprenticeship* (free), send a self-addressed label to:

Women's Bureau
U.S. Department of Labor
Washington, D.C. 20210

For special training programs, contact your local state employment office.

If you simply must get more detailed information about your skills, your aptitudes to develop skills, or areas where your skills need sharpening, you can contact a counselor at a local college, state employment office, or in private practice. You can arrange to take such tests as the *Differential Aptitude Test* (DAT) or the *General Aptitude Test Battery* (GATBY).

BACK TO WORK

You may decide to bypass further training and go directly out into the job market. Perhaps your decision-making and job-hunting skills will need to be reviewed and sharpened. For some, going back to work is a "natural." For others, it's a scary prospect. One woman had this to say:

Last fall, quaking and shaking, I had made up my mind I must not put off any longer the job-hunting ordeal. During a bridge game on a Wednesday, I announced I was going to find secretarial work. My partner announced her husband needed a secretary; she phoned him, he said, "Sure." On Thursday I made an appointment for Friday, and two weeks later I was sitting at a desk, secretary to a fine man who has been very understanding of my initial lack of self-assurance (starting to work again at age fifty-six after twenty-seven years). My 60-day performance report was a very satisfactory one (was delighted to have "initiative" get the best grading); and at six months received a 12 percent raise, but, best of all, the following remarks: "in recognition of outstanding contribution to the department." I love the work, and most of all, I love the self-assurance it's given me. Tell other women as quaking and shaking as I that it's not all that hard. Take that first plunge, and you've got it made.

I should add that my husband and family are delighted with the New Me. I hear no more complaints about what doesn't get done at home, they do the work instead. They are all being most supportive.*

SAME JOB/NEW APPROACH

If you are already employed, a brief exploration of the job market may convince you that your present job isn't so bad after all. "Then why," you wonder, "do I feel dissatisfied?" One common explanation is, "I'm not comfortable with my coworkers." Often communications problems are at the root of this discomfort. Would some fine tuning in human relations improve your work life?

Human relations can absorb much of your energy as you seek to accommodate to the various personalities you meet at work. Sometimes a change in yourself can make a vast difference. You can learn to communicate more effectively, assert yourself in a tactful way, grow in self-confidence, become more considerate and understanding of the problems of others. It will usually be necessary to strike a balance: not make a "federal case" out of every annoyance yet be able to make changes in a situation that clashes sharply with your sensibilities.

You may wish to check these items: Are you pleasant and easy to get along with? Do you overlook other people's minor shortcomings? Do your appearance and manner fit in with the style of your workplace? Do you give others credit and praise?

Sometimes asking for a change of work can alter your outlook and change the environment. For example, could you answer questions at the information

---

*Courtesy of Carol Shawhan.

If she doesn't make it as a dancer, she wants to be a dentist.

• •

window part of the time instead of answering the phone all day? A change to another department or to a slightly different job often means a new start. You might learn to manage time or the flow of work activities more efficiently, making the job more enjoyable.

If your job is beginning to call for new duties, such as public presentations or writing, some of your basic skills may need improving. Try to put energy into your job and to learn as much as you can in order to grow and develop. Your self-confidence will improve along with your skills.

Some people create a job within a job by assessing the tasks they like or dislike. Sometimes it's possible to trade tasks with others, ask for a reorganization, even hire someone to work along with you if your workload warrants it. Tackling a new project, changing departments, doing the same function in a new locale—each of these can be a creative way to get a fresh start.

Amazingly, some people are so successful they are promoted beyond the level of their own self-confidence. Suddenly they discover that everyone believes in them except themselves, and they need to grow in confidence to meet those expectations. Sometimes a step down can be a welcome change if job pressures become really unbearable. One executive, laid off and then rehired into a lower position, says, "The money doesn't add up, but for the first time in my life I don't give a damn. I haven't felt this good in years!"[2] "Stepping down" is a career direction we rarely consider, but it may be a good move toward actualizing your values. If you are dissatisfied with yourself, consider enrolling in some growth classes—or at least do some reading in the area of personal growth. If a problem is weighing on you, discuss it with a trusted friend or a counselor. Many problems have obvious solutions that we may miss when searching alone.

Even if one workplace doesn't work as a place for you, the career itself may still be a good choice. Try to separate the job from the place and people.

DECIDING NOT TO DECIDE

When you keep the status quo, you are deciding not to decide—which can be a good decision. Sometimes important decisions need time to percolate for insights to come. You might stay in the same job, take more classes, or continue to be at home with your children. You may need to do more exploring and evaluating, but try to set a time limit for your next move—say, six months to a year. If your present situation is uncomfortable for you, take some sort of action to work toward improvement—even if it is just reading or writing out a plan.

DECISION-MAKING:
A FOUR-PHASE PROCESS

Decision-making is a four-phase process that involves gathering information, weighing alternatives and outcomes, checking values, and designing strategies.

Gather information: Every decision calls for accurate information. In this book you have been gathering all the information you need to make a career decision. You have learned how to pull information from a variety of sources and resources.

Weigh the alternatives and outcomes: There are alternatives to every decision; for example, you would like to change careers and you could become a secretary or an engineer. Whichever alternative you act on, will have several outcomes. Some outcomes may seem desirable, others undesirable. Before you act on an important decision, try to imagine how it will turn out, both in the immediate future and some years down the line.

People are often only able to picture one type of outcome. Some, burdened by fears, see only disasters—major and minor. Other overly optimistic folks see nothing but grandiose positive effects. Most major decisions, however, produce a mixture of outcomes. You can take a job with a good salary, for example, but have to get extra training or work overtime. Even a dark outcome can have a light side. The extra training that you get may seem to be futile at the time, but later it turns out to provide just the background you need for another situation. Or working overtime may result in your making new friends. Hardly any decision has perfect results. Without a crystal ball, it's hard to predict exactly how a decision is going to work out.

Even the most carefully reasoned decisions can bring disappointing results. Everyone at times makes a poor decision. In such cases, try to avoid blaming yourself, but give yourself credit for having taken the risk. Some decisions that don't work do result in lost time and money, even in physical injury. But many seem risky only because they involve the approval or possible disapproval of others: What will people think? In fact, you may find yourself preserving the status quo solely out of fear of others' opinions. If so, you're giving others a great deal of power over your life. There is no way to change and grow without some risk.

Every change, however, even if it's only rearranging the garage, does have an impact on others. Caring for those around you involves bringing them along with your decision-making; that is, communicating your own needs honestly while listening to theirs, keeping them informed as you make changes. Hardly any change is perfect. There will be advantages and disadvantages to most moves. The idea is to *maximize the advantages*.

Sometimes alternatives are so clear you have no doubt which way to go. Sometimes, with just a little thought or information gathering, a decision comes easily. Sometimes decisions seem so tough that a step-by-step process can be helpful. There are many ways to weigh alternatives, all of them basically similar. We will use an exercise called Decision Point to organize and to clarify these alternatives. Using the "teetertotter" or balance principle, you will first place one of your decision alternatives in the balance, then list all the possible results, positive and negative, that might happen if you carried out that decision.

You might wish to review "Rating Values" from Chapter 1, and any other values that might possibly be affected. For example, if you were trying to decide which job to take, one in New York or Chicago, you would put the New York job in the balance first and write in such projected undesirable results as: environmentally risky company, longer work hours, hectic commute. On the desirable side, you might list: high pay, exciting work, status, closeness to family, cultural opportunities. You then rate the results on (1) how desirable (or undesirable) they are, and (2) how likely (or unlikely) they are to occur. On the positive side, you may rank high pay 5 for very desirable, but 1 on the likely scale if it doesn't look very possible.

For some people, environmental risk would outweigh other values, but perhaps, after exploring how likely that risk is, they may find the company is very careful and accidents quite unlikely. On the negative side, then, they may rank environmental risk 5, meaning very undesirable, but 1 on the likely scale, meaning only a slight possibility.

NEGATIVES						POSITIVES				
5 ___	4 ___	3 ___	2 ___	1 ___	0 ___	1 ___	2 ___	3 ___	4 ___	5

Very Undesirable   Indifferent   Very Desirable
Very Likely   Unlikely   Very Likely

Another person, for whom commuting on freeways is absolutely unacceptable, might discover that this outcome is unlikely because transit systems or car pooling are available. Next, of course, that person would need to weigh Chicago in the same way, for who knows what possible positives might turn up that would make the Windy City irresistible—such as, possibly, luxurious/affordable housing close to old college friends? Overall, the positive results of one alternative may quite outweigh any of the negatives. But you may choose to ignore the negatives and act on the decision anyway. It's up to you! What decisions have you made in the past? How have they turned out for you? Review one of these decisions as if you were just about to make it now.

In the final analysis, a decision cannot be made by numbers. Exercises help to organize and clarify your possibilities. They involve using your rational, logical self. After such a process, let your decision simmer a bit while your intuition gives voice to your sense of appropriateness and certainty about the decision. Then at some deeper level you will usually know that your choice will work for you. You will feel finished and at peace after the struggle. You will be ready to let go of the alternatives, perhaps with a twinge of regret because there are good sides to everything. You will be ready to move on and take the steps you need to reach your goals.

Check values: As you make choices, you express your value system—because values are revealed in what you do, not in what you say. As a final check, consider your decision in terms of values. If you want to live very simply, why seek a high-powered, energy-consuming job whose only reward is money? On the other hand, if money is important to you, aim for it. If you want both a family and a career, plan for it. Your decision should reflect your personal priorities.

Design strategies: This book outlines a great many strategies you can use in launching your career. How will you carry out your decision? Develop a good set of strategies, a step-by-step procedure for putting your own decision into practice. Think of each step as a goal, and set a time limit for reaching one step after the other. The time limit helps to discourage procrastination.

If time is a problem for you, learn to manage it. Some people pack their lives with so many activities that the end result is failure, frustration, or frenzy instead of accomplishment. Others take on too little and end up feeling bored and uninvolved. Here are some techniques for managing time:

- List all the tasks on your agenda and rank them in order of importance.

- Keep a "very important" list, a "so-so" list, and a "nice if I can get around to it" list of tasks that need doing.

- For one week, keep track of all your activities to find out where you are spending your time.

For further help with time management, read Alan Lakein's *How to Get Control of Your Time and Your Life.*[3]

Some people complete the entire career search process without making the big decision. If you are still unable to choose a career, you may need more time to gain confidence and clarify values. There is a point—perhaps we should call it the Great Gap—where you must cross over from process to action. No matter how much support you've had, how many inventories you do, and how many people you talk to, the decision is yours alone to make alone.

Perhaps you need to take a "dynamic rest" along the road to success. Read some books about the problem that's holding you back. Talk to a trusted friend or counselor. Paradoxically, sometimes we need to accept the status quo before we can change it, even just a little.

HOW TO DEFINE SUCCESS

As you move toward a career decision, you need to have an image of the successful you. But what is success? Some people equate it with money and prestige. The fact is, success is "all in your head"—everyone's definition is different. Failure is also whatever you choose to call it. Both success and failure are only steps in the experiment of living. Some steps work and some don't. What we learn from all this we call experience.

Success most often comes to those who set realistic goals and work hard persistently without giving up when things go wrong. Most successful people admit they have had some good luck that helped them along the way. Chances are they have had bad luck, too; they have made some mistakes but were not defeated. They were able to maintain their enthusiasm and commitment, which are the keys to success for everyone, especially those with little experience or education.

A common hazard on the road to success is the "I don't deserve it" syndrome. Since the desire for success is the strongest of all motivators, this feeling can block a good decision. If you tune into your mental conversations, you will recognize yourself as friend or foe. As Ken Keyes, Jr., says, "Beware what you tell yourself!"[4] Consider how each of these messages might affect an individual's career:

> "I don't deserve success. My goal is only to work hard."
>
> "No matter how much money I've got, it's never enough."
>
> "Everyone—including me—deserves self-actualization."

So if you ever have had a clear thought or done a brave deed or said a kind word, you can affirm it. We can choose to focus on the negative or the positive.

As surprising as it may seem, some people are afraid to succeed. Success brings more responsibility and higher visibility. It leads others to expect you to keep on performing well. Success requires a great deal of continued effort, both to get there and to stay there. The person who accepts failure no longer has to keep on trying. In some cases, failing is a way to exert independence against the real or imagined demands of others.

Some days our bad feelings send us in search of a problem. "Don't cheer me up or tell me anything good because it will ruin my misery program." Jerry Gillies, author of *Money Love,* says some people have a "poverty consciousness," others a "prosperity consciousness."[5] Margaret Anstin, in her career guide to the video series *Voyages,* says that we can use a potential salary loss as an excuse to avoid changing careers. We tend to let money indicate our value as persons and measure our success. Anstin points out, "Prosperity is much more likely to flow to and through you if you are doing work you enjoy."[6] Enjoyment of work is another way to define success.

Affirmations, both positive and negative, are so powerful that the authors of the children's book *Make It So!* have children speculate, "So—I've been wondering—could most of my problems be caused by me?"[7]

In this book, you have been learning good things about yourself: your interests, values, skills. You've learned how to find or make a place for yourself in the job market. You've learned to assess jobs and workplaces and how to network effectively. Now it's time to "own" all the good things about yourself by positive affirmations. Affirmation can change outcomes because they change attitudes and feelings. When you believe in yourself as a capable person, you are on your way to further growth and fulfillment. Fulfillment is another word for success.

Both success and failure are only temporary. The excited, enthusiastic, newly hired graduate, the forty-year company man, and the secure civil servant may have a hard time recognizing themselves as people in transition. But the fact is that *all* people are in transition. No one stands still on the same job forever. Growth, promotion, transfers, new technology, layoffs, cutbacks, mergers, reorganization, changes of management, company bankruptcy, life transitions, illness, disability, and retirement are just a few of the changes that affect careers.

• • • • • • • • • •

PERSON WHO SAY

it cannot be done
should not interrupt
person doing it!

Updated Old Chinese Proverb

• • • • • • • • • •

DECISION-MAKING AND UNEMPLOYMENT

Perhaps you have made a good career decision but now find that things are changing. You may have put a great deal of energy into your job. You may have earned a degree and learned new skills in preparation for your career. Still your job doesn't seem to be working out well, so you (or your employer) decide to call it quits. Suddenly you are jobless and worried about where to go next. It is hard to feel successful when you are unemployed. But you are also sleeping in some mornings, catching up on errands, enjoying an occasional walk on the beach. That's good: the more you can enjoy your new leisure, the better you'll be able to plan your next step. Be open to new ideas at times like this.

Some questions you need to answer are: Do I want to do almost exactly the same job in a similar setting? Do I want to get out of the old line of work or into another type of workplace? Do I want to make a career change, create my own career, start a new business, go back to school? Most important, what changes can I make in myself to put me in harmony with my choices? What skills did I learn and develop on my last job? Did that job put me in touch with new interests? What did I dislike about that job?

If you *were* fired or laid off, evaluate the causes to see how they can be avoided in the future. As everyone knows, it can happen to anyone. Despite the very real trauma involved in being jobless, you can use the experience to advantage by preparing for your next job. Learn to pick up cues that will help you to make and keep other options open, instead of sinking into mindless security on your job. You can't always plan your career step by step, but you can adopt

The Action Tree

If you have assessed your needs, wants, values, interests, and skills, made decisions, set goals, and determined strategies—then your next step is effective action.

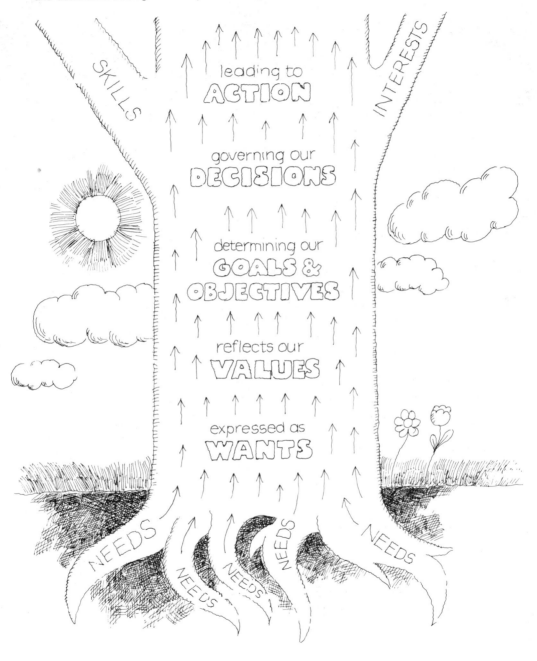

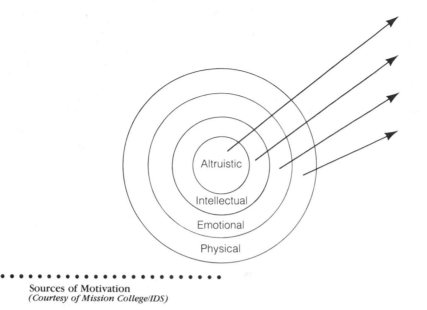

Sources of Motivation
(Courtesy of Mission College/IDS)

a game plan that provides alternatives. Ask for help from friends, relatives, and neighbors without hiding your job loss.

Even if you plan to stay at the same place in the same job for a lo-o-o-o-ong time, chances are that some day job burnout or boredom will prompt you to wonder, "Is this all there is?" You may have assessed yourself and found out exactly who you are. You have found that dream job that embodies your most important values and interests and is encouraging you to develop your skills. You have a growing family and a hefty mortgage. You seem to "have it all," but still you experience a nagging discontent. You feel "stuck," as if there were nowhere else to go. Now it's reassessment time — time to renew the career search and look for new directions. Also time to look at the balance in your life in its physical, emotional, intellectual, and altruistic/spiritual components. Which of these need levels motivates you most? The more you grow, the more your lower needs will be fulfilled and the more you will become a self-actualizing person who acts out of concern not only for self, but for other persons and the planet as well. Everything you do will express what is finest in human nature.

You will find a workplace where your skills are needed and appreciated. Knowing that your skills are needed, you will have the confidence to take action. Having proved yourself as a capable person, you will be on your way to further growth and self-fullfilment.

The steps you take create your life. May your career choice make you a "true person." May your dreams be actualized.

Self-Assessment Exercises

1. Decision-Making Style

You make many decisions every day. It's helpful to reflect on how you do it. Check (√) the appropriate columns. Then mark plus (+) in front of item numbers indicating areas you'd like to improve.

	Usually	Sometimes	Rarely
1. I make decisions after considering many alternatives.	_____	_____	_____
2. I make decisions easily, without undue agonizing, and on time.	_____	_____	_____
3. I base my decisions on "reasoned judgment" of the information available.	_____	_____	_____
4. I base my decisions on feelings and intuition.	_____	_____	_____
5. I tend to think my decisions will turn out to be disasters.	_____	_____	_____
6. I tend to imagine that results from my decisions will be spectacular.	_____	_____	_____
7. I make my own decisions, not shifting responsibility to others.	_____	_____	_____
8. I consult with others, but my decisions are my own.	_____	_____	_____
9. I compromise when the needs of others are involved.	_____	_____	_____
10. I make some decisions to fulfill my own needs.	_____	_____	_____
11. I "test out" major decisions ahead of time where possible.	_____	_____	_____

"YOU'LL HAVE TO DECIDE — DO YOU WANT TO BE TOP MANAGEMENT IN A SMALL POND, OR BOTTOM MANAGEMENT IN A BIG POND?"

12. I take responsibility for the consequences of my decisions.   _____ _____ _____

13. If a decision doesn't work, I try another plan, without great regret.   _____ _____ _____

2. Decision Point: Selecting Alternatives

If you are on the verge of a decision but are having trouble choosing which alternative would work best for you, list them here:

Alternative 1_____

Alternative 2_____

Alternative 3_____

Alternative 4_____

3. Decision Point: Weighing Alternatives

A. Write one of the alternatives you are considering on the Decision Point, Line A:

B. List the possible negative results of your decision. Include related values from "Rating Values," Chapter 1:

C. List the possible positive results of your decision. Include related values from "Rating Values," Chapter 1:

D. Rate each result on a scale of 1–5 as *desirable* or *undesirable* (on the negative side, 5 means *very undesirable*).

E. Rate each result on a scale of 1–5 as *likely* or *unlikely* (on the negative side 5 means *most unlikely*).

F. Add up the negative columns, D and E. Then add the negative D and E totals. Add up the positive columns, D and E. Then add the positive D and E totals.

G. If you are having a difficult time with decision-making, use this exercise to review an important and successful though difficult decision you made in the past.

A. <u>DECISION POINT</u>: _____

NEGATIVES   POSITIVES

−5 ____ −4 ____ −3 ____ −2 ____ −1 ____ 0 ____ ±1 ____ ±2 ____ ±3 ____ ±4 ____ ±5

Very Undesirable   Indifferent   Very Desirable
Very Likely   Unlikely   Very Likely

B. <u>POSSIBLE NEGATIVES</u>   (D)   (E)
                                            Desirability   Likelihood

_____   _____   _____

_____   _____   _____

_____   _____   _____

_____   _____   _____

_____   _____   _____

_____   _____   _____

_____   _____   _____

                        <u>Totals:</u>   _____   _____

           Total of D + E Negatives: = − _____

C. <u>POSSIBLE POSITIVES</u>   (D)   (E)
                                            Desirability   Likelihood

_____   _____   _____

_____   _____   _____

_____   _____   _____

_____   _____   _____

_____   _____   _____

_____   _____   _____

_____   _____   _____

                        <u>Totals:</u>   _____   _____

           Total of D + E Positives   = + _____

H. Compare Results:

- Do the desirables outweigh the undesirables?_____
- Is the likelihood of the negative results greater than the positive results?_____
- Does the total positive score outweigh the total negative score?_____

I. Repeat this procedure for each of your alternatives. Then write a paragraph comparing your results and how they may affect your final decision.

J. Ten years down the path, is this decision the one you would like to have made? What results might only occur later? Add your insights to the paragraph in I.

4. Goals and Strategies

Write down the decision you've chosen to carry out. State four steps or strategies you would take to accomplish this goal. In the righthand column, set the time line. How soon would you like to accomplish this change and its related strategies?

Decision or goal:_____

Is this goal realistic?_____ Does it agree with your values?_____

Steps I must take   Date to be accomplished

a. _____   _____

b. _____   _____

c. _____   _____

d. _____   _____

e. _____   _____

5. Time Management

How will you manage your time in order to reach your goals?

a. State the number of college credits you plan to carry in your next term: _____

b. Allow at least two hours of study for each credit or unit (units × 2). _____

c. State the number of hours you will work per week. (Include family care.) _____

d. Total the number of hours each week you have committed so far:

e. Estimate the number of hours per week you devote to:

Sleeping _____

Eating _____

Commuting _____

Household chores _____

Business (bank, dentist, shopping, etc.) _____

Communicating with family and friends _____

Exercise _____

Recreation/leisure _____

Miscellaneous/unexpected _____

Add the total

f. Add the total in boxes d and e to see how many hours per week you spend in all activities—the big total!

g. Remember, there are only 168 hours in a week. Do you have too much scheduled? _____ Too little? _____ Just enough? _____

6. Your Weekly Schedule

Once you have chosen some goals and strategies, it's important to fit them into your time schedule. Are you trying to do too much? Do you let too much time slip away? To find out, fill in the schedule chart on the next page for a week. At the end of the week, cross out the unnecessary activities that are overcrowding your schedule, and fill empty spaces with things you would like to do. Don't crowd every minute of every day. Try to schedule only the activities that have value for you.

Weekly Schedule

Time	Monday	Tuesday	Wednesday	Thursday	Friday	Saturday	Sunday
6:30							
7:00							
7:30							
8:00							
8:30							
9:00							
9:30							
10:00							
10:30							
11:00							
11:30							
12:00							
12:30							
1:00							
1:30							
2:00							
2:30							
3:00							
3:30							
4:00							
4:30							
5:00							
5:30							
6:00							
6:30							
7:00							
7:30							
8:00							
8:30							
9:00							
9:30							
10:00							
10:30							
11:00							
11:30							
12:00							

7. Back to School

If going to college is on your list of possibilities, check ($\sqrt{}$) the answers that explain why. If college isn't for you, check any other training alternatives that appeal to you.

Why college?

_____ Not sure, but wish to explore and find out about it

_____ Personal enrichment

_____ Hope to improve basic skills

_____ Would like to finish high school work and earn a diploma

_____ Wish to earn a career program certificate

_____ Plan to earn a two-year degree at a community college

_____ Want to earn a BA or BS degree from a four-year college or university.

_____ Want to do graduate work.

_____ My mother/father/boss/spouse made me come to college!

Other training alternatives?

_____ Apprenticeship programs with unions in various crafts

_____ Adult education through local school district

_____ Proprietary schools (private schools that teach a special job skill)

_____ On-the-job training programs or management training programs

_____ Off-campus or extension college work by TV, job experience, weekend college, and other options for the busy person

8. School Subjects

a. Check ($\sqrt{}$) the columns that describe your feelings about school subjects.

	Like	Dislike	Did Well	Did Not Do Well	Avoided
Reading	_____	_____	_____	_____	_____
Writing	_____	_____	_____	_____	_____
Speech/Drama	_____	_____	_____	_____	_____
Math	_____	_____	_____	_____	_____
Science	_____	_____	_____	_____	_____

	Like	Dislike	Did Well	Did Not Do Well	Avoided
Social Studies	___	___	___	___	___
Art/Crafts	___	___	___	___	___
Music	___	___	___	___	___
Industrial/Technical	___	___	___	___	___
Business	___	___	___	___	___
Health	___	___	___	___	___
Agriculture	___	___	___	___	___
Physical Education	___	___	___	___	___
_____	___	___	___	___	___
_____	___	___	___	___	___
_____	___	___	___	___	___

b. Circle the subjects you'd like to study further.

c. Now look at your "worst" subjects. Are there any you'd like to try again? Few people have the time and energy to become good at everything. But often our work is poor only because we don't want to make the effort to improve. Getting rid of the "excess baggage" that says we *should* try to excel at everything can be a liberating experience.

9. Some College Majors Arranged by Personality Type and Job Group

Place a check (√) in front of any college majors that interest you at this time. Check college catalog for alternate titles.

R REALISTIC

Mechanical
___ Aero Maintenance/ Operations
___ Air Conditioning/ Refrigeration/Solar Technology
___ Air Traffic Control
___ Anaplastology
___ Automotive Technology
___ Biomedical Technology
___ Construction Technology
___ Diesel Mechanic

___ Electronics Technology
___ Food Service
___ Industrial Administration/ Engineering/ Technology
___ Laser/Microwave Technology
___ Machine/Tool Technology
___ Quality Control
___ Radiologic Technology
___ Robotics/Computer-Assisted Manufacturing (CAM)

___ Semiconductor Management
___ Shoe Rebuilding
___ Technological Drafting/ Modelbuilding/ Illustrating
___ Telecommunications
___ Transportation
___ Watch Repair
___ Welding Technology
Industrial: No majors
Nature
___ Agriculture
___ Animal Health Technology

___ Nursery Management
___ Park Management Technology
___ Wildlife Management Technology
Protective
___ Administration of Justice
___ Fire Science
___ Safety Engineering
Physical Performance
___ Physical Education/ Kinesiology

I INVESTIGATIVE

Scientific/Analytic
- Biological science
  - Agriculture
  - Animal/Avian Science
  - Bacteriology
  - Biology
  - Botany
  - Conservation
  - Enology
  - Entomology/ Pest Science
  - Environmental Science
  - Food Science
  - Forest Science
  - Genetics
  - Kinesiology
  - Marine Biology
  - Microbiology
  - Nutrition
  - Soil/Water/ Wood Science
  - Toxicology
  - Zoology
- Cybernetics
- Engineering
  - Aeronautical/ Aerospace
  - Agricultural
  - Bioengineering
  - Civil
  - Computer Science
  - Electrical/ Electronic
  - Environmental
  - Material Science
  - Naval Architecture
  - Nuclear
  - Science
  - Systems
  - Transportation
- Linguistics
- Mathematics/ Statistics/Applied
- Medical
  - Dentistry
  - Optometry
  - Pharmacy
  - Medicine/ Surgery

- Veterinary Medicine
- Physical Sciences
  - Chemistry
  - Geology/Earth Science
  - Meteorology
  - Oceanography
  - Physics/ Astronomy
- Social Sciences
  - Anthropology
  - Consumer Economics/ Science
  - Ethnic Studies
  - Geography
  - History
  - Psychology
  - Sociology
  - Urban/Rural Studies
  - Women's Studies

A ARTISTIC

Applied Arts
- Architecture
- Commercial Art
- Computer-Assisted Design (CAD)
- Film/Photography
- Fashion Design
- Interior Design
- Industrial Design
- Graphics
- Journalism
- Landscape Design/ Ornamental Horticulture
- Media Specialty
- Modelbuilding
- Radio/TV
- Technical Illustrating

Fine Arts
- Art/Art History
- Dance/Drama
- English
- Foreign Language
- Humanities
- Literature

- Music
- Philosophy
- Speech

S SOCIAL

Human Services
- Community Health Worker
- Counseling
- Dental Assistant/ Hygiene
- Dietician
- Health Science
- Inhalation Therapy
- Nursing RN, LVN, Assistant
- Occupational Therapy
- Pediatric Assistant
- Physical Therapy/ also Assistant
- Primary Care Associate
- Psychiatric Technician
- Psychology— Clinical
- Public Health
- Social Service
- Speech Pathology and Audiology

Accommodating
- Cosmetology
- Food Service
- Gerontology
- Leisure/Travel Careers

S/E SOCIAL/ ENTERPRISING

Leading/Influencing
- Advertising
- Business Administration
- Convalescent Hospital Administration
- Education

- Health Care Management
- Insurance
- Labor Studies
- Law
- Library Science
- Management/ Supervision
- Manpower Administration
- Office Administration
- Public Relations
- Recreation
- Volunteer Administration

E ENTERPRISING

Persuading
- Fashion/Retail Merchandising
- International Trade
- Law
- Marketing/Sales
- Political Science
- Purchasing
- Real Estate
- Speech/ Communications

C CONVENTIONAL

Business Detail
- Accounting
- Attorney Assistant
- Banking/Finance
- Court Reporting
- Data Processing
- Insurance
- Secretarial
  - Administrative
  - Clerical
  - Medical Assistant/ Records
  - Legal
  - Unit Clerk
  - Word Processing

10. Blocks and Barriers: Finding the Keystone

To find out what is holding you back, ask yourself if you are dealing with barriers within yourself. Place a check (√) in front of the dots of any that apply:

Blocks Within You

- Locked into your stereotypes
- Too complacent to change the status quo
- Lacking confidence/awash in fear
- Weak skills
- Negative attitudes
- Caught in health or emotional problems
- Bogged down in transitions like divorce, death of spouse, immigration adjustment
- Longing for improved personal relationships
- Afraid to make a commitment
- In the habit of procrastinating
- Overresearching—losing yourself in the library
- Experiencing conflicts about values
- Too many "shoulds"

Barriers Outside You:

- A really poor job market/economy
- Societal expectations
- Imperative roles such as parenting
- Physical realities such as illness

What steps can you take to overcome these blocks and barriers?

_____

_____

_____

11. Affirmations

Everyone is a mixture of faults, foibles, and failings along with skills, successes, and strengths. Check (√) the statements that match your thought patterns. Select one *positive* statement and say it many times a day over a week's time. Know that attitudes and feelings can be changed.

Negatives	Positives
_____ I don't think I'll ever figure out what I want to do.	_____ I can take steps to figure out what to do.

Negatives (*continued*)	Positives (*continued*)

_____ I'm not interested in anything.

_____ I'm interested in many things.

_____ Nothing is much fun.

_____ I enjoy many of my activities.

_____ I'm dumb.

_____ I can learn.

_____ If my first choice doesn't work out, I'm stuck.

_____ I can plan alternatives.

_____ I'm tired of trying because nothing works.

_____ I have the energy to make things happen.

_____ I'm afraid.

_____ I can be courageous.

_____ I never have fun.

_____ I can create a good time.

_____ I can make a good decision!

Group Discussion Questions

1. Share your educational plans.
2. Discuss the concept of lifelong learning and what form it can take in your own life.
3. If you are working (or going to school), what new approaches could you take to improve your situation?
4. What factors might cause someone to "decide not to decide"?
5. Describe the steps you take in making decisions.
6. How do values relate to decisions?
7. Define success for yourself.
8. Define failure for yourself.
9. What values might prompt a manager to "step down" to a lower job status?
10. What values might take the place of work in your life?

WORK AFFECTS THE SOUL: THE FINAL ANALYSIS

FOCUS

Review the career decision-making process.

Gather personal information into one place.

Set goals that fit this portrait of you.

The self-assessment exercises in this book were designed to help you focus on the personal qualities you will bring to the workplace and the rewards you hope to receive from it. "The Final Analysis" is a place to summarize this information. It will give you an overview of most of the areas of your life affected by work. It will help you assess your career search process and how effectively this process has helped you choose the career that will lead to your personal growth and self-fulfillment on all levels. It will help you make those final decisions and provide a handy future reference.

To complete "The Final Analysis," review the self-assessment exercises and summarize the data here. Feel free to add additional information about yourself and the career you are considering.

Chapter 1   Needs, Wants, and Values: Spotlighting YOU

1. Review "Tapping into Feelings" (p. 24) and "Life Problems Checklist" (p. 25). Then list areas you would like to expand and those you would like to change or eliminate.

I want to develop: I want to change:

_____   _____

_____   _____

_____   _____

_____   _____

2. Review "Needs and Wants, Shoulds, and Values," a–g, p. 27. Check the balance in your life. Do you have enough? What do you need or want on these four levels?

	I have enough of:	I want:
Physical level	_____	_____
Emotional level	_____	_____
Intellectual level	_____	_____
Altruistic level	_____	_____

Is your life in balance on these four levels? Yes _____ No _____

If not, how can you improve the balance?_____

_____

_____

_____

3. Review "Rating Values," a–g (p. 28) and write ten of your most important values here:

a. _____   e. _____   h. _____

b. _____   f. _____   i. _____

c. _____   g. _____   j. _____

d. _____

4. Review your autobiographical data. Summarize what you learned about yourself in the two exercises in "Drawing a Self-Portrait" (p. 31), and "Creating an Autobiography" (p. 35).

_____

_____

_____

5. Review "Candid Camera—3-D" (p. 33). List the five activities you enjoy the most.

a. _____   d. _____

b. _____   e. _____

c. _____

CHAPTER 2   ROLES AND REALITIES: SINKING THE STEREOTYPES

Review the roles you play and the roles of others, 1a–c, 2a–c (p. 64). Then complete the following:

1. I enjoy being a _____ because _____

_____

2. I would like to improve my role as a _____

3. I'd like to be more accepting of people who are _____

_____

4. Review "Identifying Major Components of Your Life" (p. 65). List those you would like to improve.

_____   _____   _____

_____   _____   _____

CHAPTERS 3 AND 4   JOB SATISFIERS

1. Review the Personality Mosaic (pp. 71–83); then list your types and scores for each type in order from highest to lowest.

First _____   _____   Fourth _____   _____

Second _____   _____   Fifth _____   _____

Third _____   _____   Sixth _____   _____

2. Which level of involvement with Data, People, and Things do you enjoy? See page 92.

DATA: High level _____   Modest level _____   Little or none _____

PEOPLE: High level _____   Modest level _____   Little or none _____

THINGS: High level _____   Modest level _____   Little or none _____

3. Circle the numbers of the ten qualities that represent important skill areas for you. On the line before each skill indicate M if you prefer a moderate level, H for high level of ability. Then circle the numbers of the work qualities that you prefer (see p. 100).

KEY QUALITIES

Data/People/Things Qualities
_____ 1. Logical intelligence
_____ 2. Intuitive intelligence
_____ 3. Verbal ability
_____ 4. Numerical ability
_____ 5. Precise detail
_____ 6. Multidimensional awareness
_____ 7. Businesslike contact with people
_____ 8. Influencing people
_____ 9. Finger/hand agility
_____10. Whole body agility

Work Qualities
_____11. Repetition
_____12. Variety
_____13. Physical risk
_____14. Status

4. From the "Personal Responsibility Skills Checklist" (p. 96), list your best personal skills and the ones you could improve.

Best Skills: Could Improve:

_____   _____

_____   _____

_____   _____

5. List your work-specific skills.

_____

_____

List the work-specific skills you wish to acquire.

_____

_____

6. List three job groups by decimal code and title from the Job Group Chart (p. 118) in the order of your own interests.

a. Decimal code_____ Title_____

b. Decimal code_____ Title_____

c. Decimal code_____ Title_____

7. Tell how your top job group matches your personality, skills, interests, and work qualities. Use a separate sheet of paper if necessary.

_____

_____

_____

_____

_____

_____

_____

8. List the job title you would like the most._____

9. Do you want a career or "just a job"? Explain your answer.

_____

_____

10. How does your career choice match your values?

_____

_____

_____

CHAPTER 5   THE JOB MARKET: FACTS, TRENDS, AND PREDICTIONS

1. Of the five major trends (pp. 124–25), which would you like to change? How would you change it?

_____

_____

_____

2. Consider your altruistic feelings. What contribution would you like to make to the world?

_____

_____

_____

3. What does the *Occupational Outlook Handbook* or similar references say about the employment outlook for the career of your choice?

_____

_____

_____

4. What is the salary range for the career of your choice?_____

Would this career support your lifestyle? Yes_____ No_____

5. List five alternate careers that you would consider. List one positive and one negative feature of each.

Career	Positive Feature	Negative feature
a. _____	_____	_____
b. _____	_____	_____
c. _____	_____	_____
d. _____	_____	_____
e. _____	_____	_____

CHAPTER 6   WORKPLACES AND WORK STYLES: SCANNING THE SUBTLETIES

1. Use findings from your research to describe the ideal workplace. Consider size and complexity, type of environment, and emotional rewards you would like to receive.

   _____

   _____

   _____

   _____

   _____

   _____

2. Review the Career Ladder (p. 156). How far up the ladder do you want to go? Explain your answer.

   _____

   _____

   _____

3. Would you like to help plan your own work routine? If so, explain how.

   _____

   _____

4. Review "Researching Workplaces" and "Workplace Checklist" (pp. 184–86). Then list the four corporate values that are most important to you (see "Workplace Values," p. 186). Put a plus (+) next to any values you must have.

a. _____

b. _____

c. _____

d. _____

5. Describe your ideal job.

_____

_____

_____

_____

6. Describe your ideal boss.

_____

_____

_____

7. Describe your ideal work day.

_____

_____

_____

8. Describe your ideal balance of work and leisure.

_____

_____

_____

9. If you were to decide to open your own business, what steps would you take first?

a. _____

b. _____

c. _____

d. _____

10. What does work mean to you? Describe your personal work ethic.

_____

_____

_____

_____

_____

Chapter 7   The Job Hunt: Tools for Breaking and Entering

1. To prepare for the job hunt:

Name the title of a job you might apply for: _____

List ten of your characteristics that relate to that job:

_____

_____

_____

_____

_____

_____

_____

_____

_____

_____

2. What is the most important thing you've learned in this book?

_____

_____

_____

FENWICK VELEY
Courtesy of Mal Hancock. Reprinted with permission from the Saturday Evening Post Society, a division of BFL&MS, Inc. ©1987.

Chapter 8   Decisions, Decisions: What's Your Next Move?

1. What is your next move in the career search?

_____

_____

_____

2. Educational planning sheet:
   a. Do you now have the skills and training you need to obtain a job in the field of your choice? Yes_____ No_____

   If you need more preparation, which of the following do you need (see p. 251)?

   _____ Apprenticeship

   _____ On-the-job training

   _____ Workshops or seminars

   _____ Other: _____

b. If you need more education, which of these alternatives are you considering (see p. 251)?

_____ A few courses _____ A BA or BS degree

_____ A certificate _____ Graduate school

_____ An AA or AS degree _____ Other: _____

c. List an appropriate major (or majors) for your career choice (see p. 252).

_____ _____

d. What kind of college do you plan to attend?

_____ Two-year _____ Out-of-state

_____ Four-year _____ Public

_____ Local _____ Private

_____ In your state

e. List colleges or universities that offer the major you have chosen. (Use the educational reference section of your library and ask for assistance from a college counseling center.)

_____

_____

_____

f. Obtain catalogs for colleges of interest to you. To gather as much information as possible, visit the campuses, talk to people who are familiar with each school. For example, will you need:

_____ Financial aid _____ Housing

_____ Special entrance tests _____ A specific grade point average

_____ Other _____

g. Begin course planning here:

Major requirements	General or graduation requirements	Electives
_____	_____	_____
_____	_____	_____
_____	_____	_____
_____	_____	_____

3. Complete the botton line: I plan to be employed in the job of my choice by (date): _____

4. Review all the inventories you have taken. Read your autobiography again. Check each item in "The Final Analysis" to make sure there are no contradictions.

5. Does it hang together? Yes _____ No _____

· ·

Hang Loose
Michele F. Bakarich
I'm
just
going
to
hang
loose

,
that's
the
best
way
to
go

A P P E N D I X

SAMPLE RÉSUMÉS AND LETTERS

The sample résumés and letters in this Appendix are those of real job seekers ranging from college student to senior citizen, from engineer to housewife returning to work. Each résumé is unique to one person, as your résumé will be unique to you. But you can use these sample résumés in a number of ways. Notice the variety of forms and styles. Select the ones that seem to fit your situation best, and use them as models to create your own unique résumé.

The sample résumés can also be used for role playing. As you read them, pay attention to the person behind the résumé as an interviewer would. Think of questions you might ask the owner of each résumé, and use these questions in mock interviews.

The letters that accompany résumés are called *cover letters*. In addition to "covering" your résumé, letters may be used to thank people who have interviewed you and to maintain contact with them until you are actually employed.

269

• •
FIGURE A-1 Letter Maintaining Contact with a Prospective Employer.

5096 W. Monroe Street
South Bend, Indiana 46637
May 22, 1988

Mr. William A. Cline
U.S. Department of Forestry
II5 E. Birch Bark Lane
Sault Ste Marie, Michigan 49783

Dear Mr. Cline:

This is to let you know that I am still interested in working with the Forest Service in the Michigan area. I expect to be in touch with you around November regarding the jobs of recreation assistant and resource assistant that you mentioned to me for next year.

By the way, I applied for (and got) the spotted owl project job at Gifford Pinchot National Forest last summer. Thanks for notifying me about it. (It was never listed with Civil Service.)

If you know of any promising late-opening summer jobs in your area this year, I would appreciate it if you would let me know.

Thanks again.

Yours truly,

Daniel P. Magee

Daniel P. Magee
(2I9) 555-I2I2

. . . .

FIGURE A-2 Chronological Résumé and Cover Letter of a College Student.
Kathleen Neville is the college student whose work skills
provided the example in the "Candid Camera--3-D" exercise in
Chapter 1. Her limited work experience is amplified by high
school activities. Her brief statement of qualifications emphasizes
education and transferable and personal responsibility skills. Her
cover letter mentions her commitment to use her skills in the
desired position.

791 Peony Lane
Aptos, CA. 95003
September 17, 1988

Mr. Archibald Manx
The Elegant Cat
1000 Main Street
Los Gatos, CA 95030

Dear Sir:

Recently your accountant, Bruce McDougall, said that you are beginning the search for
someone to fill a managerial position.

I have had four years supervisory experience working in various phases of the
restaurant business. My intention is to continue in this field. The excellent quality of The
Elegant Cat is well known. I feel that I could be of assistance in maintaining this fine level of
service.

Enclosed is a copy of my resume. I will call you next week for an appointment to
discuss this with you further.

Sincerely
yours,

Kathleen M. Neville

Kathleen M. Neville

• •

Figure A-2 (continued)

KATHLEEN M. NEVILLE
79l Peony Lane
Aptos, CA. 95003
(408) 555-l730

POSITION OBJECTIVE: Restaurant Management Trainee

QUALIFICATIONS IN BRIEF:

AA In Restaurant Management
BA candidate in Business Management
Supervisory experience
Good human relations skills
Reliable, responsible, creative worker

EDUCATION:

SAN JOSE STATE UNIVERSITY, San Jose, CA.   Present
Major: Business Management

FOOTHILL COMMUNITY COLLEGE   l988
  AA Degree in Restaurant Management (Core Courses at Mission College)

WORK EXPERIENCE:

LINDA'S DRIVE-IN, Santa Cruz, CA.   August l985 to Present
Supervisor/Cook

Inventory, order, prepare, and stock food supplies. Settle employee and customer
problems and complaints. Orient/train new employees; evaluate employee
performance. Do minor repairs/maintenence. As occasional acting manager, open and
close shop, handle cash/cash register.

Babysitting and housekeeping throughout junior high and high school.   Previous

ACTIVITIES:

GIRL SCOUTS   l976-l986
Supervised day camp; planned activities, taught games, arts and crafts. sports,
camping skills, and first aid. Solved conflicts. Received art award.

MUSIC   l980-l988
Foothill Youth Symphony, Jazz, Symphony, Marching/Pep Bands at various times from
elementary school through community college. Toured Expo l988, Brisbane, Australia

DRAMA-AWALT HIGH SCHOOL   l985-87
As Assistant Director supervised making costumes, sets, props. Performed in Summer
Theatre Workshop.

REFERENCES: Provided upon request.

- -

FIGURE A-3 Functional Résumés and Chronological for the Same Person. The functional résumé shows just two work-specific areas, secretarial/clerical and inventory. In this case, the chronological résumé highlights the broader experience more impressively. It's good practice to prepare both types to see which works for you.

RUBY F. GARCIA
404 Lark Drive
Honolulu, Hawaii 96815
(808) 555-1212

POSITION OBJECTIVE: Manager of Small Office

QUALIFICATIONS IN BRIEF:

Twenty-two years of secretarial experience. Responsible, efficient, organized, careful of detail, tactful, and supportive of co-workers.

EXPERIENCE:

SECRETARIAL/CLERICAL: Both general and technical. Took dictation, typed, kept books. Operated addressograph, did monthly mailing. Typed church bulletins, letters, resumes, theses, and manuscripts.

INVENTORY: Took stockroom inventory. Ordered, checked, and delivered supplies.

HUMAN RELATIONS: Interacted with engineers and job analysts doing technical reports, registered students, supervised/taught children in a variety of settings. Cooperated with groups in fund raising.

EDUCATION:

HEALD'S BUSINESS COLLEGE, Honolulu, Hawaii
BALDWIN HIGH SCHOOL, Wailuku, Maui

REFERENCES: Available upon request.

• •

Figure A-3 (continued)

RUBY F. GARCIA
404 Lark Drive
Honolulu, Hawaii 96815
(808) 555-1212

POSITION OBJECTIVE: Manager of Small Office

EXPERIENCE:

RUBY'S TYPING SERVICE   Present
Professional Typist/Word Processor
Manuscripts, resumes, term papers, theses, letters typed and edited.

ST. PATRICK'S CATHOLIC CHURCH, Honolulu, Hawaii   11 years
Addressograph Operator
Typed names and addresses on plate machine. Operated addressograph. Kept files up to
date with changes of address; registered new parishioners. Mailed out monthly bulk mail.
Substituted for the parish secretary when needed.

McKINLEY HIGH SCHOOL, Honolulu, Hawaii   I year
Secretary to Vice-Principal and Textbook and Supply Clerk
Took dictation, typed, filed. Delivered and picked up textbooks for teachers. Filled out
supply orders and ordered new suplies as needed.

BUREAU OF RECLAMATION, Honolulu, Hawaii   I year
Secretary Pool
Took dictation from engineers and typed their reports.

HICKAM AIR FORCE FIELD, Honolulu, Hawaii
Secretary   I year
Took dictation from job analysts and typed their reports.

BALDWIN HIGH SCHOOL, Wailuku, Maui   I year
Secretary to Night School Principal
Registered students. General office work for night school.

LAWRENCE CHRYSLER, PLYMOUTH DEALER, Wailuku, Maui   2 years
Secretary
Took dictation, typed, bookkeeping, made out payroll, worked with parts manager in
checking supplies ordered and received.

HALEAKALA REALTORS, Wailuku, Maui   3 years
Secretary
General office work, took dictation, and typed for three realtors.

EDUCATION:

HEALD'S BUSINESS COLLEGE, Honolulu, Hawaii
BALDWIN HIGH SCHOOL, Wailuku, Maui

COMMUNITY SERVICE ACTIVITIES:
Leader in Brownies, Girl Scouts. Den Mother for Cub Scouts. Helped in fund-raising
affairs for PTA, Patron's Guild, Little League. Volunteer in special education classes.

REFERENCES: Available upon request.

• •

FIGURE A-4 Chronological Résumé and Cover Letter of Career Woman Moving Up. Barbara Cline's résumé shows the career path of a clerical person moving into professional management. She carefully selects "other experience" that shows her involvement both in her profession and community. Her cover letter indicates her awareness of the center's planned reorganization. She indicates how her skills and experience fit in.

409 Long Island Drive
College Point, NY 11356
June 10, 1984

Ms. Margaret Moss
Personnel Director
Deerpark Medical Center
Boulder, CO 80301

Dear Ms. Moss:

It was enjoyable meeting your representative, Dr. William Cane, at the Health Care Management Association Conference on June 6. I was interested to learn that you are looking for an administrator with computer capability.

I feel that my background would prove valuable in the reorganization and expansion that you are planning for your center. My experise lies in two areas. The first is in the way health care is actually planned for, scheduled, and delivered in an outpatient ambulatory care or HMO setting. The second area, and my most recent experience, has been in setting up a complete computer system to handle doctor and patient appointment scheduling, patient needs and flow, and statistics.

Since I am planning a visit to Boulder this summer, I look forward to getting together with you to review my qualifications for the administrative position. I will call you in about ten days for an appointment.

Sincerely yours,

Barbara A. Cline

Barbara A. Cline
(212) 555-3600

Résumé enclosed

• •

Figure A-4 (continued)

BARBARA A. CLINE
409 Long Island Drive
College Point, NY ll356
(2l2) 555-3600

POSITION OBJECTIVE: Administrator of Ambulatory Health Care Facility

EXPERIENCE SUMMARY:

FASHION MERCHANDISE WORKERS HEALTH CENTER, New York, N.Y.   1977-present
Assistant Administrative Director

Administer ambulatory care health center serving 900 patients daily. Personnel
administration: recruit, administer salary, negotiate contracts for two unions, counsel l65
lay staff. Coordinate 20 administrative department supervisors and their activities. Key
role in development of computerized appointment and pharmacy system for HP 3000
on-line; all related MIS activities. Plan, evaluate, and administer $5 million budget.
Purchase supplies. Prepare annual report text. Direct physical plant maintenance, repair,
and renovation. Do publicity and patient relations including articles, personal
appearances, and health fair.

Executive Secretary to Administrative Director   1972-77
Supervised and trained clerical personnel. Secretarial responsibilities.

NATIONAL CAMPING AND HIKING ASSOCIATION, New York, N.Y.   1971
Convention Coordinator/Administrative Assistant

Maintained membership; planned convention and publicity and employment referral service
for members. Coordinated and implemented NCHA l97l convention in Waterville Valley, New
Hampshire.

JUICE & BEVERAGE MAGAZINE, New York, N.Y.   1970
Administrative Assistant to Managing Editor

Supervised department secretaries in editorial unit; researched articles; wrote NEW
PRODUCTS section of magazine (60 items/month).

BIOKEM INSTITUTE, Pittsburgh, PA   1968-69
Administrative Secretary for Research Scientists and Professors

Prepared grant proposals to NIH, NSF, USAF. Coordinated convention hosting ACS.

EDUCATION:

FORDHAM UNIVERSITY: MBA   1982

EMPIRE STATE COLLEGE, SUNY, New York: BS in Business Management, GPA/3.6
1980

OTHER EXPERIENCE:

Free-lance writing. Community activities: teen counseling, volunteer ambulance corps,
church groups. Member APHA, GHAA, NYPHA, and NY Pers. Mgt. Assoc. Invited Paper,
GHAA l980 on computerized patient appointment system. Member, Hewlett-Packard
Users' Group.

REFERENCES: Available upon request.

• •

FIGURE A-5 **Chronological Résumé and Cover Letter of Housewife Entering the Job Market.** Deborah P. Anderson, a housewife entering the job market, uses her extensive volunteer experience to good advantage, carefully relating each activity to her position objective. Her letter shows that she is "in charge" of the hiring process.

42991 Mountain Drive
Crestview, MA 02109
June 1, 1989

Ms. Maggie Katz
Seacliff Neighborhood Community Action Center
133 Harrison Road
Boston, MA 02109
Dear Ms. Katz:

Thank you for the excellent overview and tour of the Community Action Center. After visiting several such centers, I've concluded that yours is one of the best.

I've decided to apply for the newly created position of program director that you mentioned. My experience in community action and program development, along with my paralegal education, give me the background that you indicated would be of value.

My resume and application are enclosed. If I don't hear from you, I will call next month regarding the position.

Sincerely yours,

Deborah P. Anderson

Deborah P. Anderson
(617) 555-1212

● ●

Figure A-5 (continued)

DEBORAH P. ANDERSON
42991 Mountain Drive
Crestview, Massachusetts 02109
(617) 555-1212

EMPLOYMENT OBJECTIVE: Program Director

EXPERIENCE:

CHILD ASSAULT PREVENTION PROJECT (CAPP)
Facilitator/Coordinator

Give one hour classroom safety presentations to children from kindergarten through 6th grade. Use role playing/brainstorming, private time for concerns/questions. Referral to police/other agencies. Arrange presentations, give parent and teacher inservice workshops.

VOLUNTEERS AT MISSION (VAM)   Coordinator

Developed a high school resource center for information on local agencies needing volunteers. Contacted agencies, posted information, scheduled volunteers, wrote letters of recommendation, solicited donations for scholarships.

SENIOR ADULT LEGAL ASSISTANCE (SALA):   Legal Counsel

Assisted attorney; worked with senior citizens regarding wills and other legal matters. Contacted various agencies, mainly Social Security about legal problems re: benefits.

PARENTS WHO CARE: Co-coordinator

Organized school administration, city staff, police, parents, and youth to work together in creating a wholesome, drug-free environment. Coordinated patrol of problems areas of the city. Reviewed school's drug curriculum and films.

DIABETES SOCIETY OF WALDEN VALLEY: Member Board of Directors. Director/Coordinator

MAYFLOWER ESTATES HOMEOWNERS ASSOCIATION: President

Planned with City Council, city, home builders, and homeowners to change streets. Worked with Alcoholic Beverage Control, Convenience Markets, homeowners/city toward settlement of liquor license acquisition. Coordinated citizen petitions.

POLITICAL CAMPAIGN: Co-Coordinator for City of Crestview

Organized campaign and workers of City of Crestview. Arranged for speakers and coffee hours, gave talks, leafleted, talked door to door, did publicity, contacted city officials.

CREATIVE DYNAMICS FOUNDATION: Regional Coordinator and Group Discussion Leader

Developed programs and curriculum, planned budget. Directed groups in communication and interpersonal relationships. Participated in personal growth/leadership training seminars.

EDUCATION: UNIVERSITY OF SANTA CLARA: Paralegal Program
            CITY COLLEGE OF BOSTON: AA Degree, Social Science; Honor Society
            BOSTON STATE UNIVERSITY; SIMMONS COLLEGE

PERSONAL PARAGRAPH: I enjoy working with people and have skills and experience in organization, communication, and peer counseling. Exercise initiative and responsibility.

REFERENCES: Will be provided upon request.

. . . .

FIGURE A-6 Chronological Résumé of a Professional Engineer.

LARRY ANDERSON
3288l Amazon Drive
Silicon Valley, CA 94040
(4l5) 555-7218

POSITION OBJECTIVE:

Management Facilitator in Manufacturing/selling of Complex Electronic Devices

QUALIFICATIONS IN BRIEF:

BSEE and graduate work. Twenty-one years of management/engineering experience.
Excellent human relations skills.

WORK EXPERIENCE:

INTERNATIONAL MICRO PRODUCTS, Santa Clara, CA.   September l983-Present
Vice President/Manufacturing

Responsible for complex-custom ICs in two to five micron CMOS/NMOS; also technology
R&D, product and test engineering, and corporate procedures.

Vice President/Customer Design Products

Assessed manufacturing feasibility of customer design semiconductor devices.
Managed technical/business relationships with customer and company.

Director of Engineering Services

Managed test/product engineering, fab tooling procurement, customer designed products.

FUTAMI SEMICONDUCTORS, Mountain View, CA.   l979-l983
Director of Test Operations

Responsible for wafer sort, final test and burn in for 64K DRAMs and ROMs. Did
product and test engineering, equipment maintenance.

Director of Manufacturing Services

Directed personnel, budgets, and procedures for mask making, factilites, and line
maintenance.

ELECTRONIC SYSTEMS, Mountain View, CA.   April, l968-September, l983
Manager of Manufacturing Engineering

Manage product engineering, instrumentation, and test data processing.

Also: Product Line Manager, Instrumentation Manager, Section Head, Senior Engineer

NATIONAL MICROELECTRONIC DIVISION   May l965 to April l968
Supervisor of Instrumentation

EDUCATION:
SAN JOSE STATE UNIVERSITY, San Jose CA.: BSEE Degree   1965
                                          Sixteen units of graduate work   l965-67
 REFERENCES: Provided upon request.

• •

FIGURE A-7 Chronological Résumé (Arranged Under Two Functional Headings) of a Housewife Who Returned to School.

BOBBIE CLARK
5l0 S. 39th Street
Escanaba, Michigan 49829
H - (906) 555-I2l2
W - (906) 555-I3l3

JOB OBJECTIVE: Personnel Interviewer in Private Sector

QUALIFICATIONS:

Ability to: Organize and promote programs and activities
Perform effectively under pressure
Use tact and diplomacy with people
Speak extemporaneously with originality
Implement suggestions and findings

PERSONNEL EXPERIENCE:

BAY DE NOC COMMUNITY COLLEGE, Escanaba, Michigan   Present
Placement Interviewer

Interview applicants to determine their suitability for employment; advise applicants in interview preparation techniques and assist students in completing job applications. Contact employers concerning job openings and refer properly qualified applicants. Develop new job listings.

JOB SERVICE/MICHIGAN EMPLOYMENT SECURITY COMMISSION,Escanaba, MI
Employment Interviewer

Interviewed job applicants to select persons meeting employer's qualifications. File-searched job orders, and matched applicant's qualifications with job requirements and employer's specifications. Performed reference and background checks and often referred applicants to vocational counseling and testing services. Followed up with employer or interviewer for hiring results and future recommendations. Developed jobs through contacts with employers.

PUBLIC RELATIONS EXPERIENCE

8TH ASSEMBLY DISTRICT OFFICE, Green Bay, Wisconsin

WINNEBAGO FOUNDATION, Green Bay, Wisconsin
Public Relations Representative

Liaison between State Capitol and Assembly District Office reviewing constituent problems applicable to state jurisdiction. Representative for the Assemblyman. Wrote press releases. Effective in establishing rapport with media personnel to obtain coverage. Promoted community and civic programs by speaking to groups. Coordinated scheduling of activities. Made presentations on philosophy of foundation. Recruited for workshops and taught related classes. Managed funds for budget. Counseled clients.

REFERENCES: Available and provided upon request.

• •
FIGURE A-8 Chronological Résumé of a Vietnamese Student.

HUONG-MAI VAN
369 Rose Lane
Monte Sereno, California 95030
(408) 555-1212

POSITION OBJECTIVE: Employee Trainer in Pharmaceutical Industry

QUALIFICATIONS IN BRIEF: Excellent in human relations, communications, organizational leadership. Extensive pharmaceutical experience. Speak Vietnamese, French, and English. Chemistry-English education equivalent to AA degree. Dedicated worker.

EDUCATION:
    UNIVERSITY OF CALIFORNIA, San Francisco, CA: BS/ Pharmacy   1985
    WEST VALLEY COLLEGE, Saratoga, CA. AS: Chemistry   1982
    SAIGON UNIVERSITY, Saigon, Vietnam Two years English Education/Chemistry Major

EXPERIENCE SUMMARY:

    PHARMTECK, Palo Alto, CA.   1985-Present
    Pharmaceutical Chemist
    Develop appropriate media and packaging for new products. Involves surveying literature, researching, testing various materials for safety, stability, usability, cost effectiveness.

    WEST VALLEY COLLEGE, Satatoga, CA.   1980-85
    Educational Opportunity Program Student Advisor

    Recruited, oriented, motivated students. Developed and implemented tutoring system and schedule. Founder/ President: Vietnamese Student Association. Organized cultural events.

    Chemistry Student Lab Assistant   February 1979-1980

    Prepared materials for laboratory classes.

    EQUAL OPPORTUNITY COMMISSION, San Mateo County.   October 1977-January 1979
    Health Training Coordinator

    Organized training for low-income parents as child care provider. Interviewed, evaluated, trained, supervised 52 participants.

    PARKE DAVIS CORPORATION, Washington, D.C.   February 1977-October 1977
    Pharmaceutical Representative

    Visited medical offices, pharmacies, hospitals to present new products and take orders.

    INDOCHINA CENTER (U.S. CATHOLIC CONFERENCE)   April 1976 - January 1977
    Case Aide

    JOHNS HOPKINS UNIVERSITY, Baltimore, Maryland   February 1976-April 1976
    Medical Transcriber

    RED CROSS, Baltimore, Maryland   February 1976-April 1976
    Receptionist Volunteer

    PHAM HONG THAI PHARMACY, Saigon, Vietnam   February 1968-April 1975

REFERENCES: Available upon request.

● ●
FIGURE A-9 Chronological Résumé of a Divorced Parent.

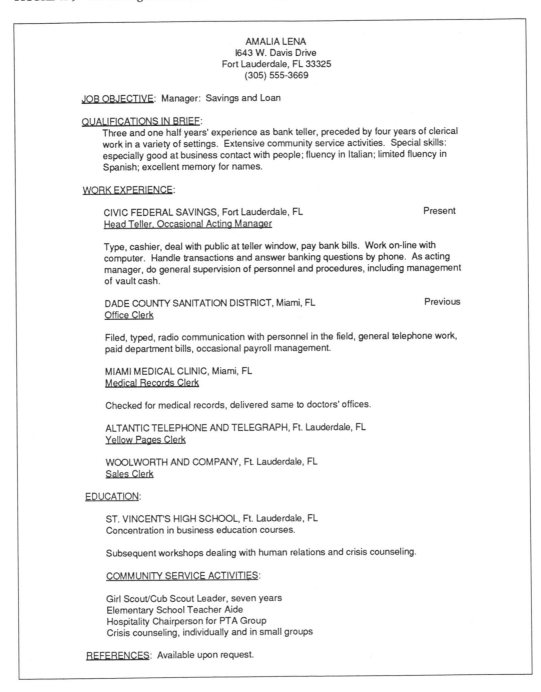

AMALIA LENA
l643 W. Davis Drive
Fort Lauderdale, FL 33325
(305) 555-3669

JOB OBJECTIVE: Manager: Savings and Loan

QUALIFICATIONS IN BRIEF:
Three and one half years' experience as bank teller, preceded by four years of clerical work in a variety of settings. Extensive community service activities. Special skills: especially good at business contact with people; fluency in Italian; limited fluency in Spanish; excellent memory for names.

WORK EXPERIENCE:

CIVIC FEDERAL SAVINGS, Fort Lauderdale, FL   Present
Head Teller, Occasional Acting Manager

Type, cashier, deal with public at teller window, pay bank bills. Work on-line with computer. Handle transactions and answer banking questions by phone. As acting manager, do general supervision of personnel and procedures, including management of vault cash.

DADE COUNTY SANITATION DISTRICT, Miami, FL   Previous
Office Clerk

Filed, typed, radio communication with personnel in the field, general telephone work, paid department bills, occasional payroll management.

MIAMI MEDICAL CLINIC, Miami, FL
Medical Records Clerk

Checked for medical records, delivered same to doctors' offices.

ALTANTIC TELEPHONE AND TELEGRAPH, Ft. Lauderdale, FL
Yellow Pages Clerk

WOOLWORTH AND COMPANY, Ft. Lauderdale, FL
Sales Clerk

EDUCATION:

ST. VINCENT'S HIGH SCHOOL, Ft. Lauderdale, FL
Concentration in business education courses.

Subsequent workshops dealing with human relations and crisis counseling.

COMMUNITY SERVICE ACTIVITIES:

Girl Scout/Cub Scout Leader, seven years
Elementary School Teacher Aide
Hospitality Chairperson for PTA Group
Crisis counseling, individually and in small groups

REFERENCES: Available upon request.

• •
FIGURE A-10   Functional Résumé of a Military Retiree.

GEORGE R. URCIUOLI
462 Great Plains Drive
Waco, Texas 76701
H (817) 555-6060
W (817) 555-2211

CAREER OBJECTIVE:

Management Position in the area of materials planning and control for manufacturing firm.

CURRENT STATUS:

U.S. Army Officer completing 20 years of active duty with rank of Lt. Colonel. Leaving military service to start second career in business.

EXPERIENCE:

MATERIALS CONTROL: Stored and allocated $4.5 million inventory of food, fuel, ammunition, repair parts, construction material. Coordinated resupply operation for 22,000 combat troops. Commanded 127 men providing supplies and services to 2,000 combat troops. Directed 90-person team furnishing materials and electronic instrumentation for R & D project. Implemented supply and service program for 800 logistics personnel. Scheduled and coordinated use of ranges, classrooms, training areas, drill fields, test facilities.

OFFICE ADMINISTRATION: Managed administrative services for command group. Coordinated projects between senior executives, section chiefs, subordinate commanders. Participated in forming organizational directorate and organization training center.

HUMAN RELATIONS: As Inspector General, conducted inspections, inquiries, surveys. Reported allegations, complaints, requests of military personnel and families. Recommended corrective actions. Advised Commanding General on activities, attitudes, status of the organization. Performed internal audits/reviews. Personnel officer for 2,500-person task force.

BUDGETING/ACCOUNTING: As Central Accounting Officer, prepared $1 million annual budget for Command Sport and Recreation Fund. Administered $600,000 budget for R & D support group. Raised and distributed $20,000 for relief program. Raised $14,000 for Red Cross drive. Formulated policies and accounting procedures for various post clubs.

INSTRUCTION: Wrote lesson plans for and conducted weapons training for 18,000 recruits. Directed committee of 104 instructors. Initiated two training innovations now accepted as standard throughout entire U.S. Army. Taught management and economics part-time at community college level.

EDUCATION:

GOLDEN GATE UNIVERSITY, San Francisco, CA: MBA	1978
US ARMY COMMAND AND GENERAL STAFF COLLEGE: MMAS	1974
UNIVERSITY OF THE CITY OF NEW YORK: BBA	1959

• •
FIGURE A-11   Functional Résumé Slanted Toward Achievements of Career Woman Moving into Public Relations from Secretarial Work.

LAURIE REAUME
36l l/2 Calle de Florencia
Santa Fe, New Mexico 8750l
(505) 970-9l20

POSITION OBJECTIVE: Public Relations

ACHIEVEMENTS:

WRITING/PUBLICITY

- Compiled and published public service directory.
- Coordinated and edited corporate newsletter.
- Designed publicity brochure and employee handbook.
- Wrote and placed employment advertising.
- Gave presentations on company's innovative policies.

ADMINISTRATION AND ORGANIZATION

- Hired, supervised, and trained contract employees.
- Established and maintained resource/reference library.
- Planned, organized, and promoted company picnic.
- Developed and conducted new hire orientation program.
- Coordinated and presented work effectiveness seminar.

EDUCATION:

GOLDEN GATE UNIVERSITY, San Francisco, CA,   MBA Candidate.

UNIVERSITY OF WISCONSIN, Whitewater, WI, BA Cum Laude.

QUALIFICATIONS SUMMARY:

Self-starter, excellent organizer, resourceful, team player.

• •
FIGURE A-12 Letter of Resignation.

378 Hames Road
Corralitos, CA. 95076
March 17, 1988

Ms. Gladys C. Penner, Chancellor
University of the Trees
369. Dogwood Blvd.
Bowling Green, KY 42101

Dear Ms. Penner:

After considerable thought, it has become clear that a career change is appropriate for me at this time. As of June 1, 1988 I will be resigning from the University of the Trees as Career Center Coordinator and Counselor.

I have enjoyed and greatly profited from my years of teaching and counseling at UOT. Your considerable expertise, openness to innovation, and general professionalism have been a significant factor in my job satisfaction.

Perhaps on occasion I might return to teach a short course or a night class -- for I plan to stay in the field of Career Development. I will be expanding my private practice and my consulting in that area.

I wish to express my appreciation to the college community for the many years of support it has given me, for its commitment to excellence, and dedication to students.

Sincerely yours,

Allison E. Stevenson

Allison E. Stevenson

NOTES

Introduction

1. Studs Terkel, *Working* (New York: Avon, 1972), p. 233.

Chapter 1
Needs, Wants, and Values: Spotlighting You

1. Victor Frankl, *Man's Search for Meaning* (New York: Washington Square Press, 1963).

2. Nena O'Neill and George O'Neill, *Shifting Gears* (New York: Avon, 1974), p. 140.

3. See Gary Carnum, "Everybody Talks about Values," *Learning* (December, 1972); S. B. Simon, S. W. Howe, and H. Kirschenbaum, *Values Clarification* (New York: Hart, 1972).

4. Edward Goss, "Patterns of Organizational and Occupational Socialization," *The Vocational Guidance Quarterly* (December 1975), p. 140.

5. Bill Cane, *Through Crisis to Freedom* (Chicago: Acta Books, 1980), p. 21.

6. IF Health Day Agenda, Freedom, California, February 1984.

7. Ken Keyes, Jr., *Handbook to Higher Consciousness* (St. Mary's, Ky.: Cornucopia Institute, 1975), p. 52.

8. Abraham Maslow, *Motivation and Personality* (New York: Harper & Row, 1954), p. 91; see also Marilyn M. Bates and Clarence Johnson, *A Manual for Group Leaders* (Denver: Love Publishing, 1972) and Keyes, *Handbook to Higher Consciousness.*

9. *The Christian Science Monitor,* January 30, 1984, p. 1.

10. *Prevention Magazine,* August 1985, p. 72.

11. Lance Morrow, *Time,* May 11, 1981, p. 94.

12. *Washington Spectator,* September 15, 1986.

13. *Statistical Abstracts of the United States* (U.S. Bureau of the Census, 1986), pp. 317, 331.

14. "Special Report," *Oxfam America News* (Winter 1983), p. 3.

15. Garrett DeBell, "A Future that Makes Ecological Sense," *The Environmental Handbook* (New York: Ballantine, 1970), pp. 153–158.

16. Terrence E. Carroll, "The Ideology of Work," *Vocational Guidance Quarterly* (December 1975), p. 154.

17. Morrow, *Time.*

18. U.S. Department of Health, Education, and Welfare, *Work in America* (Cambridge, Mass: M.I.T. Press, 1973), pp. 186–187.

19. Hans Selye, *Stress Without Distress* (Philadelphia: J. B. Lippincott, 1974).

Chapter 2
Roles and Realities: Sinking the
Stereotypes

1. Daniel J. Levinson, *The Seasons of a Man's Life* (New York: Ballantine Books, 1978), p. 229.

2. U.S. Dept. of Labor, Women's Bureau, *20 Facts on Women Workers,* 1986; *Statistical Abstracts of the United States* (U.S. Bureau of the Census, 1986), pp. 24, 393, 69, 134, 419; *Register-Pajaronian,* October 14, 1985, p. 4; U.S. Dept. of Labor, Women's Bureau, *Earnings Gap Between Men and Women* 1979; *Time,* August 4, 1980, p. 52.

3. Virginia Y. Trotter, "Women in Leadership and Decision Making: A Shift in Balance," *Vital Speeches,* April 1, 1975, pp. 373–375.

4. Ruth B. Kundsin, ed., *Women and Success: The Anatomy of Achievement* (New York: William Morrow, 1974), p. 176.

5. Carolyn Jacobson, "New Challenges for Women Workers," *The AFL-CIO American Federationist* (April, 1980), p. 3.

6. Levinson, *Seasons of a Man's Life,* pp. 20, 43–46, 158.

7. *Statistical Abstracts of the United States,* 1986, pp. 39, 450; *20 Facts on Working Women,* 1986, and *Women, Clerical Work, and Office Automation: Issues for Research,* 1986, p. 25; *The Christian Science Monitor,* March 27, 1986, p. 2; Lenore J. Weitzman, *The Divorce Revolution: The Unexpected Social and Economic Consequences for Women and Children* (New York: Free Press, 1985), pp. 37, 263, 215.

8. P. B. Walsh, *Growing Through Time: An Introduction to Adult Development* (Monterey, Calif.: Brooks/Cole, 1983), p. 237.

9. Betty Friedan, *The Feminine Mystique,* (New York: Dell, 1963).

10. *The Christian Science Monitor,* July 29, 1986, p. 26.

11. Alice Cook, "The Working Mother," address to Center for Research on Women, Stanford University, January 1976.

12. *Statistical Abstracts of the United States,* 1986, p. 45.

13. Bess Myerson, "Someday I'd Like to Walk Slowly," *Redbook* (September, 1975), p. 176.

14. Caryl Rivers, *San Francisco Chronicle,* January 1, 1975.

15. Aletha Huston Stein and Margaret M. Bailey, "The Socialization of Achievement Orientation in Females," *Psychological Bulletin 80,* no. 5 (November 1973), p. 353.

16. Hilary Cosell, "Wrong Dreams," *Ladies Home Journal,* April, 1985, p. 171.

17. *The Christian Science Monitor,* July 29, 1986, p. 26.

18. Ibid.

19. *Time,* January 21, 1980.

20. Lillian Hellman, *An Unfinished Woman: A Memoir* (Boston: Atlantic Monthly Press, 1969).

21. *The Christian Science Monitor,* February 12, 1987, p. 5.

22. National Advisory Council on Women's Educational Programs, *Working Women Speak,* pp. 5, 24.

23. Tish Sommers, "Where Sexism Meets Ageism," *Modern Maturity* (October-November 1975), p. 60.

24. John Naisbitt, "Trendnotes," *San Francisco Chronicle,* June 3, 1986, p. 2.

25. *The Christian Science Monitor,* June 7, 1982, p. 28.

26. *In Business,* January-February, 1986, p. 58.

27. *The Christian Science Monitor*, May 6, 1986, p. 17.

28. Reynolds Farley, "Assessing Black Progress," *Economic Outlook,* vol. 13, nos. 2, 3 (1986), pp. 16–17.

29. U.S. Dept. of Labor, Women's Bureau, *Women and Office Automation: Issues for the Decade Ahead,* 1985, p. 20.

30. *Statistical Abstracts of the United States,* p. 341.

31. U.S. Department of Labor, *Technical Information,* January 1987, no. 87–50, Table A-3, pp. 9, 10.

32. Terence Wright, "Liberation, My Nation, Migration," *Diaspora* (Fall, 1980).

33. U.S. Immigration and Naturalization Service, in *The Christian Science Monitor,* October 10, 1985, p. 3.

34. National Advisory Council on Economic Opportunity, "Report to the President," in *San Francisco Chronicle-Examiner,* October 19, 1980, p. A19.

35. Marilyn Power Goldberg, "The Economic Exploitation of Women," *Review of Radical Political Economics,* vol. 2, no. 1 (Spring, 1970).

36. John Kenneth Galbraith, "The Economics of the American Housewife," *Harper's* (June, 1973), p. 78.

37. Betty Friedan, *The Second Stage* (New York: Summit Books, 1981).

38. Mark Gerzon, *A Choice of Heroes: The Changing Faces of American Manhood* (Boston: Houghton-Mifflin, 1983).

39. Marilyn Ferguson, *Aquarian Conspiracy: Personal and Social Transformation in the 1980s* (Los Angeles: J. P. Tarcher, 1980).

40. Jean Houston, "The Church in Future Society," taped address to the Lutheran Brotherhood Colloquium, University of Texas, Austin, January 1979. See also Jean Houston, *The Possible Human* (Los Angeles: J. P. Tarcher, 1982).

Chapter 3
Personality and Performance: Pieces of the Puzzle

1. John L. Holland, *Making Vocational Choices: A Theory of Careers* (Englewood Cliffs, N.J.: Prentice-Hall, 1973).

2. Rose Marie Dunphy, *The Christian Science Monitor,* May 20, 1985, p. 34.

3. Compiled from the following sources: U.S. Department of Labor, *Dictionary of Occupational Titles,* vol. 2, 1965; *Guide for Occupational Exploration,* New Forum Foundation, distributed by the American Guidance Service, Publications Building, Circle Pines, MN 55014, 1984; *U.S. Army, Career and Educational Guide,* Counselor Edition, 1978.

4. Jean Houston, "The Church in Future Society."

5. See Sydney A. Fine, "Counseling Skills: Target for Tomorrow," *Vocational Guidance Quarterly* (June 1974) and "Nature of Skills: Implications for Education and Training," *Proceedings,* 75th Annual Convention of the American Personnel Association, 1967.

6. Ray A. Killian, "The Working Woman . . . A Male Manager's View," American Management Association paper, 1971.

7. Genita Kovacevich Costello, "How Women Are Recasting the Managerial Mold," *San Jose Mercury News,* April 25, 1982.

Chapter 4
The Career Connection: Finding Your Job Satisfiers

1. U.S. Department of Labor, *Dictionary of Occupational Titles,* 1978.

2. *Guide for Occupational Exploration,* 1984, (formerly by U.S. Department of Labor, 1979), National Forum Foundation, distributed by the American Guidance Service, Publications Building, Circle Pines, MN 55014.

3. Compiled from the following sources: U.S. Department of Labor, *Dictionary of Occupational Titles,* vol. 2, 1965; U.S. Department of Labor and National Forum Foundation, *Guide for Occupational Exploration,* 1979 and 1984; U.S. Army, *Career and Education Guide,* Counselor Edition, 1978; U.S. Department of Labor, *Handbook for Analyzing Jobs,* 1972.

4. *Guide for Occupational Exploration,* 1984, p. 14.

5. *Worker Trait Group Guide* (Bloomington, Ill.: McKnight Publishing Co., 1978).

Chapter 5
The Job Market: Facts, Trends, Predictions

1. *The Christian Science Monitor,* July 7, 1986, p. 2.

2. Frances Moore Lappé and Joseph Collins, *Food First: Beyond the Myth of Scarcity* (New York: Ballantine, 1978), p. 1.

3. Norris McWhirter, ed., *Guinness Book of World Records* (New York: Bantam Books, 1982).

4. *The Christian Science Monitor,* February 13, 1986, p. 5.

5. See Joseph Luft, *Group Processes: An Introduction to Group Dynamics,* 3rd. ed. (Mountain View, Calif.: Mayfield, 1984).

6. François Dusquesne, "The Making of a Sacred Planet," *One Earth,* no. 2, p. 6.

7. John Naisbitt, *Reinventing the Corporation,* quoted in Mission College *Future Line: A Newsletter for Work Experience,* Fall 1986.

8. U.S. Dept. of Commerce, Bureau of the Census, *Historical Statistics of the U.S. Colonial Times to 1970 Part 1,* 1975, p. 15.

9. *Statistical Abstracts of the United States* (Washington, D.C.: Bureau of the Census, 1986), p. 25.

10. John Peers, lecture at Mission College, Santa Clara, California, November 11, 1982.

11. Marvin Cetram and Thomas O'Toole, "Careers with a Future," *Futurist,* June, 1982.

12. "The Job Outlook for College Graduates During the 1980s," *Occupational Outlook Quarterly* (Washington, D.C.: U.S. Department of Labor, Bureau of Labor Statistics, Summer 1982); *Statistical Abstracts of the United States* (Washington, D.C.: Bureau of the Census, 1981), p. 145.

13. *The Christian Science Monitor,* January 12, 1987, p. 3.

14. Peter J. Michelozzi, "Jobs, Wages and Reading Ability," Fall, 1981.

15. *The Washington Spectator,* October 10, 1986, p. 3.

16. John Naisbitt, *Reinventing the Corporation,* from Mission College *Future Line: A Newsletter for Work Experience,* February 1987 and *The Christian Science Monitor,* February 23, 1987, p. 23, citing a recent Club of Rome Study.

17. John P. Beck, "Unions, the Economy and the 'Right to Useful Work,'" Ann Arbor: University of Michigan, Summer School on Extending Workplace Democracy, Institute of Labor and Industrial Relations, 1980.

18. Le Chef Madame de Service, Ministère du Temps Libre, Service de l'Information, 116–118 Avenue de Président Kennedy 75775, Paris, Cedex 16, France.

19. John Peers, lecture at Mission College, Santa Clara, California, November 11, 1982.

20. Alvin Toffler, *The Third Wave* (New York: Bantam Books, 1980).

21. Thomas W. Foster, "The Amish Society, a Relic of the Past, Could Become a Model for the Future," *Futurist* (December, 1981), p. 33.

22. Lappé and Collins, *Food First.*

23. *National Gardening,* March 1987, p. 18.

24. Marvin Feldman, "Work, Employment and the New Economics," Occasional Paper no. 70, National Center for Research in Vocational Education (Columbus: Ohio State University, 1981).

25. Quoted in Colin Norman, "The Staggering Challenge of Global Unemployment," *Futurist,* August 1978, p. 224.

26. Toffler, *Third Wave,* p. 350.

27. *Occupational Outlook Quarterly* (Washington, D.C.: U.S. Department of Labor, Bureau of Labor Statistics, Spring 1986), p. 31.

28. *San Jose Mercury News.* July 13, 1986, p. 4PC.

29. Cetram and O'Toole, "Careers with a Future"; also Marvin Cetron, "Getting Reading for the Jobs of the Future," *Futurist,* June, 1983, p. 15.

30. *Futurist,* December 1980, p. 4.

31. "Where Future Jobs Will Be," *World Press Review,* March, 1981, p. 21.

32. Walter Chandoha, *Book of Kittens and Cats* (New York: Bramhall House, 1973), p. 8.

Chapter 6
Workplaces and Work Styles: Scanning the Subtleties

1. *Restaurant News,* December 1984.
2. *Technical Information 87-50,* U.S. Department of Labor, February 6, 1987, pp. 22–23 and *Employment and Earning,* U.S. Department of Labor, December 1986, p. 30.
3. Robert Vahl, Small Business Assistance Service, Clymer, N.Y., quoted in *In Business,* January-February 1986, p. 15.
4. Erving Goffman, *Asylums* (New York: Doubleday, 1961).
5. Barbara Garson, "Women's Work," *Working Papers* (Fall 1973), p. 5.
6. Robert Schrank, "How to Relieve Worker Boredom," *Psychology Today* (July 1978), pp. 79–80.
7. *Time,* March 10, 1975, p. 42.
8. *The Bread Rapper,* September-October 1986.
9. Ritchie P. Lowry, "Social Investing," *Futurist* (April 1982); *Socially Sensitive Investing* (Boston: U.S. Trust Co.); Theodore V. Purcell, "Institutionalizing Ethics on Corporate Boards," *Review of Social Economy* 36, no. 1 (April 1978).
10. *The Christian Science Monitor,* September 8, 1986, p. 23.
11. Meyer Friedman and Ray H. Rosenman, *Type A Behavior and Your Heart* (New York: Fawcett, 1974).
12. John Kenneth Galbraith, "The Economics of an American Housewife," *Atlantic Monthly* (August 1973), pp. 78–83.
13. Studs Terkel, *Working* (New York: Avon, 1972), p. 4.
14. Charles McCabe, *San Francisco Chronicle,* September 1974.
15. James Michener, *The Fires of Spring* (New York: Bantam Books, 1949).
16. Part-Time Professionals, P.O. Box 3419, Alexandria, VA 22304.
17. *The Christian Science Monitor,* March 18, 1982.
18. Geoffrey Kessler, *Kessler Letter,* 1987 (11661 San Vicente Blvd., Los Angeles, CA 90049), p. 1.
19. Small Business Association, *Women's Handbook,* April, 1983, pp. 1 and 11.
20. *Working Women,* January, 1987, p. 54.
21. *The Christian Science Monitor,* January 16, 1987, p. B6.
22. *Franchising in the Economy, 1984–86* (Washington, D.C.: U.S. Department of Labor, Government Printing Office, 1986), pp. 1, 24. S/N 003-008-00199-8.
23. Jeremy Joan Hewes, *Worksteads* (Garden City, N.Y.: Doubleday, 1981), pp. 7, 5. See also Bernard Lefkowitz, *Breaktime: Living Without Work in a Nine-to-Five World* (New York: Penguin Books, 1979).
24. *Women and Office Automation: Issues for the Decade Ahead* (Washington, D.C.: U.S. Department of Labor, Women's Bureau, 1985), p. 24.
25. Marilyn Ferguson, *Aquarian Conspiracy: Personal and Social Transformation in the 1980s* (Los Angeles: J. P. Tarcher, 1982).
26. Alvin Toffler, *The Third Wave* (New York: Bantam Books, 1980), p. 387.
27. Richard Pitcairn and Susan Hubble Pitcairn, *Dr. Pitcairn's Complete Guide to Natural Health for Dogs and Cats* (Emmaus, Pa.: Rodale Press, 1982).
28. Bill Cane, *Through Crisis to Freedom* (Chicago: Acta Books, 1980), p. 8.
29. *Futurist,* February 1984, p. 28.
30. *Occupational Outlook Quarterly,* Spring 1983, p. 11

Chapter 7
The Job Hunt: Breaking and Entering

1. William L. Weiss, quoted in *Personnel Administrator* (May 1981), pp. 77–78.
2. Toni St. James, interview workshop, California Employment Development Department, 1977.
3. Ibid.

Chapter 8
Decisions, Decisions: What's Your Next Move?

1. *Statistical Abstracts of the United States, 1986* (Washington, D.C.: U.S. Bureau of the Census, 1986), p. 133.
2. *San Jose Mercury News,* October 25, 1981, p. 6E.
3. Alan Lakein, *How to Get Control of Your Time and Your Life* (New York: Wyden, 1973).
4. Ken Keyes, Jr., *"Oneness Space,"* Living Love Recording (St. Mary's, Ky.: Cornucopia Center; Ken Keyes College, The Vision Foundation, 790 Commercial Avenue, Coos Bay, OR 97420).
5. Jerry Gillies, *Money Love* (New York: Warner Books, 1978).
6. Margaret Anstin, *Voyages: A Chartbook for Career Life Planning* (Dubuque, Iowa: Kendall/Hunt Publishing, 1980), p. 115.
7. Betts Richter and Alice Jacobsen, *Make It So!* (Sonoma, Calif.: Be All Books, 1979).

INDEX